SWINDOLL
LEADERSHIP
LIBRARY

# END TIMES

Understanding Today's World Events in Biblical Prophecy

## JOHN F. WALVOORD

CHARLES R. SWINDOLL, GENERAL EDITOR

WORD PUBLISHING

NASHVILLE

A Thomas Nelson Company

END TIMES
Swindoll Leadership Library

Copyright © 1998 by Word Publishing. All rights reserved.

Unless otherwise indicated, Scripture quotations used in this book are from the
Holy Bible, New International Version, (NIV). Copyright © 1973, 1978, 1984
International Bible Society. Used by permission of Zondervan Bible Publishers.

Published in association with Dallas Theological Seminary (DTS):
General Editor: Dr. Charles R. Swindoll, President
Managing Editor: Dr. Roy B. Zuck

The theological opinions expressed by the author are not necessarily the
official position of Dallas Theological Seminary.

Library of Congress Cataloging in Publication Data:

Walvoord, John F.
End times: Understanding today's world events in biblical prophecy /
John Flipse Walvoord.
p. cm.— (Swindoll leadership library)

ISBN 0-8499-1377-2 (hardcover)

1. Bible—Prophecies—End of the world. 2. End of the world—Biblical
teaching. I. Title. II. Series.

BS649.E63W34   1998                                    98-15086
236'.9–dc21                                              CIP

Printed in the United States of America
98 99 00 01 02 03 04 05 06 BVG 9 8 7 6 5 4 3 2 1

# Contents

---

*Foreword*   v

*Preface*   vii

1

The Divine Plan for Human Destiny   1

2

Understanding Prophecy   7

3

The Blessed Hope of the Lord's Return   17

4

Our Resurrection Body   39

5

The Believer's Day of Reward   49

6

The Beginning of History and Prophecy   59

7

God's Plan for a Special People   71

8

God's Master Plan for the World   95

9

Israel's 490 Prophetic Years   109

10

The Road to Armageddon   121

11

The Second Coming of Christ   141

12

The Order of Resurrections   153

13

The Judgments   167

14

The Millennial Kingdom   185

15

The Eternal State   207

16

The Significance of Prophecy in Biblical Theology   215

*Endnotes*   223

*Bibliography*   225

*Scripture Index*   229

*Subject Index*   237

# Foreword

---

THE GOSPEL NARRATIVES picture the Pharisees and Sadducees, the official religious leaders of Judaism, coming to Jesus numerous times. But rather than drawing near to learn from the Son of God, those critics came looking for ways to trap Him in theological error or to trick Him into foolish actions. Each time, Jesus exposed their evil motives.

In one crucial confrontation the religious rebels asked Jesus to "show them a sign from heaven" (Matt. 16:2). Jesus' response cut to the heart of their spiritual insensitivity. "You know how to interpret the appearance of the sky, but you cannot interpret the signs of the times" (16:3). These self-proclaimed religious experts understood more about meteorology than they did about the Bible's clear teaching on the coming of God's Son. And the prophecies of His first coming were being fulfilled right before their eyes!

The spiritual fog that so clouded the minds of the religious leaders in Jesus' day still hangs heavy over our theological landscape today. Many teachers of the Scriptures are more at home preaching history than prophecy. Whole sections of the Bible are regularly overlooked because so many pastors and teachers feel uncomfortable treading such unfamiliar territory. Yet, to do so is to ignore vast sections of God's Word.

Candidly, some avoid prophecy because of the sensationalism and mind-numbing minutia that consume those few who have become obsessed with Bible prophecy. Wild speculation and date-setting have turned a few out-of-touch souls into "prophecy fanatics" who very foolishly set dates, read most current events into the Bible, or spend much of their time focusing on prophetic trivia.

What is needed is balance . . . a balance that sees the big picture without ignoring the rest of Scriptutre. A balance that stays true to the biblical text while demonstrating the theological unity of God's prophetic Word. A balance that avoids the extremes of obsession or ignorance. A balance that weds sound interpretation with practical application.

That is exactly what John F. Walvoord offers in the volume you hold in your hands. This gifted theologian has spent his life studying God's prophetic Word. He carefully, logically, and biblically traces God's prophetic program through the Bible. The key signposts of Bible prophecy are all clearly identified and explained. Want to understand what God says about your resurrection body? It's here. Want to know the signs the precede Christ's second coming? They are included. Confused about the differences between Christ's future kingdom and eternity future? Again, both are covered.

For prophecy to be biblical, it must also be practical. God gave His prophetic truth not just to fill our *heads* but also to change our *hearts*. Dr. Walvoord weaves the threads of practical application into the fabric of each chapter. He shares the "so What" of God's master plan for the ages.

This is not a book to be read casually . . . or to be studied superficially. Don't even try. Instead, place your Bible on the desk next to this volume. And as you read, be like the diligent people of Berea in the apostle Paul's day who "received the message with great eagerness and examined the Scriptures every day to see if what Paul said was true" (Acts 17:11). You are in for the time of your life!

—CHARLES R. SWINDOLL
General Editor

# Preface

THE CHRISTIAN FAITH by its very nature is rooted in hope. A Christian's anticipation of the future is based on faith in God, the all-powerful and all-wise Creator of the universe who has revealed in prophecy His sovereign plan for history, a plan that has been unfolding for thousands of years and will climax in eternity. In contrast to atheism, which denies the existence of God and any reasonable explanation of life and knowledge of the future, Christianity provides a comprehensive and intelligent plan for history as well as prophecy—the past as well as the future. Christianity views life as continuing after death, with every individual accountable to God. As Paul expressed it, "If only for this life we have hope in Christ, we are to be pitied more than all men" (1 Cor. 15:19). In contrast to any other comparable book on religion, the Bible alone provides a comprehensive picture of past events as well as future events. No other source looks beyond this life with any authority or intelligent details on what believers in Christ can expect. Prophecy obviously is a major portion of God's revelation; one-fourth of the Bible was prophetic when it was recorded.

Many major issues face the interpreter of prophecy. The first and most fundamental is the doctrine of the inspiration of the Bible, which teaches that God guided human authors in what they wrote, so that their writings present an accurate and comprehensive revelation of the past, present, and future, and a reliable basis for determining truth. If a person does not accept the Bible as the Word of God, it is impossible for him or her to establish a prophetic system of thought and especially to gain a comprehensive view of what the future holds for the world as well as for believers.

Some Bible prophecies have been fulfilled, some are still being fulfilled, and others are subject to future fulfillment. One of my books, *The Prophecy Knowledge Handbook* (Wheaton, Ill.: Victor, 1990), traces one thousand scriptural passages on prophecy, some of them single verses and some of them entire chapters. The book shows that half of these prophecies have already been fulfilled literally, an astounding proof that prophecy is accurate even when dealing with distant future events. This constitutes solid proof that the Bible is supernatural in its divine inspiration and that it can be trusted not only in prophecy but also in other areas of truth as well.

Undoubtedly one of the major problems in understanding prophecy is determining whether it should be understood in its natural, or literal meaning. Unless prophetic statements are taken in their normal sense, it is almost impossible to determine their meaning with any consistency. If one denies that a prophecy is to be taken in its normal sense, the door is opened to dozens of unauthorized interpretations. The nonliteral interpretation of prophecy has been a major source of confusion and contradiction.

Prophecy addresses a number of major subjects. One central focus concerns Jesus Christ. These prophecies about Christ are interwoven with many other subjects in the Bible, but the prophecies concerning His first and second comings are major revelations.

As we examine the Old Testament and the Gospels it is rather astounding that no one understood that the first coming and the second comings of Christ were separate events. Even the Jewish rabbis and Old Testament believers had difficulty understanding how Christ could be both a suffering and dying Messiah and a glorious reigning Messiah. This is mentioned in 1 Peter 1:11–12, which states that the prophets were "trying to find out the time and circumstances to which the Spirit of Christ in them was pointing when He predicted the sufferings of Christ and the glories that would follow. It was revealed to them that they were not serving themselves but you, when they spoke of the things that have now been told you by those who have preached the gospel to you by the Holy Spirit sent from heaven. Even angels long to look into these things."

The fact that there was confusion on this subject and that there is no evidence that anyone fully understood the differences between the two comings of Christ alerts us as to how easy it is to miss the point of prophetic truth if attention is not paid to its details. The first coming of Jesus Christ is obviously the center of God's purpose in the world. He is also the focus of all prophetic predictions in the Bible, which will consummate in His ultimate triumph in eternity.

Another major strand of Old Testament prophecy pertains to Israel's future. Unfortunately, like the misunderstanding of the first and second comings of Christ, this too is a subject of major difference in the interpretation of prophecy. Many scholars attempt to find fulfillment of the Old Testament prophecies of Israel in the New Testament church. But to do this, they must neglect many prophetic details and the fact that in every instance in the Bible *Israel* refers to the physical descendants of Jacob. As a major area of God's purposes and plans, the nation Israel is a significant issue in the interpretation of prophecy.

An important area of difference of opinion pertains to Genesis 12:7, which records that God said to Abraham, "To your offspring I will give this land." The tendency of many scholars to take this in a nonliteral sense not only disrupts the major focal point of prophecy concerning Israel but also results in interpreting many passages wrongly. When used in association with the nation Israel, the word *land* never means anything other than the literal land of Palestine and does not refer to the eternal state or heaven, even though it is identified as such in a number of hymns. Important also in prophecy are the unfulfilled details of Israel's future, which involve their restoration as a nation, their prominence in the millennial kingdom, and their continued identity throughout eternity. It is important not to confuse Israel with the church.

The Old Testament also contains major revelation about God's sovereign control of the gentile world. In prophecy, six major gentile nations are mentioned. In chronological order they are Egypt, Assyria, Babylon,

Medo-Persia, Greece, and Rome. Their rule will be climaxed by the world government of the end times led by the Antichrist, which will be followed by the seventh kingdom, Christ's reign, which He will usher in at His second coming.

In connection with the prophecies concerning the Gentiles, there is also the concept of the kingdom, which includes three aspects. First, Scripture often refers to God as the Creator who rules over all. Second, Christ is pictured as the Son of David, who will reign over Israel in the future millennial kingdom, as well as being King of kings and Lord of lords over the whole world. Third, in the present age the kingdom of God is a spiritual kingdom in which God rules in the hearts of those who put their trust in Him.

Also clearly distinguished in prophecy is God's plan for the church, composed of believing Jews and Gentiles, who are banded together by the baptism of the Holy Spirit. The subject of the church in prophecy has also been a source of confusion to many people; God's distinct purpose for the church in contrast to His purposes for Israel and for the Gentiles is often ignored. The church began on the Day of Pentecost and will reach its climax at the Rapture. From then on, the church will continue as a special entity in the present heaven, in the millennial earth, and in the new heavens and new earth. Again the need to observe the details of prophecy becomes most important.

The doctrine of resurrection is another central doctrine of Scripture mentioned in the Old Testament but more often in the New Testament (see chap. 12, "The Order of Resurrections"). The doctrine of resurrection is part of the concept that each person born into the world continues forever and that there is life after death. The Bible speaks of several resurrections, not one general resurrection as some have said. But in the end, everyone, whether saved or lost, is subject to God's program of resurrection.

The righteousness of God, so clearly revealed in Scripture, is also related to the doctrine of judgment (see chap. 13, "The Judgments"). Many judgments of a temporal nature are mentioned in the Old Testament, as God dealt with Israel and the nations. And today God deals in judgment with Christians who stray and to some extent with the wicked, though His purpose in the present age is not one of straightening out the moral issues of life. While everyone will be judged, they are not judged at the same time, in the same way, or on the same basis.

Prophetic Scripture also reveals that God will judge Satan and the demonic world. He will also judge holy angels. The climax of biblical prophecy is that of eternal bliss for those who are saved and eternal punishment for those who are lost.

In all these areas it is obvious that prophecy is a major part of God's revelation. Apart from prophecy, Christianity would not be the faith it is, nor would it provide an intelligent basis for understanding the past, present, and future.

In many respects prophecy is the pinnacle of God's divine revelation, for prophecy reveals many of the attributes of God, including His power, wisdom, and absolute sovereignty. A study of prophecy should bring about the willing worship of human hearts and minds, submission to God's will, and an understanding of the system of values inherent in God's prophetic program for the world.

Hopefully this presentation of prophetic truth will enrich the faith and understanding of those who study prophecy and will enable them to lead intelligent lives in view of God's program for them and for the world.

# 1
# The Divine Plan
# for Human Destiny

NO OTHER CENTURY in the history of the world has seen such rapid development as the twentieth. Each year more scientific advances are occurring than formerly took place in an entire century. It is only natural that ancient questions should now be repeated with more intensity than ever. Is there a God? Does He have a plan for the future? Is there meaning to life? What human values should we recognize as important in life?

Two world wars have torn our century apart and brought dramatic new developments. Rapid changes in the electronic transmission of knowledge have dominated life—with telephones, radios, televisions, and computers taking center stage. Rapid transportation has transformed our world and has completely changed the character of warfare. The development of nuclear weapons now holds the entire world hostage, with the prospect of millions being killed if those weapons are unleashed. These drastic changes in the world have raised new questions about the destiny of human events.

Many questions about modern life came to a head when Iraq, under Saddam Hussein, invaded Kuwait in August 1990. Many people asked if this invasion triggered the end of the world.

Few people pay much attention to the Bible; they live as if God does not exist and as if there is no future accountability for their lives.

Nevertheless whenever there is a world crisis they turn to the Bible to see if it has anything to say about current events.

In Christian theology it is standard for creeds to affirm that Jesus Christ is coming again to judge the world, whether those creeds are Roman Catholic, Greek Orthodox, or Protestant. Every Christian creed assumes this is a literal fact. The secular press, though it questioned whether this was true, nevertheless during the Gulf War published major articles in leading newspapers on whether the Gulf War was a sign of the end of the age, the approach of Armageddon, and the second coming of Christ.

The word *Armageddon* refers to a place in northern Israel, which in English means the "Mount of Megiddo." It is pictured in prophecy as the marshaling point for a great army in the end time just before the second coming of Christ. This led many to wonder if the Gulf War was the prelude to Armageddon.

Most intelligent investigators soon realized this war was not precisely what the Bible predicted, because Armageddon will occur in Israel and the Gulf War concerned the nation of Kuwait. Nevertheless there was a worldwide sense of impending climax, which soon dissipated when the Gulf War was over.

Yet events following the Gulf War have left the world in an uncertain situation, with Syria acquiring arms sufficient to destroy Israel completely. Iran and Iraq also have weapons of destruction. It would only take one attack to plunge the world into major chaos and a world conflict. Deterring all this is the fact that Israel itself is well armed with nuclear weapons and is able to reply in kind.

The United States has backed Israel with money and arms, thus enabling her to achieve a high level of military preparedness. Middle East countries obviously know that if Israel were attacked the United States would probably come to the help of Israel, and most of them do not want to risk facing such a major world power. They also realize that such a war would bring the entire civilized world to the brink of ultimate destruction. These factors serve as important deterrents, even though weapons in the Middle East are sufficient to destroy Israel. Still this highlights the tense situation of the world today, with many nations having the power to destroy millions of people by nuclear means. The forecast for our present world is certainly a troubled one.

Though some have tried to date future events, most intelligent people feel that prophetic events, though possibly imminent, cannot be accurately dated. However, impending events create tension and uncertainty as to what will happen even in the near future.

Though many teachers of prophecy make dire predictions about the destruction of the world, the fact is that Bible prophecy does not say the world will be completely destroyed by nuclear weapons. The destruction described in the Book of Revelation is largely supernatural, through earthquakes, disruption of the heavens, famine, pestilence, and so forth. Apparently God will control the evil in the world sufficiently so that the world will not destroy itself before the appointed prophetic climax.

This worldwide concern has again raised the often-asked question, Who is God? And is He in control? After all, the Bible is the only book that gives a detailed account of future events. Biblical prophetic revelation has demonstrated God's ability to predict hundreds of events that later were fulfilled literally. All this leads to the conclusion that other prophecies of future events will have similar literal fulfillment when they take place.

## THE GOD OF THE BIBLE

According to the Scriptures, God is eternal and infinite in all His attributes. As the intelligent all-powerful God, He created the universe in all its complexities. In creating the world He set the stage for the activities of human beings. But how could God predict what will happen when choice is left to His creatures? According to the Scriptures God has knowledge of everything. His understanding of all events is unsearchable (Isa. 40:28). Christ possesses "all the treasures of wisdom and knowledge" (Col. 2:3). Having knowledge of all things actual or possible, God in creating the world knew fully all that would follow from His creation.

The Scriptures also reveal that God has a plan in which He has determined what the future will hold. Having knowledge of all possible as well as all actual future events, God knows in advance any plans, regardless of how detailed they are, and He is able to predict with absolute accuracy

3

not only what He Himself will do but also what will follow from natural law and human choices. But how can God know the future without controlling it? He can predict in advance the choices human beings will make because He has perfect knowledge of what each individual will know and experience.

The supreme example of this is the death of Christ on which the whole plan of redemption hinged. God did not have to be on the sidelines and worry whether Pilate would order the execution of Christ or whether the soldiers would carry out the orders to crucify Him. God had absolute certainty from His omniscience that this would be the case. At the same time God is not responsible for the immoral acts of human beings, because they choose freely without any sense of compulsion from a higher being. Accordingly, every one of the hundreds of prophecies that have been fulfilled exactly as the Bible predicted are illustrations of the fact that God can view as certain all future events that are determined by humankind.

But how can we explain life's tragic situations and acts? Since God is perfect, He would not adopt any plan if there were a better one. Humanly speaking, God might have determined any one of several equally good plans. In one plan Mr. Black is saved, and in the other plan Mr. Brown is saved. Because of His perfection, God in keeping with His character chose the best plan—there could be none better. While we in our human limitations cannot understand tragedies and events in history that seem so contrary to what God would wish, we can only conclude that if we had the full picture and understood everything, we would choose to do exactly what God did.

A chief dispatcher of a railroad may publish a timetable. He may determine a schedule for freight times; he can also determine a schedule for passenger trains. The schedule is published, and the trains run as scheduled. If the dispatcher were omniscient, he would know in advance how many passengers would board each train. He would know whether the trains would run as scheduled. Yet he would not force anyone to board the trains. There would be certainty without compulsion. In a similar way, human choice from God's point of view can be determined without forcing anyone to do anything.

This is the argument of Romans 8:28–39. Verse 28 has often been quoted, "And we know that in all things God works for the good of those who love him, who have been called according to his purpose." Then Paul added, "For those God foreknew he also predestined to be conformed to the likeness of his Son, that he might be the firstborn among many brothers. And those he predestined, he also called; those he called, he also justified; those he justified, he also glorified" (8:29–30). His foreknowledge, as well as the doctrines of election and predestination, are all part of God's plan in which He included all aspects of human determination. Romans 8 concludes triumphantly with the statement that nothing can separate us from God's love. "For I am convinced that neither death nor life, neither angels nor demons, neither the present nor the future, nor any powers, neither height nor depth, nor anything else in all creation, will be able to separate us from the love of God that is in Christ Jesus our Lord" (8:38–39).

## THE AUTHORITY AND ACCURACY OF THE BIBLICAL REVELATION

The concept of fulfilled prophecy, however, depends on accepting the Bible as a supernaturally inspired book in which God perfectly expressed what He wanted human beings to know. As a product from God, the Bible is without error and states the truth in absolute and eternal significance. The Bible also, however, is a human book written by human beings who obviously were limited in their knowledge and understanding. Sometimes even the writers, as God guided them, did not understand what they themselves wrote; the Bible, generally speaking, was not dictated. But God guided the human writers so that what they wrote is absolutely true and expresses what He wanted to communicate. In the writing of the Scriptures God combined divine will and foreknowledge.

## WHY IS THERE CURRENT UNBELIEF IN PROPHECY?

Scripture states in emphatic terms that humans are accountable, that there is life after this life, and that God will judge every person. This is stated pointedly in Hebrews 9:27, "Just as man is destined to die once, and after that to face judgment." It is only natural that people, desiring to avoid the implication that they will ultimately have to face God in one way or another, try to avoid God's prophecies about the future. Even in the church, Bible interpreters have tended to ignore the pointedness of these prophecies; they have frequently questioned important prophecies of the Bible concerning Israel, the church, and the world, and have tended to ignore warnings about the second coming of Christ. They have done this because they ignore the many facts that prove clearly that the Bible is a supernatural book that contains revelations from God. That so many prophecies have been fulfilled already should lead to the conclusion that there is no explanation for their accuracy other than that the prophecies were divinely given by God Himself.

All this forms a background for the task of interpreting the Bible correctly and understanding the major events that crowd on the scene of future world events. It cannot be emphasized too much that the Bible is absolutely accurate in its predictions and that God intends for us to understand the major events of prophecy, even though some things remain obscure. The prevalent theory that prophecy cannot be taken seriously is not supported by the Bible or by the evidence of hundreds of prophecies already fulfilled.

# 2
# Understanding
# Prophecy

---

Aɴʏ sᴛᴜᴅᴇɴᴛ ᴏғ ᴘʀᴏᴘʜᴇᴄʏ soon becomes aware of the widespread confusion that exists in understanding the prophecies of the Bible. This has greatly hindered some and has caused many to turn away from the study of prophecy. Yet as already stated, it is remarkable that about one-fourth of the Bible was prophetic when it was written and about half of these hundreds of prophecies have already been fulfilled literally. Obviously God intended to give us information about His plans for the world and for believers.

## PROBLEMS IN TEACHING PROPHECY

In many churches today, however, little attempt is made to study and understand the prophetic Word, and most people who attend church regularly are quite uninformed on what the Bible teaches about the future. Part of the problem is that many church leaders feel they are not qualified to speak on the subject. Some college and seminary graduates received no instruction on prophetic subjects, and so to attempt to preach on it would show their ignorance. Others seem afraid of preaching on prophecy because some teachers have abused the subject, attempting to be sensational and often giving incorrect explanations of the prophetic

Scriptures. Others feel that prophecy, with its numerous details, is difficult to understand. Some preachers avoid prophetical sermons because they feel that doing so will label them as fundamentalists. Many pastors are struggling with contemporary problems in the church, both moral and relational, and the subject of prophecy does not seem to be an immediate area of concern. Some also view prophecy as controversial because there are so many different views, and they would rather preach or teach subjects on which there is more agreement. Whatever the reason, many churches today do not feature prophecy as a major area of study and the result is that people in local churches often go without any teaching on even the basics of prophetic truth.

### The Need for Clarity and Simplicity

Those who attempt to present prophetic truth to others should remember they are talking to many people who have very little background on the subject. Often teachers of prophecy tend to deal with what is new or unusual rather than tracing the most important aspects of our Christian hope.

When I listened as a teenager to some of the great prophecy teachers of that time, I was totally bewildered by what I heard. The teachers often dealt with some minute areas of prophecy that were of importance to advanced students of prophecy but unintelligible to individuals just beginning the study. Frequently they made no attempt to draw practical conclusions from what was being taught or to show how it affected those of us who were listening.

In preaching prophetic truth it is important to consider the viewpoint of the listeners; every attempt must be made to clarify terms and facts so they can be readily understood. If possible, such presentations must also include information that might be of interest to advanced Bible students, many of whom have not properly related all the facts and need to have an overall view of what the Scriptures present.

### The Importance of Literal Interpretation

Probably the most important issue in understanding prophecy is the question of whether it should be understood literally. One widespread assumption is that while ordinary Scripture can be interpreted in a literal manner, with terms retaining their natural meaning, prophetic portions of the Bible should be treated as a special case, with the literal or natural meaning no longer applicable.

During the first two centuries the early church tended to interpret prophecy literally. Thus they expected Christ to return to earth to establish His kingdom and reign for a thousand years, after which new heavens and a new earth would be established.

A school of theology that sprang up in Alexandria, Egypt, about A.D. 190 attempted to combine biblical interpretation with the idealism of the Greek philosopher Plato. This resulted in those leaders taking the Bible as an extensive allegory and not literally.

Refuting this position, the early church was able to restore the church as a whole back to the normal, grammatical, historical, literal interpretation of the Bible. However, in the area of prophecy this was more difficult since there were prophecies that had not yet been fulfilled, and so the church was unsuccessful in completely defeating the nonliteral interpretation of prophecy. The result was that while North Africa had been committed to the premillennial position, when that generation of leaders died, the amillennial position moved in. It is significant that for centuries thereafter Christianity in northern Africa was sterile.

The early church floundered somewhat in its approach to prophecy and its interpretation. This was brought to a head to some extent by the teachings of Augustine (354–430). He held that while the Bible should be interpreted in its normal, literal sense in most areas, in the area of prophecy it was not to be taken literally. This view was then adopted by the Roman Catholic Church, and unfortunately the Protestant Reformers also built on Augustine's view instead of on the views of the early church.

Yet many of these same theological leaders said some prophetic events will be fulfilled literally. For example, the Roman Catholic Church believes in a literal hell, a literal Second Coming, and literal judgments from God, but it denies a literal, future millennial kingdom. Perhaps this is because in the millennial kingdom Israel will be an important factor, and since the church consists mainly of Gentiles there has been unconscious resistance to the idea that the Jews have an important future. This problem of denying a literal fulfillment of prophecy and especially a literal millennial kingdom still persists in many churches today.

If a person does not interpret the plain statements of prophecy literally, there is no rule by which any consensus of meaning can be established; the existence of a wide diversity of interpretations shows the failure of this approach. As many as fifty different interpretations can be offered for just one passage in Revelation that could be easily understood if interpreted in its natural way.

### The Interpretation of Symbols

It is true that prophecy sometimes is presented in an "apocalyptic" or symbolic way, as in Daniel, Ezekiel, and Revelation. But often the Bible itself provides clues to what these symbols mean. For instance, the ten horns in Daniel 7:7 are interpreted in verse 24 to mean ten kingdoms or kings. When this is understood, the passage's meaning becomes clear.

It is wrong to say that because symbols are included in Revelation, all of the book should be taken symbolically. Many facts are to be accepted in their literal sense (e.g., the stars mentioned in the fourth trumpet judgment are literal, Rev. 8:12), but others are clearly symbolic (e.g., a star in Rev. 9:1 is personified as a person receiving a key).

Interpreting the Bible in its normal, literal way means we recognize figures of speech. And those figures—similes, metaphors, personifications, hyperboles, symbols, and many others—are "word pictures" that present literal truths in a picturesque way.

Since the Books of Daniel and Revelation are companion volumes, understanding one helps in understanding the other. Much of the preliminary revelation given in Daniel is more extensively developed in Revelation.

### Obscure Passages

Besides trying to interpret passages in their natural meanings, it is also important to observe the rule that obscure passages should be interpreted in light of passages that are clear. Fortunately most of the important items of the prophetic Word are stated plainly and clearly in some other place in Scripture, and this should serve as a guide to passages that are not clear.

## THE EXTENT OF BIBLICAL PROPHECY

I was once asked by a publisher to produce a book that would interpret all the prophecies of the Bible from Genesis to Revelation. This resulted in my book *The Prophecy Knowledge Handbook*, which discusses a thousand passages on prophecy, some of which are single verses and some of which are paragraphs or entire Bible chapters. The fact that half of those passages—approximately five hundred—have been fulfilled in the normal sense gives us intelligent reason for interpreting yet-to-be-fulfilled prophecies the same way. Interpreting prophecy in its natural or literal meaning yields a system of prophetic truth that is self-consistent and noncontradictory.

## THE PRACTICAL APPLICATION OF PROPHECY

Interpreters of prophecy should understand that prophecy is not an end in itself but has many applications to questions that naturally arise about the future. Accordingly, prophecy should be studied for its answers to these questions, such as whether the coming of Christ is imminent or whether Israel has a future in which she will possess her Promised Land. The relevance of prophecy to individual believers should be considered when presenting prophetic truth.

## MAJOR AREAS OF PROPHECY

The prophetic Word gives revelation in three broad areas: prophecies about the gentile world, prophecies about Israel, and prophecies about the church. What is ahead for Christians becomes vital information for anyone seeking to live consistently with what God has planned for his or her future. This is a major subject of revelation in the New Testament.

## Prophecies about World Events

Both the Old and New Testaments contain many prophecies that affect the world as a whole. Old Testament Scripture records six major world empires, Egypt, Assyria, Babylon, Medo-Persia, Greece, and Rome. This gives a prophetic outline of world events as God sees them and enables us to approach the question of what will happen to the world in the future. Many of these prophecies have already been fulfilled with remarkable accuracy.

## Prophecies about Israel

Another often-neglected area of prophecy is what God has revealed about Israel. Beginning with Abraham, God unfolded a program for Israel that involves His care for her throughout the Old Testament period as well as her future restoration and possession of her Promised Land. While this fact is not of immediate benefit to believers today, it is obviously a major portion of God's prophetic plans and gives insight on what is happening in Israel today and what will happen to Israel in the future.

## Prophecies about the Church

Two aspects of prophecy concerning the church are Christendom or the professing church, and the church, the body of Christ—that is, those who are true believers.

The capstone of prophecy for true believers is the doctrine of the Rapture, Christ's coming to take His church from earth to heaven. The Rapture will introduce for the true church the important events of heaven, which will be outlined later, such as her being joined to Christ in a symbolic marriage, her rewards at the judgment seat of Christ, and her challenging role of serving Christ throughout eternity. This will involve her being with Christ in heaven during the tribulation, being with Him on earth during the thousand-year millennial kingdom, and ultimately being in the new heavens, the new earth, and the New Jerusalem for all eternity.

When the Rapture of the church occurs, every true believer will be removed to heaven. All unbelievers, including those in the "professing church," will enter the time of tribulation. In chapter 3 the question of whether the Rapture occurs before the Tribulation or in connection with the Second Coming will be considered. It is important to note here that while the true church, the body of Christ, will be raptured before the Tribulation, the apostate or professing church will continue on the earth after the church is raptured and will persecute those who do come to Christ during the Tribulation. The professing church will be destroyed and will be replaced by the satanic religion of the end time, in which people will worship Satan and his world dictator.

This destruction of the professing church will occur in the middle of the last seven years leading up to the second coming of Christ, as described in Revelation 17:16–17: "The beast and the ten horns you saw will hate the prostitute. They will bring her to ruin and leave her naked; they will eat her flesh and burn her with fire. For God has put it into their hearts to accomplish his purpose by agreeing to give the beast their power to rule, until God's words are fulfilled." This will pave the way for the final form of satanic religion. For Christians, however, the great truths regarding the church, the body of Christ, occupy center stage in the study of prophecy.

## Prophecy about Angels

Along with these three major fields, some prophecies pertain to the devil and his angels, which usually relate to one of the three other major areas of prophecy. Though the Bible does not enlarge on the details of the judgment of fallen angels, 1 Corinthians 6:3 states that the church will judge angels: "Do you not know that we will judge angels?" Matthew 25:41 further reveals that the lake of fire is especially prepared for judgment of evil angels: "Then he will say to those on his left, 'Depart from Me, you who are cursed, into the eternal fire prepared for the devil and his angels.' " According to Revelation 20:10 the devil, after his final rebellion at the close of the millennial kingdom, will be cast into the lake of fire. "And the devil, who deceived them, was thrown into the lake of burning sulfur, where the beast and the false prophet had been thrown. They will be tormented day and night for ever and ever." It is probable that the wicked angels will also join him at that time in their final judgment. From then on there will be no demonic activity or satanic power. Today, according to Jude 6, some fallen angels are already bound, awaiting judgment since they fell in eternity past: "And the angels who did not keep their positions of authority but abandoned their own home—these he has kept in darkness, bound with everlasting chains for judgment on the great Day." It is important to recognize that in due time God will judge every evil work.

## Life after Death

The Bible gives clear revelation concerning the fact of life after death. Physical death does not terminate an individual's existence. This has significance for Christians, for it means that we will participate in the major events of God's future program. It is important for Christians to understand the scope of God's revelation and how this challenges us to prepare for God's plan for life after death.

The modern view that pictures man's existence as ending at death nullifies what the Bible teaches about the importance of serving the Lord in this life and preparing for the life to come. No one has sufficient reason to deny life after death; the Bible gives ample evidence that Jesus Christ was resurrected and is alive in heaven, and that everyone, believers and unbelievers alike, will have continued existence in the world to come.

## Major Facts about Prophecy Are Clear

Preachers and teachers of prophecy should try to make prophecy simple, understandable, and applicable to the hopes and fears of individuals. Even though prophecy is complicated in a number of its details, the main facts can still be presented in such a way that even a beginner in Bible study can understand what will confront him in the future according to God's prophetic Word.

## THE IMPORTANCE OF PROPHECY

The study of prophecy is not an end in itself; God intends for it to give us hope and guidance for the future. Just as a farmer cannot plow a straight course unless he keeps his eyes on a distant reference point, so we believers cannot plan adequately for the future unless we have some idea of what that future entails. In studying the Scriptures we discover that our lives will be reviewed and rewarded according to what we have done for Christ. Along with this, however, is the wonderful prospect of future joy and peace as recipients of God's grace throughout all eternity. This gives us hope in times of crisis, guidance in moral decisions, and a system of values consistent with what God has planned for the future.

Paul called the anticipation of the Lord's return "the blessed hope" (Titus 2:13), that is, it will be a joyful experience. While this hope should create a seriousness about the issues of life today, it can lift Christians above the sorrows, disappointments, and frustrations of this life and enable us to sense God's goal of presenting each believer faultless in His presence throughout eternity, as the objects of His wonderful grace.

# 3

# The Blessed Hope of the Lord's Return

---

THE CENTRAL THEME OF PROPHECY for believers today is the coming of Christ for His own in what is called the Rapture, or the "catching up" of the church. While many prophecies of the Old Testament do not directly concern us, the immediate question is, How can we be ready for the coming of the Lord today?

This and the next chapters consider the blessed hope of the Lord's return—what will happen immediately after the Rapture. Then with these facts before us we will consider how God has prepared the way for all this in the hundreds of other prophecies found in the Old and New Testaments.

The Rapture of the church is one of the most important practical prophecies in Scripture for believers today. It is an essential part of the many other prophecies in the Scriptures. Though the Rapture is only a small fraction of the large body of prophetic Scripture, it stands out as one of the most important. In this study of the Rapture a central question is whether Christ is coming soon.

## IS CHRIST COMING SOON?

If someone could state with certainty that Christ will come back to the earth to take believers out of the world one year from today, what effect would it have on us? Obviously it would change our whole perspective, and we would plan our lives accordingly.

If someone could state with certainty that Christ is coming one month from today, it would probably have an even more dramatic effect on us. We would concentrate almost entirely on things that would prepare us for the life to come. Actually the Scriptures present the prophecies of the coming of Christ as a *daily* expectation. We are waiting for it to happen at any moment; the Rapture is imminent—it could occur at any time.

Through the centuries some leaders have asserted that Christ would come on a certain date. In each case people who believed those leaders prepared extensively for the event—but, of course, the prediction was not fulfilled.

In the 1980s one Bible teacher thought he had proof that Christ would return on a certain day in September 1988. He sold two million copies of his book, listing eighty-eight reasons for his beliefs. Many Bible students felt he had convincing arguments in support of his prediction. Some people sold their houses and gave away their money. Some terminated their employment in order to spend all their time getting ready. Some of his followers even had their pets put to death because they did not want to leave them behind when the Lord came. However, the day came and went and nothing occurred.

The Scriptures do not give us specific information on the date of the Lord's return. This is wise, because by being aware that it could occur *any* day, we are encouraged to be ready *every* day. Unfortunately, although almost two thousand years have passed since the prophecy of the Rapture was given, many Christians do not know much about it because their churches do not teach it. Even among those who understand and believe the truth of the Rapture, some make little preparation for this dramatic event.

A practical approach is to have a plan of life that makes sense if Christ came today but also would make sense if He did not come for many years. This is what Paul did. On the one hand, he believed the Lord could come any time, and that is what he taught the Thessalonian church in 1 Thessalonians 4. On the other hand, he made plans for the future if the Lord did not come, and he carried out an extensive ministry of missionary work and Bible teaching. In his later years, however, Paul was told that he would die a martyr's death, and he knew that this, rather than the Rapture, was God's plan for him. In 2 Timothy 4:6, Paul wrote, "For I am already being poured out like a drink offering, and the time has come for my departure." He then described his fate in the coming judgment when God would reward him for his labors (4:8).

The first step a person should take to prepare for the Lord's coming is to receive Christ as his or her Savior from sin. Then as a child of God he or she will be with that company of the redeemed whom the Lord will take to heaven. Another step of preparation is to spend our lives in keeping with eternal values. Expecting the Lord's imminent return should affect what we do, what we think, and what we plan.

## THE COMING OF CHRIST IN THE OLD AND NEW TESTAMENTS

The Old Testament predicted the first coming of Christ and His sufferings, death, and resurrection. The Old Testament also includes predictions about the second coming of Christ, His return to reign over the entire earth in triumph over evil. These truths are found in many passages in the Old Testament. Isaiah 53 is one of the outstanding passages on the death of Christ, and His future kingdom reign is a frequent subject in the Book of Isaiah and in the Psalms. However, everyone in Old Testament times viewed these two aspects together; they did not separate the first and second comings or place a time period between them.

### Misunderstanding of Old Testament Prophecies

As mentioned earlier, Jewish rabbis in studying the Old Testament puzzled over the seeming contradiction of a Messiah who would suffer and die and a Messiah who would have a glorious reign. Peter mentioned this in 1 Peter 1:11, where he referred to the prophets as "trying to find out the time and circumstances to which the Spirit of Christ in them was pointing when he predicted the sufferings of Christ and the glories that would follow." Some Jewish leaders said the sufferings of "the servant" referred to the sufferings of the nation Israel. As far as we can ascertain, no one in Old Testament times or the Gospel period except Christ Himself understood there would be two comings, the first for His suffering and death, and a later coming for His glorious reign. They regarded the two events as occurring at the same time, and therefore they believed that when Christ came to earth He would bring in His glorious kingdom.

In following Christ sincerely, the disciples recognized Him as the Messiah and the Son of God, but they also thought He would deliver Israel from the oppression of Rome and exalt them as individuals in His kingdom. This was somewhat confirmed when Christ told them they would sit on thrones judging the twelve tribes of Israel (Matt. 19:28). The disciples did not understand, however, that this related to His second coming and not to His first.

### The Disciples' Failure to Understand Christ's Predictions of His Death

Even when Christ on several occasions predicted His death and resurrection, the disciples brushed it aside as impossible. And when He actually died, none of them remembered these predictions, and they were astounded when they were shown the evidence of His resurrection. By contrast, His enemies remembered that Christ had said He would be raised from the dead, so they set a guard over the tomb to prevent anyone from stealing His body and creating support for the idea of His resurrection. Only gradually did the disciples understand what happened; and they did not fully comprehend the distinction between Christ's first and second comings until after they saw Him ascend into heaven. Then it dawned on them that His sufferings and death were past, but His glorious reign would have to wait until He returned. They probably did not understand that it would be a long period of time, for Christ nowhere told them how long the interim would be between His first and second comings.

### The First Revelation of the Rapture

On His last night with the disciples before His crucifixion, however, Christ revealed for the first time that His purpose in coming back would be to take the disciples to be with Him in heaven (John 14:2–3). While many commentators try to find the coming of Christ for the church in passages in Matthew, Mark, and Luke, it simply is not there. Since the disciples did not understand the difference between the first and second comings, they certainly could not understand the difference between the coming of Christ at the Rapture and the Second Coming.

### The Rapture Distinct from the Second Coming

Though no one in Jesus' ministry on earth even understood the difference between His first and second comings, thousands of Christians today recognize the difference between the hope of the Rapture, when Christ will come for His own to take them to heaven, and the second coming of Christ, when He will come back to earth with the angels and saints from heaven to reign over the earth in His thousand-year kingdom. These entirely different events should not be confused. The Rapture is a movement from earth to heaven, whereas the Second Coming is a movement from heaven to earth with an entirely different purpose. It is obvious that the disciples did not understand the words of Christ as He announced for the first time that He will return for His own, as recorded in John 14:2–3: "In my Father's house are many rooms; if it were not so, I would have told you. I am going there to prepare a place for you. And if I go and prepare a place for you, I will come back and take you to be with me that you also may be where I am." Only later would further revelation be given to the disciples about this great event.

## REVELATION OF THE RAPTURE TO PAUL

The major passage on the Rapture is 1 Thessalonians 4:13–18. Years elapsed—perhaps two decades—between Christ's announcement in John 14 and this revelation given through Paul. In the course of God's dealings with the church Paul was saved on the road to Damascus and was subsequently given special revelation from God concerning the doctrines of grace, the church, the Rapture, and others. These doctrines were incorporated in his ministry and his epistles or letters to the churches.

Two major subjects dominated Paul's missionary messages as he went from place to place and established churches, including a church in Thessalonica. First, he preached that Christ died on the cross for our sins and rose again and that individuals can be saved only by trusting in Him as their Savior. He then announced, even to young Christians, that this same Jesus who came once is coming again. When He comes, He will take believers out of the world and take them to heaven. This is uniformly presented in the Bible as an immediate event, and no passage in the Bible predicts that any event need be fulfilled before the Rapture. Thus believers in Thessalonica who heard his message were looking each day for the return of Christ. This is the background of the Thessalonian passage.

According to Acts 17:1–9 Paul encountered opposition while preaching in the synagogue at Thessalonica and was forced to leave after only a few weeks of ministry. He left behind a small band of believers who had the wonderful joy of salvation as well as the hope of Christ's return. They were under terrible persecution, however, and because Paul could not go back to Thessalonica he sent Timothy to see how they were getting along (1 Thess. 2:17–3:5). Timothy visited them, encouraged them, and then reported back to Paul. He told the apostle that the Thessalonians were standing firm in spite of persecution (3:6–9) and were looking for the Lord's return. But they had a number of theological questions; this was understandable in view of the short time they were under Paul's instruction. One of these questions was occasioned by the fact that some of their number had died since Paul had left.

### Death in Relation to the Rapture

Death immediately confronts us with the questions of whether there is life after death and whether believers will see their loved ones again. In Thessalonica some of the believers had died after Paul left there. This led the living Christians to wonder if they would have to wait for some future time in God's program for those dead loved ones to be resurrected. We do not know exactly what they had in mind, but possibly they understood the difference between the Rapture and the Second Coming and thought that the resurrection of their dead loved ones would not take place until the Second Coming. Timothy could not clarify this problem, and so he brought it back to Paul, along with other theological questions.

In writing 1 Thessalonians Paul was overjoyed that the Thessalonians were standing true to the faith, and he wrote to answer some of their questions and to reinforce them in their Christian living. Of interest is the fact that each of the five chapters of 1 Thessalonians includes a reference to the Rapture.

In 1 Thessalonians 1:10 Paul described believers as those who "wait for his Son from heaven, whom he raised from the dead—Jesus, who rescues us from the coming wrath." In verses 3, 5, 8–9 the apostle had spoken of their Christian walk of faith, beginning with salvation and continuing until the Lord's return.

In 1 Thessalonians 2:19 he asked, "For what is our hope, our joy, or the crown in which we will glory in the presence of our Lord Jesus when he comes? Is it not you?" Paul said that at the Rapture he will rejoice because the Thessalonians will be rising to meet the Lord.

In 1 Thessalonians 3:13 Paul prayed, "May he strengthen your hearts so that you will be blameless and holy in the presence of our God and Father when our Lord Jesus comes with all his holy ones." He was concerned that when Jesus returns He would find these believers blameless before others and holy toward God. Some say Jesus' "holy ones" are angels, but they may be the souls of saints who died and are now with Jesus, and whose bodies will be resurrected when He comes (4:16).

After discussing the Rapture and its details in 4:13–18, Paul said in 5:1–10 that Christians are "sons of the day," looking for the coming of Christ, in contrast to the world, which after the Rapture will be left in the "night" of the Tribulation. In 5:23 he prayed, "May God himself, the God of peace, sanctify you through and through. May your whole spirit, soul and body be kept blameless at the coming of our Lord Jesus Christ." It is most significant that in dealing with young Christians, Paul's message on the Rapture was prominent and was an essential part of what he taught them.

Regarding their particular question, Paul gave them a chronological account of what will happen at the time of the Rapture, a truth that is found in detail only here in the Bible. He assured them that they would not have to wait for their dead loved ones to be resurrected later. He said their loved ones will be resurrected moments before they themselves are caught up with the Lord.

## Prophecy Is Intended to Give Hope

In writing about the Rapture Paul addressed his readers as "brothers": "Brothers, we do not want you to be ignorant about those who fall asleep, or to grieve like the rest of men, who have no hope" (1 Thess. 4:13). A person becomes a Christian because he believes in the first coming of Christ and His death and resurrection, but he may not necessarily be informed about the Rapture. Thousands of Christians will be raptured who have never been instructed in this doctrine of Christ's coming for them. Paul, however, wrote here that it is not God's plan for them to be ignorant or uninformed. God wants us to know the future, and that is the secret behind all of the prophetic Word. While some prophecies may be obscure and not every question answered, the main points are clear: God wants us to know we have a glorious future ahead.

## The Rapture in Relation to Sorrow

One of the main reasons for Paul's teaching on the Rapture is that he did not want Christians to sorrow as the world does without any hope (1 Thess. 4:13). The Bible is absolutely clear that unless a person is saved by Christ, he or she is living without God and without hope no matter how religious and moral he or she may be. But those who believe in Christ have the wonderful hope that they will see their believing loved ones again and will be restored to them forever in the world to come.

## The Certainty of the Rapture

In verse 14 Paul declared the certainty of the Rapture and what will be a major aspect of it. "We believe that Jesus died and rose again and so we believe that God will bring with Jesus those who have fallen asleep in him."

Before Jesus' first coming His death and resurrection were a matter of prophecy. But now they are historical facts. They are absolutely certain, and they comprise the heart of the gospel. The Thessalonians believed that Christ had died and rose again. Now Paul was saying to them that the truth that Jesus is coming again—though a future event—is just as certain as His past death and resurrection. One is as sure as the other.

### The Resurrection of Believers

When a Christian dies, a medical doctor may examine the body and declare the person dead. Physical life has departed. But when a believer dies, his soul leaves his body; he is "away from the body" but "at home with the Lord" (2 Cor. 5:8). His soul goes immediately to heaven where he is in the presence of Christ, rejoicing in the wonder of his salvation. While his body is placed in a casket, his soul is not there but is in heaven.

At the Rapture, when Christ comes back, God will bring with Him those who have died so that their souls can reenter their resurrection bodies. It is important to observe that Christ will come bodily. In His deity Christ is omnipresent, that is, present everywhere. That is how He can indwell every believer and can assure us He will never leave us or forsake us (Matt. 28:20; Heb. 13:5). But bodily He is in only one place at a time. Today He is bodily at the right hand of the Father interceding as our High Priest (Rom. 8:34). At the Rapture Christ will leave His position in heaven and come back to the air above the earth to participate in the Rapture.

The exact order of events in the Rapture is recorded in 1 Thessalonians 4:15–18. "According to the Lord's own word, we tell you that we who are still alive, who are left till the coming of the Lord, will certainly not precede those who have fallen asleep. For the Lord himself will come down from heaven, with a loud command, with the voice of the archangel and with the trumpet call of God, and the dead in Christ will rise first. After that, we who are still alive and are left will be caught up together with them in the clouds to meet the Lord in the air. And so we will be with the Lord forever. Therefore encourage each other with these words."

In using the phrase "by the word of the Lord" (literal translation), to introduce these verses, Paul was saying that the Lord gave this truth to him by direct revelation. He did not quote the Old Testament because this doctrine was not taught in the Old Testament. He asserted that Christians who are alive at the time of the Lord's return will not precede those who have died. These dead believers are said to "have fallen asleep in Him" (4:14) or to "have fallen asleep" (4:15). This does not suggest an unconscious existence after death, often called "soul sleep." Instead, this is "body sleep," for a corpse looks as if the person is sleeping (see Matt. 9:24; John 11:11; 1 Cor. 15:51). These same ones are said to be "the dead in Christ" (1 Thess. 4:16), those who "have fallen asleep in Christ" (1 Cor. 15:18). The souls of dead believers are with Him in heaven. The bodies of those who have died will be resurrected and united with their souls, which have been in heaven from the time of their death. The resurrection at the Rapture is part of the series of resurrections that began with the resurrection of Christ and will conclude with the resurrection of the wicked after the Millennium (see chap. 12, "The Order of Resurrections").

### The Transformation at the Rapture

At the Rapture "the Lord Himself will come" (1 Thess. 4:16). He will not send someone else to take us to Himself. He will come bodily, visibly, physically, and in the clouds, just as the apostles saw Him ascend to heaven. "This same Jesus," two angels told them, "will come back in the same way" He left for heaven (Acts 1:11). Though this verse refers to the Second Coming, not the Rapture, it does support the physical nature of Christ's coming.

When the Lord returns at the Rapture, He will issue a shout, that is, a command (1 Thess. 4:16). He will command Christians all over the world who have died to be instantly resurrected, their souls reentering their bodies. "The dead in Christ will rise first." Then immediately after that, in a split second, He will command every living Christian to be instantly changed. Together, living and resurrected believers will rise from the earth and meet the Lord in the air.

Added revelation of this tremendous event was given later to Paul in 1 Corinthians. After a long discussion on the subject of the resurrection in 1 Corinthians 15, Paul declared in verses 51–53 the grand exception to the normal sequence of death and resurrection. "Listen, I tell you a mystery: We will not all sleep, but we will all be changed—in a flash, in the twinkling of an eye, at the last trumpet. For the trumpet will sound, the dead will be raised imperishable, and we will be changed. For the perishable must clothe itself with the imperishable, and the mortal with immortality."

When the Lord comes for Christians who have died, they will be instantly changed, receiving resurrection bodies patterned after His resurrection body. Living Christians on the earth will experience an immediate transformation from their present bodies to bodies suited for heaven. As "imperishable" bodies, they will not be subject to decay and age. And mortality will be exchanged for immortality, so that they cannot die. According to 1 John 3:2, when the Lord comes, believers "shall be like him, for we shall see him as he is." In other words, our sin nature and all tendency to sin will be removed forever, and we will be as perfect in our spiritual state as our position in Christ is perfect now. While we are declared righteous in the act of justification, obviously Christians in this life still fail and tend to sin. This failure would not be suitable for those who live in the light of God's presence in heaven, and so there will be an instantaneous change. He "will transform our lowly body [lit., 'our body of humiliation'] that it may be conformed to His glorious body" (Phil. 3:21, NKJV).

The resurrection of believers is a resurrection from among the dead (Phil. 3:11). Old Testament saints and all the unsaved will be resurrected later at different times (see chap. 12, "The Order of Resurrections"). Eventually everyone will be resurrected in the order revealed in Scripture.

### The Voice of Michael

Accompanying the loud command of Christ will be the voice of the archangel Michael, the head of all the holy angels (Dan. 12:1; Jude 9). Michael has been engaged in ceaseless warfare with the devil and the demon world as they have sought to spoil Christians, to keep people from being saved, and to defeat God's purposes. Now here, in spite of what Satan has done, Michael is entitled to rejoice in the triumph of the church now made perfect and going to heaven. Michael is later mentioned in Revelation 12:7–9 as fighting with the devil and the demon world (Satan's "angels"); in the middle of the seven-year period preceding the Second Coming he will cast them out of heaven. At the present time Satan is allowed to enter heaven and criticize the saints as he did Job (Job 1:6–12; 2:1–7). He is "the accuser" of believers (Rev. 12:10). The battle between Michael and the satanic world demonstrates the power of God working through Michael, who has participated in the battle with the unseen powers mentioned in Ephesians 6:12: "For our struggle is not against flesh and blood, but against the rulers, against the authorities, against the powers of this dark world and against the spiritual forces of evil in the heavenly realms." The triumph of the Rapture is a triumph for Michael as well.

### The Trumpet of God

The Lord's return will be signaled by what is called "the trumpet call of God." This is also called "the last trumpet" (1 Cor. 15:52). This reference to the last trumpet confuses some people because they try to link it with the seven trumpet judgments in the Book of Revelation. In Bible times trumpets were blown as a signaling device. In Israel a trumpet sounded when the nation began its marches in the wilderness. Another trumpet sounded when they stopped marching. Each series would have a first trumpet and a last trumpet. But the last trumpet for one event would not be the last trumpet for another. So here, the last trumpet of the church is not the last trumpet ever to be sounded in history, because seven trumpets blown by angels will signal great catastrophes God will pour out in judgment on the earth (Rev. 8:6–9:21; 11:15–19). Later the "loud trumpet call" in Matthew 24:31 will signal the gathering of all the saints to enter the millennial kingdom.

While the trumpet that will be sounded at the Rapture will be the last trumpet the church will hear, it is not the last trumpet ever to be blown. The Rapture trumpet will call all Christians to rise from the earth to meet the Lord in the air and from there they will go to heaven, as Christ promised in John 14:3. The last trumpet for the church may be analogous to the last trumpet used in the Roman army. Soldiers were awakened by a first trumpet blast early in the morning, which served as their alarm clock. A second trumpet assembled them for instructions for the day. At the third and last trumpet they marched off to their assignments.

Similarly, receiving salvation is like hearing a trumpet call. Then God's call to service is like hearing a second trumpet. And at the third or last trumpet believers will go to heaven. And wherever Christ is, whether in heaven or on earth, or in the new earth or the new Jerusalem, believers will be with Him forever. Paul captured this in his statement, "And so we will be with the Lord forever" (1 Thess. 4:17).

Some say these three sounds at the time of the Rapture—Jesus' loud command, the archangel's voice, and the Lord's trumpet call—refer to one sound, as if the verse read, "Jesus' command that will sound like the archangel blowing a trumpet." However, the Greek construction of verse 16 most likely points to three separate sounds.

## THE MEANING OF THE RAPTURE

Some have asserted that the Rapture is not a biblical doctrine because, they argue, the word *Rapture* is not mentioned in the English Bible. However, the word *Rapture* comes from the words "caught up" in 1 Thessalonians 4:17. This verse could be translated, "Then we who are alive and remain shall be *raptured* together with them in the clouds." The important point is that the verse says Christ will come for believers and take them from the earth to heaven, where they will be in His presence till they return with Him to the earth to reign. The Rapture will mean that all believers "will be with the Lord forever," enjoying Him and His presence for all eternity. As Paul wrote to the Colossians, "When Christ, who is your life, appears, then you also will appear with him in glory" (Col. 3:4). This will be in answer to the Lord's prayer in John 17:24, "Father, I want those you have given me to be with me where I am, and to see my glory."

## THE IMMINENCE OF THE RAPTURE

Throughout this discussion of the Rapture and related prophetic subjects it has been stated that the Rapture is an imminent event, that is, that it could occur any day as far as our knowledge of this is concerned. This is intrinsic in the basic revelation of 1 Thessalonians 4:13–18, where it is clear that the Thessalonian believers, on the basis of Paul's revelation, were expecting the Rapture at any time. This is part of the problem they had in facing the deaths of some of their fellow believers; their deaths had raised the question of when the dead would be resurrected if the living church was already raptured.

Because many Bible interpreters throughout church history have questioned the imminence of the Rapture one way or another, it is important to summarize the evidence that will be supported in part by later chapters on the resurrections and the judgments (chaps. 12 and 13), and the doctrine of the Second Coming itself.

It is important to note what is often obscured in the Old Testament. As noted earlier in this chapter, two major aspects of the Messiah's coming were predicted: one was His sufferings and death and the other was His glorious reign. To many, these seemingly contradicted each other. As mentioned previously, it is amazing that in the Old Testament and the Gospel period no one other than Christ Himself understood that He would become incarnate and would suffer, die, and be raised from the dead, and that a time period of considerable length would exist between this first coming and His second coming when He will come back to reign. None of the Scripture writers seem to have comprehended this, though when they wrote Scripture they were guided by the Holy Spirit to such an extent that they never denied this. Part of the problem was that the first and second comings were often stated in the same passage as if there were no time period between them, as in Isaiah 61:1–2, which Christ quoted in the synagogue at Nazareth. In His quotation, however, He read the first part dealing with His first coming but stopped before He got to the phrase "the day of vengeance of our God" in verse 2, which relates to His second coming. Why did this universal misunderstanding of the first and second comings of Christ exist?

There are two fundamental reasons. First, many people tended not to take the prophecies literally, and in fact the Jews apparently thought the sufferings of "the servant" were the sufferings of the nation Israel instead of the individual Savior. Second, many did not pay attention to the details of the prophecy. Obviously if the Messiah came and suffered, died, and rose again, that is totally different from the Messiah coming to reign gloriously as King of kings and Lord of lords. First Peter 1:10–11 records the difficulty Old Testament interpreters had in understanding these dual predictions of Christ. As a result, the Jewish nation, including the twelve disciples, expected that when the Messiah came He would deliver them from Roman rule, which seems to be promised in Isaiah 61:2b. Not aware that this verse was related to His second coming, not His first coming, the disciples followed Christ under this misguided conclusion.

The confusion on the two advents or comings of Christ in the Old Testament casts significant light on the problem of whether the second coming of Christ and the Rapture of the church will occur at the same time. These two events are confused for the same reason there was confusion on the first and second comings. In the history of the church probably most Christians have not distinguished the two events but have believed the Rapture was simply a part of the Second Coming. In arriving at this conclusion, they have made the same mistake as the interpreters in the Old Testament in not paying attention to the details and not interpreting the prophecy as literal revelation. In contrast, however, today many interpreters of the Bible are aware of the difference between the Rapture, in which the church will be taken from the earth to heaven, and the Second Coming, when Christ will return to earth with all the saints. They are convinced that the two events cannot be the same and are never presented that way in the New Testament.

For Bible students who come to grips with this problem, there is a confusing array of contradictory interpretations to choose from. The popular view (inherited from the school of theology at Alexandria, Egypt, in the third century), namely, that prophecy cannot be interpreted literally, has derailed most of the church in her understanding of the distinction between the Rapture and the Second Coming. The idea that there are still two future comings is often ridiculed even though in the Old Testament, as we have seen, there was a prediction of two comings, though in a different context.

The problem of proving that the Rapture is an imminent event is complex enough to call for special volumes on this theme. One is my book *The Rapture Question* (rev. ed.; Grand Rapids: Zondervan, 1979), which consists of three hundred pages of discussion on various major views on when the Rapture will occur. Other significant volumes have contributed to this discussion as well, such as *Things to Come,* by J. Dwight Pentecost (Grand Rapids: Zondervan, 1958), which deals with the whole subject of prophecy. *Kept from the Hour,* by Gerald B. Stanton (4th ed.; Miami Springs, Fla.: Schoettle, 1991), contains another incisive discussion in its more than four hundred pages. Tim LaHaye has published *No Fear of the Storm* (Sisters, Oreg.: Multnomah, 1992), another solid and significant work and *Come Quickly, Lord Jesus,* by Charles C. Ryrie (Eugene, Oreg.: Harvest, 1996), is another excellent book on the Rapture. Those vitally interested in this issue would do well to study these and other books on the subject. To summarize this doctrine is an exceedingly difficult task but at least certain facts should be mentioned.

Many hold to the *pretribulational* view, the doctrine that the Rapture will occur before the prophesied end-time Tribulation. Probably the most popular view is the *posttribulational* view, which says that the Rapture and the Second Coming will occur at the same time. A compromise is the *midtribulational* view, which holds that the Rapture will occur in the middle of the last seven years preceding the Second Coming. A view held by comparatively few is the *partial-Rapture* position, the view that the Rapture will include only those spiritually prepared and that others will be raptured later. A recent view is the *pre-wrath Rapture* view, which says the Rapture will occur toward the end of the Great Tribulation, based on the idea that there is allegedly no wrath mentioned in the Book of Revelation before the bowl judgments in chapter 16.

The fact that there are so many views held by godly people, often competent scholars, is confusing to many students of prophecy. And yet the fact remains that these views are contradictory and are either true or false. It is possible to approach this subject from a theological view, as I do in many of the chapters in my book *The Rapture Question.* Another approach is to go through the New Testament asking the question, "Is there any passage that teaches the posttribulational rapture?" This was attempted in the latter chapters of *The Rapture Question.*

Before World War II the common position of posttribulationists was that the Great Tribulation refers to the troubles the church has experienced since the first century and is largely past; in other words, the Tribulation is not a distinct period of a limited number of years. This is contradicted, however, by the express statements of Scripture that the Great Tribulation is a specific time of three and a-half years without parallel in world history. That "will be a time of distress such as has not happened from the beginning of nations until then" (Dan. 12:1). Jesus made a similar statement that the Great Tribulation will be "a great distress unequaled from the beginning of the world" (Matt. 24:21). The destruction of much of the human race as described in Revelation, the destruction of gentile civilization, and the massive disruptions of nature have never occurred, so these predictions have not been fulfilled.

Posttribulationists, generally speaking, dismiss the whole idea of pretribulationism. But after World War II, when atomic weapons with their destructive power were developed, many posttribulationists took a 180-degree turn and began to admit that there will be a specific time of trouble immediately before the Second Coming. This, however, introduced new problems for them.

According to Paul's first epistle to the Thessalonians, the time of God's wrath is not part of God's plan for Christians. According to 1 Thessalonians 1:9, "Jesus . . . rescues us from the coming wrath," and in 1 Thessalonians 5:9, Paul wrote, "for God did not appoint us to suffer wrath but to receive salvation through our Lord Jesus Christ."

Most significant, however, are the graphic prophecies given in the Book of Revelation, which picture the Great Tribulation as a time of wrath. The word *wrath* appears many times in Revelation in relation to end-time events.[1] The Second Coming itself will express "the fury of the wrath of God Almighty" (19:15). All these statements of wrath tend to be ignored by the posttribulationists, and to some extent their neglect of these passages is shared by the pre-wrath view that the Tribulation will not start until the bowl judgments of Revelation 16.

Posttribulationists answer that God is able to protect Christians and carry them through this time unscathed. No one disputes the fact that God has the power to do this, as the 144,000 Israelites will be protected by God in the Great Tribulation (7:1–8). However, this chapter then states that great numbers of believers from every nation, tribe, people group, and language will be martyred in the Great Tribulation (7:9–17). The number of martyrs will be "a great multitude that no one could count" (7:9). This passage is almost totally neglected by posttribulationists because it directly contradicts their position. While God can protect, many times He does not do so but allows countless numbers of people to be martyred.

When Satan will be cast out of heaven, he will be "filled with fury" (Rev. 12:12), and as "the dragon," he will be "enraged" against Israel (12:17). Revelation 20:4 indicates that many who reject the rule of the world ruler will be beheaded. To sum up, the possibility of believers surviving the Great Tribulation is actually less than that of nonbelievers, as they will be subject not only to all the catastrophic judgments but also to the persecution of the world ruler.

In tracing the doctrine of the Rapture through Scripture it is most important to note that there is no evidence whatever for a posttribulational Rapture. Posttribulationists argue that the Rapture is referred to in Matthew 24. But when pressed for a particular verse they come up empty-handed because the Rapture, including both a resurrection and a translation, is never mentioned. Matthew 24:40–41, which refers to one being taken and the other left, is just the reverse of the Rapture, because in these verses the one taken will be put to death while the one who is not taken will enter the millennial kingdom saved and thus worthy to enter that age. This is confirmed by Luke 17:34–36, which says the one taken will be eaten by the vultures. Posttribulationists also usually neglect John 14:1–4, in which Christ specifically said He is coming back to take the disciples to heaven. This is a prediction of the Rapture, not of the Second Coming. Nor does it refer to death, as some have held. Jesus' words about His return were totally new to the disciples, who did not understand them at the time.

First Thessalonians 4:13–18 is in many respects the bulwark and center of the whole doctrine of the Rapture. Significantly, posttribulationists do not pay much attention to this passage because it gives no indication whatever that the Rapture will follow the Great Tribulation. Instead the Thessalonians were anticipating the Rapture at any time.

In 1 Thessalonians 5, immediately after the Rapture passage, Paul wrote that the Day of the Lord will follow the Rapture. The Day of the Lord is identified in the Old Testament as the period of time that includes the end-time Tribulation. (For a discussion of the Day of the Lord, see chapter 11.) The Day of the Lord is a day of "darkness" (1 Thess. 5:4), but believers "belong to the day" (5:8), that is, the light.

This is confirmed in 2 Thessalonians 2. The Thessalonians were contending with the false doctrine that they were already in the Day of the

Lord. This alarmed them because Paul had taught them they would be raptured before the Day of the Lord would occur. So they wondered if they had missed the Rapture.

Paul gave them two arguments to show that they were wrong to conclude this. First, he pointed out that the man of lawlessness had not been revealed (2 Thess. 2:3). Since he will not be revealed before the Rapture, the Rapture had not yet occurred. This man of lawlessness, also referred to as "a man of sin" (NKJV), is the leading character of the end times, the Antichrist, the world ruler. He will be revealed in the sequence of important prophetic events that occur at the end time in the Tribulation, including the revival of the Roman Empire, his conquering ten countries, and then his making a covenant with Israel that will supposedly bring peace to the Middle East for seven years (Dan. 9:27). He obviously will be identifiable once he conquers ten countries, which will occur at least seven years before the second coming of Christ. If the Rapture were to occur in the middle, second half, or end of the seven-year period before the Second Coming, then it would occur after the Antichrist is revealed. And that would contradict 2 Thessalonians 2. So we can see that all views of the Rapture are automatically eliminated except the pretribulational view.

Second, Paul called attention to the fact that the one who was restraining sin had not been taken away; he was presently holding back evil in the world (2:6–7). There has been much dispute on the identity of this "restrainer"; views include the gospel, the Roman Empire, human government, Satan, and others. But the only power that really holds back evil is the Holy Spirit, and the presence of the Holy Spirit in the church is God's present method of reaching the world with truth and righteousness. The fact that the Holy Spirit has not been taken out of the church is evidence that the Day of the Lord has not begun. His removal, however, will mean that the Holy Spirit will be with believers but not in them (John 14:17). The Holy Spirit, who indwells the church, could not be removed unless the church itself is taken out. In other words, the Rapture will have to occur first. While some dispute these conclusions, taking the passage in its ordinary meaning points clearly to the Rapture occurring before the Day of the Lord. Thus these are solid proofs that the Rapture will occur before the seven-year period preceding the Second Coming.

This is further confirmed by the Book of Revelation, which nowhere associates the Rapture of the church with the Second Coming. Only one of the several resurrections in Scripture (discussed in chap. 12, "The Order of Resurrections") mentions dead believers in the church being resurrected. And no Rapture of living believers is mentioned except the Rapture of the church.

This is consistent with Matthew 25:31–46, which refers to sheep and goats, representing the saved and unsaved, still being mingled some time after the Second Coming. This would not be true if the Rapture had occurred at the Second Coming and the saved had been taken out. The same is true in Revelation 20:4–6, describing the resurrection of the martyred dead of the Tribulation, which also will take place several days after the Second Coming. If the Rapture had taken place these would have already been resurrected, and the fact that they had not been raised shows that the Rapture will not occur at the Second Coming.

While arguments can be greatly extended, as they are in various works on this subject, the fact is there is no scriptural evidence for a post-tribulational Rapture. All evidence in the Scriptures points to the conclusion that the Rapture will come before the final outbreak of trouble described in familiar terms as "the Tribulation," referring to the whole period of seven years. The belief that the Rapture is imminent, even though it has already been delayed for almost two thousand years, continues to be the hope of the church today. Obviously whatever date God has set for this future event, each day brings us closer to it. Other evidence can be added to show that not only is the Rapture possible but also that the world stage is being set for the events that will follow the Rapture. This is another indication that the Rapture may take place soon.

## THE APPLICATION OF THE RAPTURE FOR CHRISTIANS

In 1 Thessalonians 4:18 Paul exhorted Christians to "encourage each other with these words," that is, with the facts pertaining to the Rapture. Besides being an important theological and biblical truth, the Lord's return for His church has tremendous practical applications.

*The Important Question of Salvation*

The fact that Christ will return for His own underscores the need for each person to be sure he or she is saved. Only those who are "in Christ" (1 Thess. 4:16) will be caught up in the Rapture. All unbelievers will be left on earth. Everyone who is "in Christ" has been baptized into (or "placed into") the body of Christ, the church, by the Holy Spirit at the moment of salvation. "For we were all baptized by one Spirit into one body—whether Jews or Greeks, slave or free—and we were all given the one Spirit to drink" (1 Cor. 12:13). Beginning at Pentecost, this is something that takes place for for each of us at the moment of salvation. It is a matter of our position spiritually: It speaks of our relationship to Christ as a member of His church, His body of believers. Unfortunately a person may have religion, morality, culture, education, or refinement, and still be lost. If we are saved, however, we are in Christ. The baptism of the Holy Spirit marks those who are to be raptured. (Since this includes those who were saved from the Day of Pentecost to the time of the Rapture itself, it probably excludes Old Testament saints, who will be raised later.)

The outstanding illustration of the necessity of the new birth is the story of Nicodemus. Nicodemus was apparently a pious individual, one of the rulers of the Jews. As a faithful Jew, he attended the synagogue every Sabbath, tithed, brought offerings, and sought to observe the moral rules of the Jewish faith. But he was troubled because some of his peers said that Christ was performing miracles by the power of Satan. This did not make sense to Nicodemus because he did not see how these miraculous works could be accomplished by an evil person dominated by Satan. As he said to Jesus, "For no one could perform the miraculous signs you are doing if God were not with him" (John 3:2).

In seeking an answer to this question, he came to Christ at night— probably because he wanted to avoid being seen in His presence in the daytime. Christ abruptly told him, "I tell you the truth, no one can see the kingdom of God unless he is born again" (3:3). This astounded Nicodemus, for he could not comprehend how a person could be born twice (3:4). Later, though, he apparently came to trust in Christ as his Savior, for he helped Joseph of Arimathea bury Jesus' body (19:39). (Also, he came to Jesus' defense one of the times when Jesus was accused by the Jews in 7:50–51).

When a Christian is born again, he receives eternal life. While undoubtedly Old Testament saints were born again and received eternal life, they were not baptized into the church, the body of Christ, and they were not necessarily indwelt by the Holy Spirit, because these divine works—the Spirit's baptizing and indwelling—began on the Day of Pentecost. Nicodemus, however, should have understood, even on the basis of the Old Testament, that to receive eternal life a person must be born again (Ezek. 36:26–27).

### The Question of Christian Commitment

The Rapture not only confronts individuals with the challenge to receive Christ before it is too late; it also challenges Christians to live with eternal values in view. Since the Rapture can occur at any moment, and believers' lives on earth will thus be cut short, we need to maximize our commitment to Christ, doing all we can for the Lord in upright living and service to Him and others.

The Rapture is important both theologically and practically. Those who understand and believe this great truth will be energized and transformed by the expectation of Christ's glorious return. While many prophetic truths are of great importance, the Rapture is the most important for believers in Christ.

# 4
# Our
# Resurrection Body

---

**W**HEN THE LORD COMES at the Rapture, all church-age believers will be introduced to new experiences far different from the present life. As noted previously, each believer will receive a resurrection body, a body without sin, aging, or death.

## THE RESURRECTION OF BELIEVERS MAY BE SOON

At the Rapture those who have already died and whose souls are in heaven ("the dead in Christ," 1 Thess. 4:16) will return with Christ and will be given resurrection bodies instantaneously. Then immediately after those graves are opened, believers "who are still alive" (4:15) will be suddenly relieved of the infirmities and difficulties suffered in this world. As they are caught up to be with the Lord, each will receive a radiant new body.

Our present bodies are not suitable for heaven; they need a dramatic change. As Paul wrote in 1 Corinthians 15:50, "I declare to you, brothers, that flesh and blood cannot inherit the kingdom of God, nor does the perishable inherit the imperishable." The doctrine of our future physical resurrection rests on the certainty of the resurrection of Christ. If Christ were not raised, our whole Christian faith would collapse and the future would become unknown (15:14–19).

Christ's resurrection—a historical fact—opens the way for those who believe in Him to receive resurrection bodies. Paul said the death and resurrection of Christians is like planting a seed in the ground. The seed dies, but as a result it produces a plant. "But someone may ask, 'How are the dead raised? With what kind of body will they come?' How foolish! What you sow does not come to life unless it dies. When you sow, you do not plant the body that will be, but just a seed, perhaps of wheat or of something else. But God gives it a body as he has determined, and to each kind of seed he gives its own body" (15:35–38).

Similarly, when Christians die our bodies decay, but in the resurrection we will be given new bodies. Paul put it this way: "So will it be with the resurrection of the dead. The body that is sown is perishable, it is raised imperishable; it is sown in dishonor, it is raised in glory; it is sown in weakness, it is raised in power; it is sown a natural body, it is raised a spiritual body. If there is a natural body, there is also a spiritual body" (15:42–44). The new, resurrected body is spiritual not because it is immaterial but because it is suited for spiritual worship and service of God.

With this as a background, however, Paul revealed a grand exception to the normal rule of death and resurrection. Since our present bodies are not suited for eternity, the transformation of living saints at the time of the Rapture will come not from death and resurrection but from what may be called "translation," an instant change in our bodies: "Listen, I tell you a mystery: We will not all sleep, but we will all be changed—in a flash, in the twinkling of an eye, at the last trumpet. For the trumpet will sound, the dead will be raised imperishable, and we will be changed. For the perishable must clothe itself with the imperishable, and the mortal with immortality. When the perishable has been clothed with the imperishable, and the mortal with immortality, then the saying that is written will come true: 'Death has been swallowed up in victory.'" (1 Cor. 15:51–54).

One way to help understand the doctrine of our future resurrection is to study facts about Jesus' resurrection body as it is portrayed in the Gospels and Acts, along with later comments elsewhere in Scripture.

## THE RESURRECTION OF CHRIST

When Christ died, His body was prepared for burial by winding strips of cloth saturated with ointment around it, as described in Luke 23:53. "Then he [Joseph of Arimathea] took it down, wrapped it in linen cloth and placed it in a tomb cut in the rock, one in which no one had yet been laid" (see Matt. 27:59–60; Mark 15:46). John wrote that Nicodemus, who had interviewed Christ (John 3:1–21), brought a mixture of myrrh and aloes. "He was accompanied by Nicodemus, the man who earlier had visited Jesus at night. Nicodemus brought a mixture of myrrh and aloes, about seventy-five pounds. Taking Jesus' body, the two of them wrapped it, with the spices, in strips of linen. This was in accordance with Jewish burial customs" (19:39–40).

The Scriptures do not record the actual time of Jesus' resurrection, but possibly He left the tomb shortly after sundown on Saturday, which was the beginning of the first day of the week according to Jewish reckoning. The walls of the tomb could not confine Christ in His resurrection body.

Sunday morning, however, several women, including Mary Magdalene, went to the tomb carrying additional spices, hoping to apply them to Jesus' body though they were aware that the tomb was closed. To their surprise, when they arrived at the tomb the stone was rolled away. Soldiers stationed there to guard the tomb had seen an angel of the Lord roll back the stone. "There was a violent earthquake, for an angel of the Lord came down from heaven and, going to the tomb, rolled back the stone and sat on it. His appearance was like lightning, and his clothes were white as snow. The guards were so afraid of him that they shook and became like dead men" (Matt. 28:2–4).

The guards fled in terror. When they reported this occurrence to the chief priests, they were bribed to say that Jesus' disciples stole the body while they slept (28:11–15). (This also saved the soldiers from execution for having failed to guard the body in the tomb.)

The angel standing by the tomb informed the women that Christ had risen. "The angel said to the women, 'Do not be afraid, for I know that you are looking for Jesus, who was crucified. He is not here; he has risen, just as he said. Come and see the place where he lay. Then go quickly and tell his disciples: "He has risen from the dead and is going ahead of you into Galilee. There you will see him." Now I have told you.' So the women hurried away from the tomb, afraid yet filled with joy, and ran to tell his disciples" (Matt. 28:5–8).

As the account of that resurrection unfolds in the four Gospels, it seems that the women, though they were told He was risen from the dead, did not fully comprehend what was said. Mary Magdalene went back a second time to the tomb, thinking that someone had stolen the body of Jesus. According to Luke 24:11–12, the disciples did not believe the women's report: "But they did not believe the women, because their words seemed to them like nonsense. Peter, however, got up and ran to the tomb. Bending over, he saw the strips of linen lying by themselves, and he went away, wondering to himself what had happened."

Meanwhile Mary and the other women went to the tomb a second time, and the Scriptures record that Mary was weeping. "But Mary stood outside the tomb crying. As she wept, she bent over to look into the tomb and saw two angels in white, seated where Jesus' body had been, one at the head and the other at the foot. They asked her, 'Woman, why are you crying?' 'They have taken my Lord away,' she said, 'and I don't know where they have put him' " (John 20:11–13). When Mary saw Jesus, she thought He was the gardener. So she said, "Sir, if you have carried him away, tell me where you have put him, and I will get him" (20:15).

### Individual Identity Retained in the Resurrection

Jesus replied to Mary by simply calling her name (20:16). She immediately recognized His voice and responded, "Rabboni!" This is a remarkable revelation because many people wonder whether believers in heaven will retain their identity. Clearly Christ did, and even though He was marvelously resurrected in newness of life and power, He still was recognizable as the same person who had been on earth before His death. So believers, whose bodies will be like that of Jesus' resurrected body (1 John 3:2), will retain their individual identity, presumably including having voices that sound like their voices in this world.

In her joy at seeing Christ, Mary embraced Him. She did not grab at air but held on to a real body, which He later said was a body of flesh and bones (Luke 24:39). A little later the other women came to the tomb a second time and Jesus met them, and they held Him by His feet (Matt. 28:9). Since the nail prints were still in His feet (John 20:25–27), by embracing His feet they lovingly recognized He was the One who had died on the cross.

### Jesus' Resurrection Appearances

The nail prints in Jesus' hands and feet, as well as the wound in His side, are everlasting memorials to His sacrificial death and His glorious triumph over it. This is evident in His appearance to his disciple Thomas (John 20:24–27). His resurrection body was identified with the body that was laid in the tomb.

Regarding Christ's appearance to Peter, Luke 24:34 simply states that the Eleven and others were saying, "The Lord has risen and has appeared to Simon."

A next significant appearance of Christ was to the disciples on the road to Emmaus, mentioned briefly in Mark 16:12–13 and in more detail in Luke 24:13–35. The two unnamed disciples were going from Jerusalem to Emmaus, a town about seven miles west of Jerusalem, and they were talking about what had happened that weekend in connection with Jesus. While they were talking, Jesus Himself joined them (24:15). They, however, were prevented from recognizing Him (24:16). They discussed with him how the Old Testament had anticipated the death and resurrection of Christ, and Christ interpreted this to them (24:17–27). "And beginning with Moses and all the Prophets, he explained to them what was said in all the Scriptures concerning himself" (24:27). How tremendous it would be to have a record of what Christ said in that exposition!

When the three got to the village of Emmaus, the two disciples invited Jesus to have supper with them. At the meal He revealed Himself to them: "When he was at the table with them, he took bread, gave thanks, broke it and began to give it to them. Then their eyes were opened and they recognized him, and he disappeared from their sight" (Luke 24:30–31). Apparently for the first time they saw the nail prints in His hands. Forgetting their supper, the two rushed back to Jerusalem, where they found Jesus' disciples and others that night gathered in a room (24:33) because they were fearful they might be arrested and crucified (John 20:19). As they discussed the previous appearance to Peter and their experience on the road to Emmaus, suddenly Christ stood in their midst, apparently without the door having opened. He greeted them with the words, "Peace be with you," but they were frightened, assuming they had seen a spirit (Luke 24:36–37).

The fact that Christ could enter a room without opening the door shows that His resurrection body, while physical, was unique. To make clear that He was there bodily, Christ showed them His hands and feet, and said, "A spirit does not have flesh and bones as you see I have" (Luke 24:39, NKJV). Jesus then asked for food, so they gave Him a piece of a broiled fish, which He ate (24:43). Following this, He gave them a discourse on how His sufferings, death, and resurrection were a part of God's plan revealed in the Old Testament (24:44–47).

A week later Christ appeared again to the disciples, this time with Thomas:

> Now Thomas (called Didymus), one of the Twelve, was not with the disciples when Jesus came. So the other disciples told him, "We have seen the Lord!" But he said to them, "Unless I see the nail marks in his hands and put my finger where the nails were, and put my hand into his side, I will not believe it." A week later his disciples were in the house again, and Thomas was with them. Though the doors were locked, Jesus came and stood among them and said, "Peace be with you!" Then he said to Thomas, "Put your finger here; see my hands. Reach out your hand and put it into my side. Stop doubting and believe." Thomas said to him, "My Lord and my God!" (John 20:24–28).

When Thomas saw the Lord, he forgot all about his need for proof and immediately recognized Him as resurrected. Apparently Thomas never carried through on having to touch the nail prints and the wounds to prove to himself that Jesus had a physical resurrection body.

*The Fact of Resurrection Proved by Jesus' Appearances*

Christ made five appearances on the day of His resurrection: (1) to Mary Magdalene (Mark 16:9–11; John 20:11–17); (2) to the other women returning to the tomb the second time (Matt. 28:8–10); (3) to Peter (Luke 24:34; 1 Cor. 15:5); (4) to the disciples on the road to Emmaus (Mark 16:12–13; Luke 24:13–35); and (5) to the ten disciples, without Thomas (Mark 16:14; Luke 24:36–43; John 20:19–23). (Luke 24:33 says the two Emmaus disciples found the Eleven. However, since Thomas was not with them the term "the Eleven" may be a technical term used for the group even though only ten were present.)

Following this there were twelve other appearances of Christ, all of which offer abundant proof of the certainty of His resurrection.

6. To the eleven disciples a week later, with Thomas present (John 20:26–29)

7. To seven disciples by the Sea of Galilee (John 21:1–14)

8. To more than five hundred believers (1 Cor. 15:6)

9. To James, the Lord's brother (1 Cor. 15:7)

10. To eleven disciples in Galilee (Matt. 28:16–20)

11. To the eleven disciples at His ascension (Mark 16:19–20; Luke 24:50–53; Acts 1:3–9)

12. To Stephen at his martyrdom (Acts 7:55–56)

13. To Saul on the road to Damascus (Acts 9:3–7)

14. To Paul in Arabia (Gal. 1:12)

15. To Paul in the Jerusalem temple (Acts 22:17–21)

16. To Paul in prison at Caesarea (Acts 23:11)

17. The final appearance of Christ to the apostle John (Rev. 1:12–20)

These seventeen appearances of Christ confirm the doctrine of the resurrection in general and Christ's resurrection in particular. Christians' bodies will be transformed (Phil. 3:21) to be like Jesus' resurrected body (1 John 3:2). This means that our future bodies will be similar to our present bodies—that is, bodies of flesh and bones that look like human beings. In fact, each believer will continue to look as he did in this world. Yet each one may have remarkable abilities, like Jesus' ability to appear in a room without going through a normal entrance. It is probable that in the resurrection our bodies will be improved, and older people will be returned to comparative youth. Some have suggested that the apparent age of people in heaven will be about thirty years of age, the ideal borderline between youth and maturity, illustrated in the fact that Old Testament priests were thirty years of age when they began their ministry and Christ was a little more than thirty when He began His public ministry.

## THE DOCTRINAL SIGNIFICANCE OF THE RESURRECTION

The resurrection of Christ is tremendously significant doctrinally because it demonstrated His deity (Rom. 1:4). His resurrection is also related to His three offices of Prophet, Priest, and King.

He was obviously the greatest of the prophets, and His teachings, remarkably, touch the important areas of prophetic revelation. As Priest, He is our Advocate and Intercessor in heaven (Rom. 8:34; Heb. 7:25–26). As King, He rules over God's spiritual kingdom now, and in the future He will reign over Israel and the entire world.

The resurrection of Christ, of course, is key to all His present work in heaven. Because He is resurrected, people are justified in believing in His death on the cross as the basis of their salvation. His resurrection also guarantees and undergirds all His future works, including returning for His own in the Rapture, blessing all those who are the objects of His saving grace, resurrecting everyone in their proper order, reigning on the throne of David in the Millennium, and ultimately triumphing over the world in delivering the conquered world to God the Father. His resurrection also adds proof to the inspiration of the Bible and constitutes a tremendous fulfillment of prophecy recorded by inspiration of the Holy Spirit.

All these factors concerning the resurrection make it clear that the resurrection and translation of Christians at the Rapture will be a tremendous event, an event worthy of our constant expectation. Knowledge of our future life helps to cast light on our present life goals, encouraging us to consider how our actions will be seen from the viewpoint of eternity.

# 5

# The Believer's Day
# of Reward

---

THE GRAND EXPERIENCE of being raptured at the time of Christ's coming is obviously a major aspect of a believer's expectation of future events. The transformation that will take place as believers exchange our present bodies for bodies suited for heaven and leave our present abode on earth for the glories of being in the presence of Christ in heaven is completely beyond description. Unfortunately many believers know little about the Rapture, or else are not living in anticipation of its fulfillment.

## LOVING HIS APPEARING

The early church, according to 2 Timothy 4:8, was described as those "who have loved His appearing" (NKJV). They loved, or looked forward to, Christ's appearing because they loved Him, and it is only natural for those who love each other to look forward with keen anticipation to the time when they can be in each other's presence, seeing each other face to face. For a person who loves Christ there can be no greater experience than to be caught up in His presence and to see Him in all His glory.

As we have seen, some Bible interpreters have difficulty accepting the view that the Rapture is the next event in God's prophetic program. More disturbing, however, is the fact that many Christians who believe the Lord could come at any moment are indifferent to that truth and do not live accordingly.

Many believers get tangled up in the events and activities of this world without genuinely anticipating going to heaven as a glorious experience. However, if a person is walking in fellowship with Christ, experiencing His wonderful love and fellowship, it is most natural for that believer to anticipate His coming as a wonderful, eagerly welcomed event. Failure to appreciate the Rapture is not simply a theological problem; it is also a spiritual problem. It points to something lacking in a Christian's walk with the Lord.

Following the Rapture, God will reward those who have served Him faithfully. Thus when the Rapture takes place believers will not only experience a transformation in their bodies (as discussed in chap. 4); they will also face an entirely new kind of life.

### The Bridegroom and the Bride

Jesus' coming for His church will be like a bridegroom coming for his bride. Second Corinthians 11:2 speaks of Christ as a husband and believers as His virgin bride, and Ephesians 5:22–24 compares the husband-wife relationship to that of Christ's relationship to the church. Revelation 19:7 also refers to Jesus' bride. In Jewish customs of Jesus' day, the parents of a bridegroom would contact the parents of their son's intended bride and pay a dowry. The payment of this dowry affirmed the marriage legally. However, the couple would usually wait for a year before the next step. Following this betrothal period, the groom would take his bride from her house to his home, where a banquet would be held.

The parable of the ten virgins in Matthew 25:1–13 describes a bridegroom claiming his bride. This passage focuses on the bride's attendants being ready for the wedding. This refers to those who after the Rapture and before the second coming of Christ will become believers. They will not be part of the bride of Christ, the church, but nevertheless they will be saved, as illustrated by the wise virgins awaiting the wedding feast that will take place following the Second Coming.

*Preparing for His Coming*

When Christ delivered the "Olivet Discourse" recorded in Matthew 24–25, the Rapture had not yet been revealed. Matthew 25, then, does not deal with the Rapture but rather with the preparation of believers on earth for the wedding feast that follows Christ's claiming His bride at His second coming. Actually in Matthew 25 the bride is not mentioned, because here the emphasis is on others preparing for the coming of the bridegroom in connection with the wedding feast, as we have seen.

After the customary betrothal period, the bridegroom would come for his bride. The groom's male friends would lead a procession through the city at midnight, carrying torches on the way to the bride's home. She would know he was coming and would be ready with her maiden attendants. They would join the procession from her home to the bridegroom's home. This would begin a new relationship as the bride and bridegroom assumed the responsibilities of marriage and prepared for the wedding feast (Rev. 19:7–9), attended by the "wise" virgins (Matt. 25:1–13).

In a similar way believers are referred to as a betrothed young woman waiting for her future husband to claim her as his wife (2 Cor. 11:2). The present age is the time of the betrothal. Believers can enjoy the wonderful intimacy of fellowship with Christ while on earth. But when he, the Groom, comes for His church, a new relationship will begin and they will dwell together in this new relationship forever.

## THE JUDGMENT SEAT OF CHRIST

After the Bridegroom presents His bride to the heavenly host, the bride—the church—will then stand before the judgment seat of Christ to be evaluated and rewarded. "For we must all appear before the judgment seat of Christ, that each one may receive what is due him for the things done while in the body, whether good or bad" (2 Cor. 5:10).

Several unusual things characterize this judgment. First, everyone standing before Christ will be saved. This means they will be transformed—holy and without sin. They will all have been justified by faith in Christ, that is, declared righteous.

The fact that a believer is justified by faith (Rom. 5:1) means more than just being forgiven. If a person overdraws his bank account, the bank may advance the money but it will also notify him of his overdraft. If he deposits the amount of the overdraft, he will be forgiven. But if a friend, hearing of his problem, deposits a huge amount of money to his account, that not only wipes out the deficit but also leaves the balance of credit to the individual. So it is in the believer's relationship to Christ. Not only are our sins forgiven, but God has also declared us righteous because the believer, being in Christ, is seen in light of the perfections of the person and work of Christ.

Therefore the judgment seat of Christ will in no way be an evaluation of our sins. Because a Christian is justified, he is forgiven and stands before God in the perfection of Christ's righteousness. Believers in Christ will not suffer any penalty for their sins: "Therefore there is now no condemnation for those who are in Christ Jesus. ... Who will bring any charge against those whom God has chosen? It is God who justifies. Who is he that condemns? Christ Jesus, who died—more than that, who was raised to life—is at the right hand of God and is also interceding for us" (Rom. 8:1, 33–34). Paul added that nothing can separate believers from the love of God (8:35–39). The purpose of the judgment seat of Christ, then, will be to determine not the extent of believers' sins but rather the quality of their service for God while on earth.

This is supported by the fact that at the judgment seat the question will pertain to "what is due him for the things done while in the body, whether good or bad" (2 Cor. 5:10). In this judgment the deeds that are good in God's sight will be subject to reward, and the deeds that are bad or worthless will be discarded.

In verse 11 Paul spoke of the "fear" of the Lord. What is this fear of God? It is a reminder that everyone will have to appear before Christ sooner or later. The fear for Christians at the judgment seat of Christ is not that of condemnation but of failure to give a good account of what God has entrusted to us. Paul used three illustrations to explain what will happen at the judgment seat of Christ.

*Building a Life for Eternity*

In 1 Corinthians 3:10–15 Paul used the illustration of a building. The foundation of the building is the believer's salvation. Paul wrote, "I laid a foundation as an expert builder, and someone else is building on it. But each one should be careful how he builds" (3:10). On this foundation of salvation in Christ the believer constructs a building consisting of either gold, silver, and costly stones, or of wood, hay, and straw: "For no one can lay any foundation other than the one already laid, which is Jesus Christ. If any man builds on this foundation using gold, silver, costly stones, wood, hay, or straw, his work will be shown for what it is, because the Day will bring it to light. It will be revealed with fire, and the fire will test the quality of each man's work. If what he has built survives, he will receive his reward. If it is burned up, he will suffer loss; he himself will be saved, but only as one escaping through the flames" (3:11–15).

The building will be tested by fire (3:13), which will reduce the wood, hay, and straw to ashes, but the gold, silver, and costly stones are not combustible. What endures judgment will be the basis of reward. What is burnt and left in ashes will be lost but will not be the basis for condemnation.

The spiritual meaning of the materials listed in the Scripture is not revealed by Paul, but elswhere in Scripture gold is typical of the glory of God as seen in the tabernacle (Exod. 25) and the temple (1 Kings 6:21–32). Gold reflects whatever a Christian does to the glory of God. Even a small act of kindness may reflect the work of God in his heart and life. Silver in Scripture is the metal of redemption (Lev. 27) and may speak of soul-winning, whether through personal testimony, gifts, or prayers. The costly stones are not itemized because there are so many other things a Christian can do that reflect God's working out of salvation in his life. The point in this illustration is that a Christian should live with eternal values in view. It is easy to be good without accomplishing much that is worthwhile in eternity. And the good is often the enemy of the best. While salvation is not based on works, rewards will be given based on what a believer has accomplished.

*Running the Race*

In 1 Corinthians 9:24–27, Paul used a second illustration, one that describes the Christian life as a race: " Do you not know that in a race all the runners run, but only one gets the prize? Run in such a way as to get the prize. Everyone who competes in the games goes into strict training. They do it to get a crown that will not last; but we do it to get a crown that will last forever. Therefore I do not run like a man running aimlessly; I do not fight like a man beating the air. No, I beat my body and make it my slave so that after I have preached to others, I myself will not be disqualified for the prize."

Races were common in Corinth, and the custom was to give a crown of leaves to the winner. Unfortunately the leaves would decay in a few days and be worthless. Paul pointed out by contrast that the victor in the Christian race will receive a reward that will not decay. Also, every Christian can win the race, while in competitive races only one person wins. A Christian in this life is competing with self, not with others. The question is whether we are running the race in such a way that we will receive a crown of victory.

The rules of running a race are quite simple. First, the runner lines up in light clothing and when the starter says "Go" or fires the gun, he takes off immediately. In my observation of track meets I have never seen a runner turn around to the referee when the starting gun goes off and say, "Do you mean me?" So often Christians are not listening, and so when God says "Go," we do not respond.

Second, runners must stay on the track. If one leaves the track, he is disqualified from the race. Christians need to be careful not to "get off the track" by sinful living.

Third, in running a race one cannot be distracted by the crowd that is watching or by anything else. A runner does not look back to see where the other runners are. A runner may stop and pick daisies, but if he does he is not running the race. It is so easy to do things that are not terribly wrong but yet do not help us win the race of life.

Fourth, running a race requires physical discipline and laying aside everything that will hinder winning the race. What a clear illustration of the importance of living for Christ!

## Life as a Trust

Paul gave a third illustration related to the judgment seat of Christ in Romans 14. "You, then, why do you judge your brother? Or why do you look down on your brother? For we will all stand before God's judgment seat" (14:10). He then quoted Isaiah 45:23, which predicts that every knee will bow before the Lord. The sad fact here is that even unbelievers will be forced to acknowledge Christ as the Savior in the final judgment, but it will be too late. For the Christian, however, confession indicates that we have come to God and we recognize God's sovereignty and our need to serve the Lord. His judgment is summarized in Romans 14:12, "So then, each of us will give an account of himself to God."

This illustration is built on the laws of a trustee. A trustee is responsible to administer something that belongs to another. He is legally bound to give an account in due time of how he managed his trusteeship. The Christian life, by its nature, is a trust from God. All we have has been made possible by God, whether it is physical life, natural gifts, spiritual talents, opportunities, environment, or education. These provisions and many others God gives us are our responsibilities, and the Lord's question to us at the judgment seat of Christ will be, "What have you done with what I have given you?"

This illustration points out several important truths. First, a Christian will not be judged competitively with other Christians. Second, believers will not be held responsible for things we did not possess, gifts we did not receive, or opportunities that were not before us. God gives every believer equal opportunity for spiritual victory. Third, we are responsible to use properly what God has entrusted to us. Thus a person with great talents or great resources is held accountable for far more than one who has few talents.

Each of these three illustrations about the judgment seat of Christ shows that believers are accountable for the use of our God-given gifts. And while we are saved by grace apart from works, we are rewarded only when our works deserve recognition, even though the works themselves are made possible by the grace of God.

*The Grace of God*

Some Christians have asked if we will be filled with remorse when we realize how little we accomplished in view of what Christ has done for us. The answer is that heaven is not a place of ongoing sorrow. It would not be heaven if we were to spend eternity in sadness because of what we did not do. Undoubtedly there will be regret, but our overwhelming emotion will be the realization of the wonderful grace of God that saved us and brought us to heaven. There will be rejoicing in heaven instead of tears.

The situation can be compared to a school graduation exercise. Some students graduate with honors or high honors, and others receive rewards for distinctive achievements. However, the overwhelming emotion of all the graduates is the joy of receiving the diploma after years of sacrifice and study; every graduate receives a diploma and thus experiences joy and fulfillment. On the one hand, the seriousness of the judgment seat of Christ should be considered; on the other hand, all believers can rejoice in the marvelous grace of God that will enable them all to be in heaven even though they are imperfect in this life.

*The Rewards of Faithfulness*

The Bible does not indicate the extent or nature of the rewards believers will receive. But whatever they will be, most likely the rewards will not be in the form of tokens of achievement such as soldiers receive for battles they have endured.

The story is told of a person who had perfect attendance in Sunday school and each year was given a card that was added to a ribbon indicating his perfect attendance. The ribbon of cards got so long that it finally touched the floor and the individual tripped on it, broke his leg, and spoiled his perfect attendance. Obviously this will not be our experience in heaven. Believers in heaven will desire to show God their love for Him and their desire to serve Him. It is entirely possible, instead, that our rewards will be in the form of privileged service.

## OUR SERVICE IN HEAVEN

The Scriptures say very little about what we will do in heaven. But the Bible does say that Christians will reign with Christ in the administration of the millennial kingdom (Rev. 20:6). It also speaks of Christians reigning with Christ in eternity (22:5). Apparently Christians will be given spheres of authority in God's government both in the Millennium and in the eternal state. These spheres of service will relate to how well we have served Christ in this life.

In athletics a person often makes the first team if he has practiced well. So the Christian who in this life serves God faithfully will be recognized in eternity and will be given larger spheres of service. The fact of the judgment seat of Christ encourages believers to consider what is genuinely important in life. On earth it encourages believers to follow God's standards of eternal values, which transcend all human systems of worth despite our falling short of what God would have us be and do. It is possible to receive the Lord's commendation, "Well done" (Matt. 25:21). The truth of the judgment seat of Christ is a reminder to evaluate our lives to be sure we are not simply avoiding evil but are also incorporating into our lives the things that will make a difference in eternity from God's point of view.

# 6

# The Beginning of
# History and Prophecy

---

$T$HINKING CHRISTIANS are naturally interested in the future. We wonder what will happen between now and the Lord's coming. How close is the Lord's return? How should we live in the light of prophecy? All these are important questions.

For believers in Christ, the most important prophecies are those that relate to them directly, such as the Rapture and the judgment seat of Christ. But much can be learned both from prophecies already fulfilled and from unfulfilled prophecies concerning Israel and the world.

## THE OLD TESTAMENT INTRODUCTION
## OF GOD'S MASTER PLAN

All prophecies in the New Testament are set in the larger context of the Old Testament in which God revealed His master plan for human destiny. The Old Testament is an amazing account of how God sovereignly has worked in gentile nations as well as in Israel to accomplish His eternal purpose. While the world's incredible wickedness may make it seem as if God is not controlling the course of events, nevertheless the Scriptures make plain that God is still on the throne, and that in His time and according to His purpose He will fulfill all He has planned. God's dealings with the world and the people of Israel, as recorded in the Old Testament, are an important framework for understanding the role of believers today in history and prophecy. Though the church, the body of Christ, as revealed in the New Testament, is one of God's major undertakings, it is only one of several major aspects of God's purpose.

Major prophecies of the Old Testament deal with the people of Israel and God's special purpose for them. Though the Old Testament does not reveal God's present role of dealing with believers, His role for Israel does stand in contrast to His purpose for the church.

One of the important points for believers in prophecy is that all these lines of prophecy and fulfillment come together in God's ultimate establishment of His eternal reign over creation.

## THE BEGINNING OF MAJOR LINES OF PROPHECY

The Book of Genesis, the book of beginnings, is a most remarkable portion of Scripture because in it all the great lines of Old Testament prophecies begin in one way or another. Moses, who wrote the Book of Genesis, recorded not only what he knew personally but also the tremendous revelation God gave him, beginning with history before man was created and anticipating the wise design of God in guiding the gentile nations as well as the nation of Israel through their various historical episodes and on into the future.

### God as the Eternal Creator

The Bible begins with the words "In the beginning God created" (Gen. 1:1). It is difficult for our human minds accustomed to beginnings and endings to comprehend the fact that God has always existed from eternity past. If God is infinite, obviously He would have to exist from eternity past and not be a created Being, and in turn He would be the Creator of everything created. Rightly the story of the world begins with God.

In our modern world the human race is desperately trying to forget that God exists. The media constantly report scientific findings that seem to show that the human race has existed for millions of years, even though alleged proof for it is highly questionable. Modern science has advanced the idea that life began with a single cell that divided and eventually developed into the complicated organisms of humans, animals, and plant life of today. Yet evolution is not supportable by any solid evidence, even though most of the scientific world accepts it as fact.

Though skeptics challenge the concept of Christ's second coming (2 Pet. 3:3–4), it is significant that they speak of Creation as the beginning: "Everything goes on as it has since the beginning of creation" (3:4). Our intelligent universe, complicated as it is in the movements of the stars and the intricate structure of organic creation—whether animals, humans, or vegetation—points to the conclusion that an intelligent Being of infinite power and wisdom created it. The only rational explanation of our universe is what is provided in the Bible in the simple statement that "God created."

Scripture dealing with creationist history forms a solid basis for prophecy and is thus the hinge by which prophecy is related to the past.

## The Time of Creation

The fact that creation occurred in time implies that before creation only God existed, as Father, Son, and Holy Spirit. There was perfect communion between the persons of the Trinity and mutual enjoyment of their infinite perfections. In the will of God, however, He decided to create the universe and in creation to set loose a series of events that will find final fulfillment in eternity.

No time element is given in the statement, "In the beginning God created the heavens and the earth" (Gen. 1:1). This could be translated, "In the beginning God was creating the heavens and the earth." The implication is that creation was carried out in a series of divine creative acts, the first act apparently being the creation of the physical heavens and the earth.

## Creation of Angels

Though the scriptural revelation on angels is limited, it seems evident that in addition to creating the material world God also created the angels, each

61

of whom was holy. Though all angels were created holy, some of them sinned and fell from their holy position. They became the demon world of which Satan is the leader. A few passages of Scripture cast light on this.

The prophecy in Isaiah 14:12–15 relating to Satan's rebellion is set in a context that deals with the destruction of the leaders of Babylon. Satan's sin was that he wanted to be like God: "I will ascend above the tops of the clouds; I will make myself like the Most High" (14:14). His sin was that of defiant pride (1 Tim. 3:6). Scripture records this rebellion as preceding the sin of Adam and Eve.

A second passage of Scripture on the fall of angels is Ezekiel 28:11–15. This passage is set in the context of judgment on the king of Tyre, but the passage goes beyond anything that could be attributed to an earthly ruler. As the true "king" (28:12) of Tyre, Satan motivated the human "ruler" (28:2) of Tyre. Satan was "anointed as a guardian cherub" (28:14), which seems to refer to him in his holy estate before he fell. He is described as being "full of wisdom and perfect in beauty" (28:12). He is also referred to as one who was "in Eden, the garden of God" and was "created" (28:13). Also he was "on the holy mount of God" (28:14), possibly a reference to his having access, with other angels, to God's presence in heaven. Of him it is declared, "You were blameless in your ways from the day you were created till wickedness was found in you" (28:15). Satan's pride led to his being expelled from the mount of God and thrown to the earth (28:16–17), though he still has access to God's presence (Job 1:6–12; 2:1–6; Zech. 3:1–2; Rev. 12:10).

Though scholars differ on the interpretation of these two passages in Isaiah and Ezekiel, the traditional view of the church is that they give insight into what happened to Satan and the resulting judgment on the demonic world. Jude wrote that the angels who sinned with Satan "did not keep their positions of authority but abandoned their own home" (Jude 6). So God confined them to "gloomy dungeons to be held for judgment" (2 Pet. 2:4). They are "kept in darkness, bound with everlasting chains for judgment on the great Day" (Jude 6). These fallen angels are demons reduced to inactivity until the time of their final judgment. Other angels who sinned with Satan are not bound and are active as his demons.

All the fallen angels, or demons, will be judged because they followed Satan when he rebelled against God. When Satan is cast into the lake of fire at the end of the Millennium, fallen angels will join him in eternal punishment: "And the devil, who deceived them, was thrown into the lake of burning sulfur, where the beast and the false prophet had been thrown. They will be tormented day and night for ever and ever" (Rev. 20:10). This lake of fire is "the eternal fire," which is "prepared for the devil and his angels" (Matt. 25:41). The sin of Satan and other angels and their being cast down from their holy estate form the background for Genesis 1, which records the preparation of the earth for the creation of the human race.

### The Creation of Adam and Eve

As described in Genesis 1, the earth was not complete before the time of the so-called Creation days. In a series of creative acts, God brought the earth to a state in which mankind could live. Beginning with the creation of light, God continued by dividing the waters and then having the earth bring forth grass and other vegetation. There followed the creation of animals, birds, and sea creatures. The final act of Creation was the creation of man and woman, recorded in Genesis 1:26–27.

Some have suggested that the creation of Adam and Eve occurred about 4000 B.C.; they base this on genealogies in the Old Testament. The problem with this is that a number of the genealogies are not complete, and in several cases an individual who is said to be the "son" of a certain person was actually his grandson or great-grandson. Some New Testament genealogies add names that are not mentioned in the Old Testament, and sometimes the Old Testament includes names not in genealogies of the New Testament. Also we should remember that God created man and woman as adults, just as he created animals and vegetation as mature organisms. Thus it is impossible to set an exact date for creation.

On the other hand, claims of evolutionists and others that mankind has lived for millions of years are totally unjustified. While the 4000 B.C. date for the creation of the first humans cannot be supported, it is doubtful that the human race was created hundreds of thousands of years ago.

The dating of the creation of Adam and Eve is not only difficult because the genealogies are incomplete, but also because of the need to account for the Flood. The written history of Egypt, which began about 3000 B.C., does not include reference to a flood. So at least several thousand years before 3000 B.C. are required to account for the probable course of events after the Flood.

After the creation of Adam and Eve, the human race had to prosper for a while and multiply, as recorded in Genesis, and this must have taken hundreds, if not thousands, of years. When the Flood came, that generation was wiped out, and then there had to be considerable time for the human race to replace those who perished in the Flood. By 3000 B.C., when writing began, there was obviously a flourishing civilization in Egypt as well as in other places. All these developments would have required an extensive length of time.

While evangelical Christians reject the evolutionists' claim that human history has gone on for millions of years, it is necessary to chart a course in which creation occurred much earlier than 4000 B.C. Some have suggested that the human race must have been created between 10000 and 6000 B.C. This is guesswork, but it still opposes the wilder guesses of evolutionists. The important point in Creation is not when it occurred but the fact that it occurred, and that God created everything after its kind. The various species of life are a result of God's creative work, not because they descended from a common source but because they had the same Creator.

### The Fall of Adam and Eve

When Adam and Eve disobeyed God by partaking of the forbidden fruit (Gen. 2:16–17; 3:1–7), it became the occasion for extended prophecy concerning mankind. God said that Satan, who appeared in the form of a serpent, was cursed. The serpent was condemned to eating the dust of the earth and to being at enmity with the woman. "So the Lord God said to the serpent, 'Because you have done this, cursed are you above all the livestock and all the wild animals! You will crawl on your belly and you will eat dust all the days of your life' " (3:14). In this connection God also predicted that Satan's head would be bruised and that he would bruise the heel of the predicted Redeemer. "And I will put enmity between you and the woman, and between your offspring and hers; he will crush your head, and you will strike his heel" (3:15). This is the first indication in Scripture of God's plan of salvation, which would require the death of Christ on the cross, Satan's "bruising" of Christ's "heel."

In Genesis 3 God revealed the law of condemnation and spiritual death because of sin, and He predicted His provision for salvation through the sacrifice of the Redeemer. Additional prophecies were given concerning the woman and her lot as the wife of Adam, including her difficulties in childbearing and her subjection to her husband (3:16).

Also Adam was solemnly informed that the ground was cursed because of him and that he would have to work hard to produce a living. God said to Adam, "Cursed is the ground because of you; through painful toil you will eat of it all the days of your life. It will produce thorns and thistles for you, and you will eat the plants of the field. By the sweat of your brow you will eat your food until you return to the ground, since from it you were taken; for dust you are and to dust you will return" (3:17–19). Because of their sin Adam and Eve were driven out of the Garden of Eden so that they could not eat the fruit of the Tree of Life (3:22–24).

## THE CONTINUED PATTERN
## OF SINFULNESS AND THE FLOOD

As the human race multiplied, it became increasingly evil. Cain's murder of Abel and mankind's wickedness is described in Genesis 4:1–6:6. As a result, the next great dimension of God's master plan came into play—the Flood that wiped out the entire human race except for Noah, his wife, and his three sons and their wives.

### The Command to Build the Ark

God instructed Noah to build a huge boat, 75 feet wide, 450 feet long, and 45 feet high. God gave minute instructions on how it should be built.

Then God told Noah He would bring a flood on the earth: "I am going to bring floodwaters on the earth to destroy all life under the heavens, every creature that has the breath of life in it. Everything on earth will perish" (6:17).

God also instructed Noah to bring animals, birds, and creeping things of the earth into the ark (6:19–20). These would serve the purpose of filling the earth again with animal life after the Flood. Noah was also told to put food on board, enough to last for the duration of the Flood.

Building the ark took more than one hundred years. God said He was giving man one hundred and twenty years before He would destroy them (6:3). No doubt Noah's generation considered him crazy for building an ark on dry land where there had never been water. But the day finally came when the ark was finished.

As people watched, something strange happened. The animals in pairs began marching into the ark. Those who looked on also saw Noah's three sons and their wives enter the ark. Then Noah and his wife entered the ark, and the door was shut (7:7–9). Everything was in place for the Flood to begin. Apparently seven days elapsed before the rain came (7:10). (These seven days may have included the time during which the animals and Noah's family were entering the ark).

Then rain fell for forty days and forty nights (7:12). Besides the rain ("the floodgates of the heavens were opened"), "all the springs of the great deep burst forth" (7:11), indicating that water sprang up from the ocean floors. As the waters rose, the ark was borne up by the water and everything in the surrounding world was drowned. "The waters rose and covered the mountains to a depth of more than twenty feet" (7:20). "Every living thing on the face of the earth was wiped out; men and animals and the creatures that move along the ground and the birds of the air were wiped from the earth. Only Noah was left, and those with him in the ark" (7:23). The waters prevailed for 150 days before they began to recede (7:24). In the entire process God's prophecy about the Flood was fulfilled literally and dramatically.

The waters receded (8:1–14), and in due time the earth was dry enough for Noah and his family to leave the ark, along with all the animals they had brought in (8:15–19).

## The Principle of Human Government

God solemnly pronounced a blessing on Noah and his family (Gen. 9:1–7). He also established a rule for government, namely, the principle that those who commit murder should be put to death. "Whoever sheds the blood of man, by man shall his blood be shed; for in the image of God has God made man" (9:6). In view of the modern debate on capital punishment for murderers, this verse makes it clear that this is a part of human government as God instituted it. In fact, under the Mosaic Law some were put to death for other offenses besides murder. Even violating the sanctity of the Sabbath by picking up sticks was considered work and was punishable by death (Num. 15:32–36). While this was an instruction given to Israel, it apparently did not violate the directive in the Ten Commandments, "You shall not murder" (Exod. 20:13; Deut. 5:17).

As a sign of God's blessing that the earth would never again be destroyed by water, He introduced the rainbow (Gen. 9:8–17). However, the Scriptures do predict that the earth ultimately will be destroyed by fire (2 Pet. 3:7, 10–12). All humankind since Noah descended from him and his three sons, his sons being patriarchs of the three major divisions of humanity.

## The Origin of the Nations

Genesis 10 is a remarkable document that describes how the nations descended from Noah, and it provides information on the origin of mankind as found in no other document. Though those who do not accept the Bible have speculated extensively about the origin of the various races, this chapter in Genesis is the only document that actually explains it. Much of the gentile world descended from Japheth, and the people of Israel descended from Shem.

## The Tower of Babel

In spite of the evidence that God judges sin, as illustrated by the Flood, the descendants of Noah nevertheless departed from God. They attempted to make a name for themselves by building a city and in it a tower that would reach to heaven (Gen. 11:4). Because of their sin, God said, "Come, let us go down and confuse their language so they will not understand each other" (11:7). As a result of this judgment diverse human languages were created and the people stopped building their tower. The city where the tower was built was called Babel, another name for Babylon, referring to the "babel" of various languages (11:9). Genesis 11:10–32 then records the genealogy of Noah's son Shem, which leads to the line of Abraham.

## THE NEW LINE OF HUMANITY
## WITH THE CALL OF ABRAHAM

The continued sin of the human race prompted God to begin another aspect of His master plan: the call of Abraham and the beginning of a new division of humanity—namely, the descendants of Abraham, Isaac, and Jacob. Remarkably, the Book of Genesis, which records the history of the world in the first eleven chapters, deals in the rest of Genesis (chaps. 12–50—thirty-nine chapters) with the history of Abraham and his immediate descendants. From God's point of view the new line beginning with Abraham is the most important. In introducing the Abrahamic Covenant, God predicted that Abraham would become the progenitor of a great people, and that from his posterity would come one who would bring blessing to the entire world (12:1–3). These promises to Abraham outline the great master plan God introduced in the Book of Genesis. This covenant also introduces a tremendous line of prophecy relating to Israel, beginning in Genesis and extending throughout the Bible and into eternity.

God's master plan revealed in the Book of Genesis forms the background and context of what God has promised the church. It illustrates how God, in predicting the future, also provides for its complete and literal fulfillment in accord with His timing. History has already fulfilled most of the promises to Abraham about his place and his posterity, including Jesus Christ, the promised Savior. This assures believers that God's yet-unfulfilled promises will be fulfilled literally in their normal sense, just as hundreds of Old Testament prophecies have been.

What all this means today is that we are living in a world that has many natural qualities and laws but nevertheless is governed by the omnipotent God who can overrule those laws, fulfill His purposes, and conclude history in its various phases exactly as He predicted. For Christians this is a marvelous reassurance that God is on the throne, and whatever problems believers face will be solved in eternity, especially in the days following the Rapture.

# 7

# God's Plan for a Special People

---

Genesis 12 RECORDS THE BEGINNING of one of God's great prophetic programs—prophecy related to the people of Israel. As noted in
the previous chapter, the first eleven chapters of Genesis record the history of the world for thousands of years from the beginning of creation
until the time of Abraham. The remaining thirty-nine chapters in Genesis concern Abraham and his descendants. In every situation though,
people failed—whether in Adam and Eve's created state of innocence in
the Garden of Eden, or those who followed Adam who were governed by
conscience, or those in the period of human government given in the
covenant with Noah. This lengthy period of world history climaxed with
people rebelling against God in their attempt to build a tower reaching to
heaven (Gen. 11:1–9). Following this, God revealed His plan to meet human needs through a special people. This plan is summarized in God's
pronouncement to Abraham recorded in the opening verses of Genesis 12.

## THE CALL OF ABRAHAM

God's process of preparing a special people to be the object of His blessings and care throughout time and eternity began with the call to Abraham
recorded in Genesis 12:1.

Abraham lived in Ur of the Chaldeans (11:28, 31; 15:7), a city not far from Babylon in the Mesopotamian Valley. It was an advanced city in many respects, with two-story houses, beautiful parks, and much to commend itself. But it was also a place where human sacrifices and the worship of idols took place.

Though located in a comfortable situation physically, Abraham was told to leave his family, live in a tent, and go to a land God would show him. (Why God chose Abraham the Scriptures do not reveal.) Abraham attempted to fulfill this command. However, in the traditions of his time he was still subject to his father, who, learning of the command to Abraham, said he would go with him. So they departed from Ur, taking along Abraham's nephew Lot. However, about halfway to the Promised Land they came to Haran and set up residence there instead of going on. Only when his father Terah died was Abraham able to obey God's command and go on to the Promised Land.

## THE ABRAHAMIC COVENANT

Genesis 12:1–3 records one of the most remarkable prophecies in the Old Testament. This far-reaching prophecy stretches all through the Old Testament in its fulfillment and on into the eternal future. God made a solemn covenant with Abraham. "The LORD had said to Abram, 'Leave your country, your people and your father's household and go to the land I will show you. I will make you into a great nation and I will bless you; I will make your name great, and you will be a blessing. I will bless those who bless you, and whoever curses you I will curse; and all peoples on earth will be blessed through you.'"

God's first prophecy to Abraham in these verses was that He would make him into a great nation. As subsequent Scripture demonstrates, Abraham became the forefather of Isaac, Jacob, and Jacob's twelve sons, who became the leaders of Israel. Abraham also fathered other nations of the ancient world (16:1–4; 25:1–4). The promise of making a great nation—that is, Israel—was literally fulfilled. God's second prediction was, "I will bless you." Abraham was indeed blessed with long life (he lived 175 years; 25:7–8), numerous descendants, and many other material and spiritual blessings from God.

God made a third promise to Abraham: "I will make your name great." Today Abraham is revered not only as one of Judaism's great patriarchs but also in the Muslim faith and in Christianity. Not many people are still in the limelight after four thousand years! Then God added a fourth prediction: "And you will be a blessing." Abraham's life and posterity have indeed been a blessing to the whole world.

The promise that God would curse those who cursed Israel has frequently been fulfilled in history. God used various nations to punish Israel for her sins, forcing her to come back to God. But He also punished the instruments of His judgment, and every nation that has persecuted Israel has suffered for it. For example, Egypt suffered great loss when Pharaoh and his host perished in the Red Sea (Exod. 14:26–31; 15:19). Assyria, which led captive the ten tribes of Israel in 722 B.C. (2 Kings 17:5–6), was defeated by Babylon in 609 B.C. Then in 539 B.C. Babylon fell in one night to the Medes and the Persians, according to Daniel 5. The Medes and the Persians, who formed the empire that followed Babylon, were relatively kind to the Jews.

The Roman Empire was cruel to Israel and in due time Rome was ultimately destroyed by God's terrible judgment, though it is destined for revival in the end times. All this makes clear that God had a special people in mind when He called the people of Israel to Himself.

God's final sweeping statement to Abraham, "And all peoples on earth will be blessed through you" (Gen. 12:3), covers all that God has provided for the world through Abraham's posterity. From Israel came the prophets of God. From Israel came all the known writers of the Old and New Testaments (except Luke, who may have been a Gentile), and the kings of Israel. From Abraham's descendants came the twelve apostles and, supremely, Jesus Christ Himself. The death of Christ on the cross provides salvation for the entire human race and great blessings that come through the grace of God.

Each of these sweeping promises has already been graphically fulfilled, and yet is subject to future fulfillment as long as the human race continues, even into eternity.

## The Promise of the Land

Another far-reaching promise God gave to Abraham is in Genesis 12:7: "The LORD appeared to Abram and said, 'To your offspring I will give this land.'" While some prophecies are difficult to understand and need to be interpreted carefully, this prophecy is obviously clear. God predicted that He would give to Abraham's descendants the land to which He had called him, namely, the land of Palestine or Israel.

In the history of the church some have denied that there will be a future Millennium with Christ reigning over Israel in her land. Many of these scholars, therefore, are forced to say this verse refers not to the land of Palestine but to heaven. Yet there is absolutely no justification for taking the word *land* in Genesis 12 in any way other than its plain, simple meaning. Throughout the Old Testament the word *land* is never used in a symbolic way to refer to heaven. Unfortunately this image of the Promised Land as heaven is used in a number of familiar hymns.

Bible students follow one of three major approaches to prophecy. First, the *premillennial* view holds that Christ will come before His reign of a thousand years on earth. He will rule over the world and over Israel in her land. Second, the *amillennial* view holds that there will be no literal Millennium, but that in one way or another it is now being fulfilled in a nonliteral sense. Third, the *postmillennial* view teaches that the thousand-year kingdom will come as the final segment of the present age, in which the gospel will be triumphant and the whole world will be Christianized. The postmillennial view was popular in the nineteenth century when evolution began to influence Christian theology, for it offered a bright future to the preaching of the gospel. However, the advent of World War I—in which Germany, the country in which Protestantism was born, was a major protagonist—devastated this view, and most of those holding the postmillennial view reverted to the amillennial view.

## The Land Is Not Heaven

Amillenarians and postmillenarians say Genesis 12:7 means Abraham's descendants will inherit heaven. But this view has no justification in Scripture. Why would Abraham think "this land" meant heaven? This promise of the land is repeated often in the Old Testament. A number of prophecies clearly refer to Israel's regathering to and installation in the Promised Land, a subject we will consider later.

The concept that the land represents heaven is built on a wrong typology—the view that Israel's crossing the Jordan River to enter the Promised Land represents the death of a Christian and his or her entrance into heaven. This, however, has no support in the Bible. If the crossing of the Jordan River pictures anything symbolically, it could refer to the death of Christ by which a person enters the Christian life, represented by the Promised Land. Thus Joshua's possessing every part of the land on which he stepped (Josh. 1:1–6) would represent the believer's walk of faith.

But the Promised Land described in the Book of Joshua was not a place of complete rest. There was failure (7:4), death (7:5), and incomplete possession of the land (13:1–17). Though Israel was given title to all the land (21:43), several portions were not conquered. Obviously this could not represent heaven but rather the life of faith today in which Christians fall short of possessing all God wants to give them.

## Confirmation of the Promise of the Land

God's promise to give the land to Israel is confirmed several times in Genesis. Abraham's and Lot's herds became so great they could not occupy the same place, because there was not enough grass and water. Abraham, although he held title to the Promised Land, graciously offered Lot his choice of the land (Gen. 13). At that time, the plain of Jordan, according to archeologists, was a luxurious place, well-watered and abundant with grass, ideal for raising cattle. Unfortunately it also was the place where Sodom and Gomorrah, two wicked cities, were located. Lot chose this valley and eventually became corrupted by the people in those wicked cities (Gen. 19). After Lot left Abraham, God reaffirmed that the land would belong to Abraham's posterity: "The LORD said to Abram after Lot had parted from him, 'Lift up your eyes from where you are and look north and south, east and west. All the land that you see I will give to you and your offspring forever. I will make your offspring like the dust of the earth, so that if anyone could count the dust, then your offspring could be counted. Go, walk through the length and breadth of the land, for I am giving it to you' " (13:14–17).

Obviously when Abraham was told by God to survey his inheritance and to walk on it, he was looking at and stepping on physical land that was before him. He would not have been seeing and walking in heaven.

Amillenarians point out that while Abraham lived in the land of promise (Heb. 11:9), it was nevertheless true that "he was looking forward to the city with foundations, whose architect and builder is God" (11:10). They say this supports their view that "the land" designates a spiritual residence, that is, heaven. But Abraham looked forward to what the New Testament calls the New Jerusalem on the new earth, described in Revelation 21–22, which will come after the millennial kingdom. This anticipation of dwelling for eternity in the New Jerusalem differs from God's promise that the patriarch's posterity would enjoy the land of Israel.

## The Testing of Abraham's Faith

The promise of the land was a test of Abraham's faith because he did not have any children to provide the posterity to claim the land. Abraham and his wife were already old, so humanly speaking the promise could not possibly be fulfilled.

Abraham suggested a compromise to God—that one of his servants, Eliezer of Damascus, be considered his son and that Eliezer and his children be the heirs of Abraham's possessions. But God told Abraham this was not His will for him, for he would have his own child (Gen. 15:4). Then God had Abraham look at the stars and said, "So shall your offspring be" (15:5). Though about three thousand stars can be identified by the unaided human eye, scientists admit that the stars are innumerable.

Then "Abram believed the LORD, and he credited it to him as righteousness" (15:6). After this, God introduced a formal sacrificial act in which the covenant of the land was confirmed by shed blood (15:8–17).

## The Land Described

At the conclusion of Genesis 15, God added a "real estate" description of the Promised Land. "On that day the LORD made a covenant with Abram and said, 'To your descendants I give this land, from the river of Egypt to the great river, the Euphrates'" (15:18). Then He named the heathen tribes inhabiting the land at that time (15:19–21), whom the Israelites would need to drive out. Again, this clearly cannot be interpreted as heaven. Rather it is a literal description of the land as it existed in the time of Abraham. And this is what God promised the nation Israel as her perpetual possession.

## The Promise of the Land Given to Isaac and Jacob

God's promise of the land was confirmed again in Genesis 26, this time to Isaac. Isaac was born long after human hope was gone; Abraham was a hundred years old and his wife Sarah was ninety. But Isaac's birth was a miraculous fulfillment of God's promise to Abraham. As Isaac grew up he desired, like many young people, to leave home and "see the world." He planned to go down to Egypt, but God told him to stay in the land of Israel and promised Isaac that his descendants would be as numerous as the stars of heaven: "For to you and your descendants I will give all these lands and will confirm the oath I swore to your father Abraham. I will make your descendants as numerous as the stars in the sky and will give them all these lands, and through your offspring all nations on earth will be blessed, because Abraham obeyed me and kept my requirements, my commands, my decrees and my laws" (26:3–5).

Later Isaac's son, Jacob, fled to the land of Haran from which his mother Rebekah had come. On the way God appeared to Jacob and passed on to him the promise given to Abraham and Isaac, assuring him that his descendants would be as numerous as the dust. In a dream the Lord told him, "I am the LORD, the God of your father Abraham and the God of Isaac. I will give you and your descendants the land on which you are lying. Your descendants will be like the dust of the earth, and you will spread out to the west and to the east, to the north and to the south. All peoples on earth will be blessed through you and your offspring. I am with you and will watch over you wherever you go, and I will bring you back to this land. I will not leave you until I have done what I have promised you." (28:13–15).

Thus God's promise to Abraham that his descendants would dwell in the land was passed on to Isaac and then to Jacob—not to Esau or any of Abraham's other children, whether Ishmael or the children of Keturah. This promise about the land will ultimately be fulfilled in the millennial kingdom.

### The Claim of Palestinians

Palestinians today claim they should possess the land, saying that God promised this to Ishmael. This claim is without scriptural support, but it is found in the Koran, on which Palestinian Muslims base their faith. The Koran, however, was written some six hundred years after Christ, in contrast to the Book of Genesis, which was written fifteen hundred years before Christ. There is no ancient evidence anywhere that God promised the land to Ishmael. The entire Old Testament contradicts this Palestinian claim. The covenant of the land is confirmed in Psalm 105:8–11 in unmistakable terms. "He remembers his covenant forever, the word he commanded, for a thousand generations, the covenant he made with Abraham, the oath he swore to Isaac. He confirmed it to Jacob as a decree, to Israel as an everlasting covenant: 'To you I will give the land of Canaan as the portion you will inherit.'" The promises of the land were given to the descendants of Jacob alone, not to the other children of Abraham.

Genesis 12–50 records the lives of Abraham, Isaac, and Jacob and of God's establishing a special people, the nation Israel, along with His larger promise of salvation to all who would trust the God of Abraham. What God promised there is confirmed all through the Old Testament. Clearly a normal, literal interpretation of Genesis is the basis for determining God's prophetic program.

## THE MOSAIC COVENANT

In keeping with God's promise to Abraham that his descendants would go into a strange land where they would be enslaved (Gen. 15:13–14), in the time of Jacob and Joseph the Israelites went to Egypt, where their descendants became slaves to the Egyptians. As the Book of Exodus records, in due time Moses led the Israelites out of Egypt and they began their journey to the Promised Land.

But Israel's journey through the wilderness was not without problems; they needed water and food. Some of them wanted to go back to Egypt where they had had a more secure food supply. God intervened to provide Israel's physical needs and He gave the Ten Commandments to Moses, which form the cornerstone of the Law of God. Many other regulations were also added to the Law. Instructions concerning the tabernacle and the sacrifices were revealed. Additional instructions in the Book of Leviticus deal mostly with the worship of God, along with many regulations concerning individual conduct. Eventually more than six hundred regulations were given as a part of the Mosaic Law, the Law of Moses.

Numbers 1–4 records the census Moses made of the people of Israel. When he sent twelve spies to survey the Promised Land, ten came back reporting that they could not conquer the land, and as a result Israel refused to trust God, rebelling against Him (Num. 13–14). God intervened, however, and sentenced Israel to forty years of wandering in the wilderness until the generation that refused to trust had died (32:9–13). This emphasized the importance of the Promised Land as it relates to Israel.

At the close of Moses' life he wrote the Book of Deuteronomy, which is the second law, the summary of all the commandments revealed earlier. Tragically it also predicts Israel's future wandering from God and God's curse on her disobedience, which was to result in her being scattered all over the world (Deut. 28:1–68).

Once the Israelites entered the Promised Land, the challenge was to accept God's invitation to possess the land by faith, and for a while they pursued this goal. After the deaths of Joshua and the high priest Eliazar, Aaron's son, however, the Israelites once again wandered from God. The dark days of the Book of Judges stand in grim contrast to the victories that were experienced under Joshua. In a series of departures from God, God's resulting discipline, and the return of Israel to the Lord, various judges were raised up to lead Israel during this time of difficulty. Still Israel grew further and further away from God.

## THE MESSIANIC LINE

During this period of the judges is set the Book of Ruth with its beautiful love story of Ruth, whom Boaz claimed as his wife, and the messianic line resulting from their union. Their son Obed became the father of Jesse, who in turn was the father of David, whose line of descendants eventually led to the birth of Christ.

### Samuel the Prophet

At the close of the period of the judges God raised up the prophet Samuel. He is a marvelous illustration of how God answered Hannah's prayers for a son who would serve the Lord. Throughout his life Samuel helped bring Israel back to God, and he also helped prepare the way for the nation's glorious years under David and Solomon.

The impact of Samuel the prophet on the people of Israel is chronicled in 1 Samuel 1:1–24:22, with his death recorded in 25:1. Samuel's ministry was a corrective to the sad era of the Book of Judges, which records one apostasy after the other, each ending in a judgment from God and a measure of repentance in Israel's return to God under a new judge's leadership. The spiral of disobedience, however, was downward, not upward. The sad conclusion is stated in Judges 21:25: "In those days Israel had no king; everyone did as he saw fit." As noted, the Book of Judges is separated from 1 Samuel by the beautiful story of Ruth, which showed God had not forgotten Israel and had a plan for her coming Messiah.

The chapters of 1 Samuel devoted to Samuel's life reveal the tremendous influence he had on the nation of Israel, preparing them in many respects for their future. Prominent in this narrative is the rise of Saul as king of Israel. At the start Saul seemed to be a choice vessel for the Lord, but his pride and lack of good judgment ultimately resulted in his downfall. This led to Samuel anointing David in 1 Samuel 16. But David's rise to power took many years. First Samuel 17 tells the story of David conquering Goliath and Saul's resulting jealousy as the people praised David's skills in battle. For many years Saul sought to kill David to prevent him from taking the throne. One blessing out of this was the deep friendship of Saul's son Jonathan and David. When Samuel died, Saul was still carrying on his attacks on David. When 2 Samuel picks up the account of Israel's history, Saul was dead and David was able to take over the tribe of Judah; later the other tribes of Israel followed him as well. Samuel's life illustrates how God answered the prayers of his mother and used this one man to change the course of a nation.

### The Kingdom of David

While 1 Samuel is devoted largely to the life of Samuel, it also records the beginnings of David's prominence in the seventeen chapters of 1 Samuel 15–31. In addition, the life of David occupies all twenty-four chapters of 2 Samuel, as well as the first two chapters of 1 Kings, which record David's death. Compared to the eleven chapters that record all the history of the world before Abraham (Gen. 1–11), it is certainly evident that from God's point of view the kingdom of David is an important centerpiece in God's program.

After God had Samuel inform Saul that he would be deposed as king, David was anointed to the throne (1 Sam. 16:1–13). However, David did not occupy the throne until much later, even as Christ who is now the appointed Son of David is not yet ruling over Israel but will reign beginning with His second coming. Over several years Saul attempted to kill David and thereby eliminate him as his successor. These were difficult days for David. His repeated escapes from Saul were all part of God's plan that David would ultimately sit on the throne. The second anointing of David is recorded in 2 Samuel 2:4, though Ish-Bosheth, Saul's son, was anointed after Saul's death. He eventually was killed, and David grew stronger and stronger (3:1). After Ish-Bosheth was murdered (4:7), David was able to rule over all the twelve tribes of Israel, who came to him voluntarily (5:1–3).

## THE DAVIDIC COVENANT

Most important in the reign of David was the revelation of God's covenant with him in which He assured David that his Descendant would reign over the house of Israel forever, meaning Christ. The covenant is stated in its essential details in 2 Samuel 7:12–16: "When your days are over and you rest with your fathers, I will raise up your offspring to succeed you, who will come from your own body, and I will establish his kingdom. He is the one who will build a house for my Name, and I will establish the throne of his kingdom forever. I will be his father, and he will be my son. When he does wrong, I will punish him with the rod of men, with floggings inflicted by men. But my love will never be taken away from him, as I took it away from Saul, whom I removed from before you. Your house and your kingdom shall endure forever before me; your throne shall be established forever."

The details of this covenant are important. God declared that David's house—that is, his posterity or dynasty—would be established, and that the throne of his kingdom would continue forever. If his descendants departed from the Lord, God would chasten them (7:14), but He would not take away His mercy as He did from Saul (7:15). Verse 16 summarizes God's assurance that He would perpetually establish David's lineage, kingdom, and throne. This covenant is restated many times in Scripture and forms one of the great purposes of God in relation to the world as well as to the nation of Israel.

One of the important confirmations of the Davidic Covenant is recorded in Psalm 89:3–4: "I have made a covenant with my chosen one, I have sworn to David my servant, 'I will establish your line forever and make your throne firm through all generations.'" And verses 29–37 state: "I will establish his line forever, his throne as long as the heavens endure. If his sons forsake my law and do not follow my statutes, if they violate my decrees and fail to keep my commands, I will punish their sin with the rod, their iniquity with flogging; but I will not take my love from him, nor will I ever betray my faithfulness. I will not violate my covenant or alter what my lips have uttered. Once for all, I have sworn by my holiness—and I will not lie to David—that his line will continue forever and his throne endure before me like the sun; it will be established forever like the moon, the faithful witness in the sky." These verses do not mean there would be an unbroken continuation of Davidic rulers in Israel. Instead, these verses indicate that when Christ is seated on David's throne (Isa. 9:7; Luke 1:31–33; Acts 2:30), His rule will never end.

While many commentators agree that these promises will be fulfilled by Christ, they attempt to see them fulfilled in the church alone, that is, the spiritual kingdom of God. From Scripture, however, it is clear that the kingdom of David is a political kingdom, not a spiritual one. While David's kingdom reflects God's rule over Israel, it nevertheless is not the same as the spiritual kingdom that relates to salvation and an individual's relationship to God as Lord and Master.

### The Davidic Covenant Fulfilled in the Millennium

Here again, the Old Testament reveals that the kingdom of David relates to the earth as a political kingdom, not to the present kingdom of God, which is a spiritual kingdom. Yet both will have spiritual qualities. Psalm 72, a psalm of Solomon, shows that the kingdom is a political kingdom on the earth. The early part of the psalm refers to the justice (72:1–4) and peace (72:5–7) that would characterize Solomon's rule. While verses 8–11 may speak of Solomon in words of hyperbole, they are ultimately true of only Christ. Verses 8–9 declare, "He will rule from sea to sea and from the River to the ends of the earth. The desert tribes will bow before him and his enemies will lick the dust." And verse 11 predicts, "All kings will bow down to him and all nations will serve him." These verses relate to the millennial earth and the fulfillment of God's plan to give the Promised Land to David's posterity.

### The Kingdom of Solomon

In keeping with God's revelation concerning His will for David's successor, David before his death appointed Solomon as king (1 Kings 1:28–53). Adonijah, another son of David, attempted to take the throne. He persuaded some important followers of David to recognize him, including Joab and Abiathar the priest and a number of other mighty men of God (1:7, 9–10). When Adonijah did this, however, Bathsheba and Nathan the prophet informed David of what Adonijah had done. David renewed his pledge to Bathsheba that her son Solomon would sit on the throne. When Zadok the priest and Nathan the prophet announced the appointment of

Solomon, Adonijah's followers immediately deserted him. Not many days later David died (2:10–12). Adonijah, however, continued his efforts to gain the throne, and the result was that Solomon ordered his execution. In the days that followed, Solomon laid the foundation for his glorious kingdom, which attained greater wealth and power than that of any of the kings of Israel. First Kings records his wisdom in handling matters of the court, and his administration was thorough and wise. The wisdom of Solomon was widely known (4:29–34).

While David had the important role of receiving the Davidic Covenant, Solomon was given the charge to build the temple. Elaborate steps were taken to provide for the temple structure and furniture, as God revealed to Solomon. Solomon's prayer of dedication of the temple, recorded in 1 Kings 8, is a magnificent document of praise to the Lord.

### God's Covenant with Solomon

Following the dedication of the temple, God acknowledged that He had accepted the consecration of the temple, and He promised Solomon that if he was obedient God would bless him and his posterity. God said to him: "I have heard the prayer and plea you have made before me; I have consecrated this temple, which you have built, by putting my Name there forever. My eyes and my heart will always be there. As for you, if you walk before me in integrity of heart and uprightness, as David your father did, and do all I command and observe my decrees and laws, I will establish your royal throne over Israel forever, as I promised David your father when I said, "'You shall never fail to have a man on the throne of Israel'" (1 Kings 9:3–5).

God, however, warned Solomon that if he failed to keep God's commandments and his children also failed, He would cut Israel off from the land and destroy the temple (9:6–9).

Solomon continued to prosper, achieving great wealth (10:14–29). Sadly, he violated God's basic commandments in two areas: He married foreign women, and he collected many horses and chariots (10:26–11:8; see Deut. 17:14–17). As a result God denounced Solomon's failure to keep the covenant and told him his rule would not be permanent, even though the throne of David would last forever. God told Solomon his rule would decline and that after his death the kingdom would be divided (1 Kings 11:9–13). After Solomon's death (11:41–43) ten tribes followed Solomon's rival Jeroboam and the two remaining tribes of Judah and Benjamin stayed loyal to the descendants of Solomon.

In the genealogies of Jesus Christ, however, it is significant that while Christ is descended from David, He is not a descendant of Solomon. Instead He is connected to David through Nathan, another son of David. This is because the line of Solomon was cursed so that no descendant of his could rule on David's throne (Jer. 36:27–31). Joseph, the husband of Mary, was a descendant of Solomon, but Mary descended from David through Nathan. Thus Jesus' virgin birth to Mary avoided the cursed line and assured Him a legitimate title as the King of Israel.

## THE DISPERSIONS OF ISRAEL

In his final message to the Israelites before his death, Moses warned them that if they did not keep the Law, God would judge them by removing them from the land, and many of them would be destroyed.

> Then the LORD will scatter you among all nations, from one end of the earth to the other. There you will worship other gods—gods of wood and stone, which neither you nor your fathers have known. Among those nations you will find no repose, no resting place for the sole of your foot. There the LORD will give you an anxious mind, eyes weary with longing, and a despairing heart. You will live in constant suspense, filled with dread both night and day, never sure of your life. In the morning you will say, "If only it were evening!" and in the evening, "If only it were morning!"— because of the terror that will fill your hearts and the sights that your eyes will see. (Deut. 28:64–67)

This prophecy of Israel being driven out of the land was partly fulfilled more than seven hundred years later. The Assyrians conquered the northern kingdom of ten tribes, with its capital, Samaria (2 Kings 17:1–6). This occurred in 722 B.C. Then later Judah and Benjamin, the southern kingdom, were conquered by the Babylonians. Nebuchadnezzar, king of

Babylon, took captives from Jerusalem in 605, 597, and 586 B.C. Jeremiah warned Judah to surrender to Babylon so that the royal family would not be killed. "Then Jeremiah said to Zedekiah, 'This is what the LORD God Almighty, the God of Israel, says: "If you surrender to the officers of the king of Babylon, your life will be spared and this city will not be burned down; you and your family will live. But if you will not surrender to the officers of the king of Babylon, this city will be handed over to the Babylonians and they will burn it down; you yourself will not escape from their hands" ' " (Jer. 38:17–18). But King Zedekiah refused to listen, and the royal family was destroyed, the treasures of the temple were carried off, the palaces were burned, and many Jews were taken as captives to Babylon (2 Kings 24:18–25:21; Jer. 25:1–11).

## THE RETURN FROM BABYLON

In the midst of this sad record of God's judgment, however, Jeremiah made the prediction that Judah would return from Babylon to her homeland after being in captivity in Babylon seventy years (Jer. 29:11). "This is what the LORD says: 'When seventy years are completed for Babylon, I will come to you and fulfill my gracious promise to bring you back to this place' " (29:10). Several decades later Daniel the prophet recorded that he had read the Book of Jeremiah and learned apparently for the first time of the seventy-year prophecy (Dan. 9:1–2). Then followed one of the most remarkable prayers of Scripture, recorded in Daniel 9:4–19.

In his prayer Daniel pleaded with God to fulfill His word, to glorify Himself, to forgive Judah's sins, and to allow the people to go back to Jerusalem. All his life Daniel had prayed for this, and now he had scriptural basis for believing this could soon be brought to pass. The reason Daniel was so thrilled by this prophecy was that approximately sixty-seven years had already elapsed (605 to 538 B.C.), and if the prophecy was to be fulfilled in seventy years, as God prophesied, the return of Judah to the Promised Land would take place soon.

In answer to Daniel's prayer and in keeping with the prophecy, almost fifty thousand returned to the Promised Land, led by Zerubbabel (Ezra 1–2).

Their plan was to rebuild the temple and Jerusalem as well as to inhabit the land. They arrived in 537 B.C.

After the Israelites settled in their towns, Jeshua and Zerubbabel built an altar to the God of Israel, and for the first time since the captivity burnt offerings were offered as commanded in the Law of Moses (Ezra 3:1–3). Following this they kept the Feast of Tabernacles (3:4) and attempted to follow the other commands of the Mosaic Law (3:5). They collected money for materials to build the temple and fourteen months after their return they laid the foundation of the new temple (3:7–13). This was in 536 B.C., exactly seventy years after the first captives were taken in 605.

However, people who were living in the land around Jerusalem suggested they help Judah and Benjamin build the temple (4:1–2). This was probably designed to forestall the project. But Zerubbabel, Jeshua, and others told them, "You have no part with us in building a temple to our God. We alone will build it for the LORD, the God of Israel, as King Cyrus, the king of Persia, commanded us" (4:3). So their enemies "set out to discourage the people of Judah and make them afraid to go on building. They hired counselors to work against them and frustrate their plans" (4:4–5).

The temple altar and the foundation had been built, but because of the enemies of Israel the work was stopped for sixteen years—until 520 B.C. Then Haggai and Zechariah, two of the so-called "minor prophets," challenged the Israelites to resume the building of the temple (Ezra 5:1). Again opposition arose, but this time when research was made of the original decree King Cyrus had issued, it was found that he had specified not only that the work be allowed but that the king's treasury should provide the materials for the temple and also for the sacrifices (5:3–17). The temple was finally completed in the year 516 B.C., exactly seventy years after the temple had been destroyed in 586. Thus the returnees arrived in Jerusalem and the altar was built seventy years after the first captives (including Daniel) were taken (605–536), and the temple was completed seventy years after it was destroyed (586–516). These important events fulfilled Jeremiah's prophecies precisely. Here again, the numbers are to be taken literally.

Later in 444 B.C. Nehemiah in Babylon secured the king's permission to go to Jerusalem to rebuild the city and its walls. Though the walls had lain in ruins for years, Nehemiah and the people rebuilt them in fifty-two days (Neh. 6:15). Once the walls were built, an edict was passed requiring one in ten of Israel's families to reside in Jerusalem (11:1) and to build houses to replace the ruined ones. Thus Christ was born in Bethlehem, near Jerusalem—and not in Babylon—as prophesied by Micah (Mic. 5:2). Israel's sojourn in Egypt fulfilled God's prediction to Abraham, and the Assyrian and Babylonian captivities literally fulfilled His predictions of her captivity. But Moses' prophecy that Israel would be scattered all over the world was yet to be fulfilled.

## THE THIRD AND FINAL DISPERSION OF ISRAEL

When Israel failed to follow Jesus Christ as her Messiah, He predicted that she would once again be scattered. Jerusalem, He said, would be left desolate (Matt. 23:38), the temple would be destroyed (24:1–2), and Israel would suffer terrible persecution (24:3–12). Christ's sad comment about Jerusalem and His heartbreak over the rebellion of Israel are stated dramatically in 23:37–39: "O Jerusalem, Jerusalem, you who kill the prophets and stone those sent to you, how often I have longed to gather your children together, as a hen gathers her chicks under her wings, but you were not willing. Look, your house is left to you desolate. For I tell you, you will not see me again until you say, 'Blessed is he who comes in the name of the Lord.' "

The disciples, perhaps feeling Jesus was unnecessarily upset, showed him the magnificent buildings of Herod's temple, which were nearing completion (24:1). Jesus responded, "I tell you the truth, not one stone here will be left on another; every one will be thrown down" (24:2). The disciples were deeply troubled by this because it did not fit with their idea of what was to happen. They continued to believe that Christ would deliver them from Rome and lead them in a triumphant restoration of Israel. However, more than three years had passed since they had joined with Christ, and the tide seemed to be going the other way, with growing opposition from the chief priests and scribes. This prompted the disciples to ask about the coming of Christ and the fulfillment of the kingdom promises.

Four of the disciples—Peter, Andrew, James, and John (Mark 13:3)—approached Jesus with three questions. "When will this happen, and what will be the sign of your coming and of the end of the age?" (Matt. 24:3). The first question was, When would the temple be destroyed? The second question was, What will be the sign of Your coming? The third question was, What will be the sign of the end of the age? The second and third questions are answered together in Matthew 24:4–28; Mark 13:5–26; and Luke 21:8–19, 25–28.

Jesus' prophecy of the temple's destruction (Luke 21:20–24) was tragically fulfilled in A.D. 70 when the Roman army surrounded Jerusalem, breached its walls, and killed hundreds of thousands of Jews who had gathered in the city for their feast. Only those who quickly fled the city escaped. Jerusalem itself was left in ruins for 150 years, and only a small portion of the nation of Israel remained in the land. For more than 1,900 years since then, Israel has been scattered all over the face of the earth in tragic fulfillment of Deuteronomy 28:64: "Then the Lord will scatter you among all nations, from one end of the earth to the other."

A significant development took place in the twentieth century (May 1948) when Israel was recognized as a political state. During the last half of this century several million Jews have returned to the land of Israel. This is necessary for the peace treaty prophesied for Israel in Daniel 9:27 (see chap. 9, "Israel's 490 Prophetic Years"). Most of these returned Jews are not believers in Christ, however, and will be driven out of the Promised Land at the beginning of the Great Tribulation, according to Matthew 24:15–22. The final restoration of Israel to her land will take place after the Second Coming.

## THE FINAL REGATHERING OF ISRAEL

In the Great Tribulation, Israel will suffer greatly (Jer. 30:5–7) and will be scattered, fleeing to the mountains (Matt. 24:15–21). But the Lord will save her out of that time of trouble, for at the second coming of Christ the people of Israel will be regathered to serve the Lord and David their king, who will be resurrected at that time. Jeremiah wrote, " 'In that day,' declares the Lord Almighty, 'I will break the yoke off their necks and will tear off their bonds; no longer will foreigners enslave them. Instead, they will serve the LORD their God and David their king, whom I will raise up for them'" (Jer. 30:8–9).

Israel will be gathered from all over the world, for God said, "I will restore the fortunes of Jacob's tents and have compassion on his dwellings" (30:18). Further details are given in 31:8–9, in which the Lord said through Jeremiah, "See, I will bring them from the land of the north and gather them from the ends of the earth. Among them will be the blind and the lame, expectant mothers and women in labor; a great throng will return. They will come with weeping; they will pray as I bring them back. I will lead them beside streams of water on a level path where they will not stumble, because I am Israel's father, and Ephraim is my firstborn son."

Ezekiel recorded an important prophecy concerning God's regathering of Israel after the Great Tribulation and His purging of all unbelievers when Christ returns.

> I will bring you from the nations and gather you from the countries where you have been scattered—with a mighty hand and an outstretched arm and with outpoured wrath. I will bring you into the desert of the nations and there, face to face, I will execute judgment upon you. As I judged your fathers in the desert of the land of Egypt, so I will judge you, declares the Sovereign LORD. I will take note of you as you pass under my rod, and I will bring you into the bond of the covenant. I will purge you of those who revolt and rebel against me. Although I will bring them out of the land where they are living, yet they will not enter the land of Israel. Then you will know that I am the LORD. (Ezek. 20:34–38)

An important fact in all these prophecies is that God's Word was fulfilled literally when the nation went to Egypt and returned, when she was taken captive by Assyria and Babylon and returned, and when Israel was scattered in the first century of the Christian era. This shows that the final regathering of Israel at the time of Jesus' second coming will also be fulfilled literally.

The fact that Israel is already now back in the land, even though in unbelief, has set the stage for some of these great prophecies to be fulfilled.

## THE NEW COVENANT

God's various covenants have been discussed, especially as they relate to prophecy. The Abrahamic Covenant was seen as a far-reaching promise of God concerning the land and Israel's ultimate possession of it. An important prophecy is the Davidic Covenant, in which God affirmed His plan to regather Israel and place the Son of David on David's throne in the millennial kingdom.

In Jeremiah's prophecy during the Babylonian captivity, another far-reaching covenant was outlined, one called the New Covenant. The essential details are stated in Jeremiah 31:31–34.

> "The time is coming," declares the LORD, "when I will make a new covenant with the house of Israel and with the house of Judah. It will not be like the covenant I made with their forefathers when I took them by the hand to lead them out of Egypt, because they broke my covenant, though I was a husband to them," declares the LORD. "This is the covenant I will make with the house of Israel after that time," declares the LORD. " I will put my law in their minds and write it on their hearts. I will be their God, and they will be my people. No longer will a man teach his neighbor, or a man his brother, saying, 'Know the LORD,' because they will all know me, from the least of them to the greatest," declares the LORD. "For I will forgive their wickedness and will remember their sins no more."

In this passage the New Covenant is contrasted with the Mosaic Covenant and promises not only the regathering of the people but also their spiritual revival when the Lord will put His Law in their hearts. This will be fulfilled in the millennial kingdom, when there will be full revelation of who God is. In addition to these details Jeremiah also declared that Israel will continue as a nation forever and that this covenant was determined by divine decree (31:36).

As Jeremiah said, the New Covenant was made specifically with the nation of Israel and is a prophetic statement of how Israel will be revived after her experiences in the Great Tribulation detailed in Jeremiah 30:5–11. The New Covenant is related to God's purpose to regather Israel (30:1–11, 18–21;

31:8–14, 23–28). This covenant assures Israel that she will again be a promi-nent people. Her prominence is related to the manifestation of God's glory in the millennial kingdom. In the New Covenant there will be forgiveness for Israel, a demonstration of God's grand promise of His unmerited blessing.

Ezekiel also spoke of the New Covenant, adding other details. He wrote, "For I will take you out of the nations; I will gather you from all the coun-tries and bring you back into your own land. I will sprinkle clean water on you, and you will be clean; I will cleanse you from all your impurities and from all your idols. I will give you a new heart and put a new spirit in you; I will remove from you your heart of stone and give you a heart of flesh. And I will put my Spirit in you and move you to follow my decrees and be careful to keep my laws. You will live in the land I gave your forefathers; you will be my people, and I will be your God" (Ezek. 36:24–28).

In the next chapter Ezekiel prophesied again about Israel's New Covenant:

> This is what the Sovereign LORD says: I will take the Israelites out of the nations where they have gone. I will gather them from all around and bring them back into their own land. I will make them one nation in the land, on the mountains of Israel. There will be one king over all of them and they will never again be two nations or be divided into two king-doms. They will no longer defile themselves with their idols and vile images or with any of their offenses, for I will save them from all their sinful backsliding, and I will cleanse them. They will be my people, and I will be their God. My servant David will be king over them, and they will all have one shepherd. They will follow my laws and be careful to keep my decrees. They will live in the land I gave to my servant Jacob, the land where your fathers lived. They and their children and their children's children will live there forever, and David my servant will be their prince forever. I will make a covenant of peace with them; it will be an everlast-ing covenant. I will establish them and increase their numbers, and I will put my sanctuary among them forever. My dwelling place will be with them; I will be their God, and they will be my people. Then the nations will know that I the LORD make Israel holy, when my sanctuary is among them forever. (37:21–28)

The nation will be spiritually cleansed; David will be resurrected to rule over Israel with Christ; and Israel will enjoy God's peace. The fact that the New Covenant is everlasting stands in contrast to the Mosaic Covenant, which was terminated at the death of Christ.

The New Covenant is also described in the New Testament. In fact, the Bible is divided into what is called the Old and New Covenants (or Testaments) because of the importance of the promises that are added in the New Testament.

New Testament references to the New Covenant are found in Luke 22:20; 1 Corinthians 11:25; 2 Corinthians 3:6; and Hebrews 8:8, 13; 9:15; 12:24. Other verses refer to it without using the word *new* (Matt. 26:28; Mark 14:24; Rom. 11:27; Heb. 8:10; 10:16). Romans 11:26–27 relates this covenant to Israel's future deliverance in the end times. Among these references, those found in Hebrews 8 are the most important for they emphasize that the New Covenant is better than the Mosaic Covenant. This is summarized in Hebrews 8:6: "But the ministry Jesus has received is as superior to theirs as the covenant of which he is mediator is superior to the old one, and it is founded on better promises." Though Hebrews 8:7–12 refers to Jeremiah's covenant (Jer. 31:31–34), the Book of Hebrews does not claim that the New Covenant is being fulfilled today in its entirety, as amillenarians suggest. The facts are that many details of the covenant are not being fulfilled today: everyone does not know the Lord today; there is no widespread spiritual revival; Israel has not reclaimed all the land God promised her; and God's laws are not in the hearts of Israel. The writer of Hebrews quoted Jeremiah 31:31–34 simply to show that the Mosaic Covenant had been abolished, and something better will come.

The attempt to understand the New Covenant in relation to the church has been variously treated by evangelicals and continues to arouse discussion. Some contend that the New Covenant is a covenant with Israel alone, and that the only element Christians share in today is the sacrificial blood of Christ on the cross. Another common view is that while the covenant is primarily with Israel, it has an oblique reference to the church as is expressed in the Lord's Supper. In yet another view, Lewis Sperry Chafer introduced the unique explanation that there are two New Covenants, one for Israel and one for the church.

I have wrestled with these theological interpretations of the New Covenant for many years and finally came to realize that what the New Covenant is all about is embraced in the concept of the grace of God.

In systematic theology it is commonly held that in eternity past God promised to provide a Savior who would die on the cross for our sins and provide salvation for all who would put their trust in Him. This is the key to understanding the New Covenant because the New Covenant—in contrast to the Mosaic Covenant—is not a covenant of works but a covenant of grace, and all grace stems from Christ's death on the cross for our sins. Accordingly, a reasonable explanation is simply that God has provided one New Covenant of grace, which has many applications. It applies to Israel, especially in the future in the millennial kingdom. It applies to the church today because church-age believers are also saved by grace. So the church does not partake in *Israel's* New Covenant, but rather both Israel and the church benefit from God's grace, which provides forgiveness, favor, and blessing that is neither earned or deserved. The New Covenant therefore remains alongside other biblical covenants as a centerpiece in God's program for the world, the church, and Israel.

## CHRISTIANS ARE ENCOURAGED TO BELIEVE GOD'S PROMISES

Because these prophecies have been fulfilled Christians can trust the promises of God that are subject to future fulfillment. God has always kept His word. He never deceives, He never gives false hopes. So Christians can rest in God's wonderful promises for use. The prediction of the coming of the Lord and our dwelling in eternity as the objects of His grace can be firmly believed. The fulfillment of prophecy is a remarkable confirmation that the Word of God is absolutely true and can be literally believed, and that our hope is built on an eternally solid foundation.

# 8

# God's Master Plan
# for the World

A NOTHER MAJOR PROPHETIC REVELATION concerns the history of the world as a whole. Many of these prophecies have already been fulfilled; some are destined for future fulfillment. The Old Testament provides a remarkable revelation of six great empires that would dominate the world. The Bible does not trace the history of Asia, nor does it deal with the Western Hemisphere. Rather it is concerned with territories and nations surrounding the nation Israel.

The first of the six great Old Testament empires that related to Israel was Egypt.. Egypt's history goes back many thousands of years before Christ, but the first important dynasty of unified Egypt surfaced around 3100 B.C. From then on, one dynasty after another rose and fell for more than two thousand years.

## ISRAEL IN EGYPT

Egypt, the first of the great empires of the Middle East, reached its peak of prominence and power about 1500 B.C., but it was conquered by Assyria in the seventh century B.C.

Egypt is mentioned in Scripture, more than seven hundred times in the Old Testament and thirty-three times in the New Testament, including

95

references to Egyptians. Many prophecies about Egypt have already been fulfilled: Only a few pertain to the future in relation to the return of Christ. When Abram went to Egypt because of a famine, Pharaoh was attracted to Sarai, Abram's wife, whom Abram had deceitfully identified as his sister. (This was partially true because she was his half-sister.) When the Lord inflicted diseases on Pharaoh because of her, Pharaoh ordered Abram out of Egypt, but not before Abram had acquired considerable wealth through gifts from Pharaoh (Gen. 12:10–20).

Though not named, Egypt is alluded to in the prophecy of Genesis 15:13–14: "Then the Lord said to him, 'Know for certain that your descendants will be strangers in a country not their own, and they will be enslaved and mistreated four hundred years. But I will punish the nation they serve as slaves, and afterward they will come out with great possessions.'" It is generally agreed that this refers to the sojourn in Egypt, but the statement that their sojourn would last for four hundred years has caused considerable debate. Apparently "four hundred" is a rounded figure, because Exodus 12:40 and Galatians 3:17 state Israel's Egyptian bondage was 430 years. This period of time probably began when Jacob moved his family from the Promised Land to Egypt in 1876 B.C., and ended with the Exodus in 1446.

Many prophecies about Egypt are found in Isaiah, Jeremiah, Ezekiel, Hosea, Amos, and Micah. Because these prophecies have been largely fulfilled, not much attention is given them in prophetic studies. A highly significant reference, however, is Hosea 11:1: "When Israel was a child, I loved him, and out of Egypt I called my son." Three other times Hosea referred to God's having brought Israel out of Egypt (12:9, 13; 13:4). When Joseph and Mary took the baby Jesus to Egypt till Herod died (Matt. 2:13–14), their return to Israel, according to Matthew 2:15, "fulfilled" Hosea 11:1. Since Hosea 11:1 was a historical reference, not a prediction, how could it be fulfilled by Christ? Apparently Matthew was pointing to similarities between Israel, God's chosen "son," and Jesus, God's Son, both of whom God summoned out of Egypt. Matthew, then, "heightened" the reference to the Exodus to a more significant event, the Messiah's return from Egypt.

Because of Joseph's prominence in Egypt, Pharaoh awarded his family a favored portion of the land of Egypt for their cattle and homes. The Israelites prospered and became a people of several million (Exod. 1:1–7). When Egypt rose to power in the Middle East, Israel fell into disfavor with their rulers, and they were made slaves (1:8–14). Eventually God brought plagues on the Egyptians, which forced them to allow the Israelites to leave (5:1–12:42).

Many of the prophecies concerning Egypt were prophecies of God's judgment on them for their persecution of Israel, which have been fulfilled. The Old Testament records considerable prophetic details about the conflicts between Egypt and nations to the north, principally Assyria, which occurred over a lengthy period of time before the coming of Christ.

One of the comprehensive prophecies about Egypt is in Daniel 11, which describes her conflict with Syria. Egypt was led by the king of the South and the armies of the north were led by the king of the North (11:5–6). Of particular interest is the reference to Antiochus Epiphanes, a ruler of Syria from 175 to 164 B.C. (11:21–32). Earlier he was victorious over the armies of Egypt, but later on this victory was erased by the rising power of Rome, which prevented Antiochus from pursuing his conquest of Egypt. He desecrated the temple in Jerusalem by setting up an idol to Zeus on the altar of burnt offering. But this was reversed even in the lifetime of Antiochus, and the orthodox religion of Israel was reinstated. In the conflict, though, thousands of Jews were killed by Antiochus, who attempted to force pagan religion on the nation of Israel.

It is particularly interesting that Antiochus seems to foreshadow the future Antichrist, who will dominate the world in the Great Tribulation. The best interpretation of these passages is that the predictions of Daniel 11:1–35 have been fulfilled in history, and that verses 36–45 relate to the end times when the final world ruler will oppose the people of God and desecrate the temple, much as Antiochus did.

In the Great Tribulation the world will come under the domination of the king mentioned in Daniel 11:36, who will claim to be God. The wars mentioned in verses 40–45 will occur "at the time of the end" (11:40), that is, they will take place in the Great Tribulation between Egypt, "the king of the South," and the Antichrist, "the king of the North" (11:40). While the descriptions of these battles are somewhat obscure, it is clear that nothing has yet occurred in history that corresponds to this conflict. Egypt will again be prominent in the days just before the Second Coming.

Egypt will have its place also in the future millennial kingdom. Isaiah 19 records a number of prophecies about Egypt's destruction, all of which have been fulfilled. Isaiah 19 also predicts that Egypt will turn to the Lord: "In that day there will be an altar to the LORD in the heart of Egypt, and a monument to the LORD at its border. It will be a sign and witness to the LORD Almighty in the land of Egypt. When they cry out to the LORD because of their oppressors, he will send them a savior and defender, and he will rescue them. So the LORD will make himself known to the Egyptians, and in that day they will acknowledge the LORD. They will worship with sacrifices and grain offerings; they will make vows to the LORD and keep them" (19:19–21).

Isaiah also spoke of a highway extending from Egypt to Assyria, which will go through the land of Israel. "In that day there will be a highway from Egypt to Assyria. The Assyrians will go to Egypt and the Egyptians to Assyria. The Egyptians and Assyrians will worship together. In that day Israel will be the third, along with Egypt and Assyria, a blessing on the earth. The LORD Almighty will bless them, saying, 'Blessed be Egypt my people, Assyria my handiwork, and Israel my inheritance' " (19:23–25). This apparently will be fulfilled during the Millennium. Most of the prophecies concerning Egypt, however, refer to her desolation at different times in her history, and these have been literally fulfilled.

## THE RISE OF ASSYRIA

The Assyrians were an ancient people in Mesopotamia for hundreds of years. Assyria began her ascent to power in the eighth century B.C., conquering a number of countries. In 732 B.C., she attacked and plundered Damascus, Syria's capital city, and in 722 she plundered Samaria, the capital of the Northern Kingdom, Israel. Isaiah related these events to the name of his first son. "Then I went to the prophetess, and she conceived and gave birth to a son. And the LORD said to me, 'Name him Maher-Shalal-Hash-Baz. Before the boy knows how to say "My father" or "My mother," the wealth of Damascus and the plunder of Samaria will be carried off by the king of Assyria' " (Isa. 8:3–4).

When Assyria conquered Israel, she took many captives (2 Kings

17:1–6; 18:9–11). Then in 701 Assyria, under King Sennacherib, moved south to Judah, conquering its fortified cities and besieging Jerusalem (18:13–19:14; Isa. 37:1–38:13). Scripture records Hezekiah's eloquent prayer (2 Kings 19:15–19; Isa. 37:15–20) and Isaiah's response: "Then Isaiah son of Amoz sent a message to Hezekiah: 'This is what the LORD, the God of Israel, says: I have heard your prayer concerning Sennacherib king of Assyria'" (2 Kings 19:20; see Isa. 37:21). In a lengthy prophecy Isaiah predicted that Assyria would not be able to conquer Jerusalem (2 Kings 19:21–34; Isa. 37:22–35). The historical account in 2 Kings 19:37 and Isaiah 37:36–38 records that 185,000 Assyrian soldiers were killed by the angel of the Lord overnight. Sennacherib went back to Nineveh, where he was later killed by two of his own sons. In keeping with this prophecy, the two tribes of Judah and Benjamin—the Southern Kingdom,— continued until the rise of Neo-Babylonia. The Assyrian Empire came to its end in 609 B.C., when Nineveh fell to the Babylonian army and the Neo-Babylonian Empire came to power.

## THE RISE OF BABYLON

The Neo-Babylonian Empire, brought to prominence by Nebuchadnezzar, was one of the most powerful governments of the ancient world. Babylon destroyed Jerusalem in 586 B.C., after two previous attacks on the city in 605 and 597. The Book of Daniel dramatically outlines the role of Daniel the prophet in Babylon, a foreign country, for almost seventy years. Amazingly, Daniel, a captive Jew, was appointed by Nebuchadnezzar to a leading political position (Dan. 2:48–49).

The Book of Daniel records the fascinating story of the relationship of the Babylonian Empire to Israel in this crucial time of her history. Daniel and his companions, many of them of royal Judean descent, were carried off as hostages shortly after Jerusalem was besieged in 605 B.C. (Dan. 1:1–3). Later they were joined by several thousand Jews who were taken as exiles to Babylon in the year 597 B.C. (2 Kings 24:10–14).

Daniel and three of his companions were trained to be servants of Nebuchadnezzar, Babylon's king. This three-year educational program consisted of the study of numerous subjects, primarily astrology and

Babylonian religion (Dan. 1:17). Daniel and his friends, however, faced the problem of eating the king's cuisine. This conflicted with their Jewish dietary laws, which prohibited them from eating what was offered in Babylon. Daniel courteously requested a different diet, which eventually was granted, and so they were able to maintain their adherence to God's laws in this matter (1:5–21). This glimpse of Daniel as a teenager reveals his faith in God, which apparently had been planted in his heart by godly parents even though they lived in times of apostasy in Israel.

## Nebuchadnezzar's Dream

Toward the end of Daniel's three-year schooling, Nebuchadnezzar had a prophetic dream (2:1). He called in his wise men, but they could not tell him the dream or its interpretation. Because they could not help him, he gave the order to have all the wise men killed. Daniel was one of the wise men, even though he was not present in this interview. But he went to the king and asked for time, and then he and his three faithful companions prayed and God gave them the secret of the king's dream.

When he reported this to Nebuchadnezzar, Daniel explained that the interpretation was not because of any unusual insight Daniel had, but by the help of God in heaven, who can reveal secrets. Daniel explained that the image in the king's dream was a representation of the future history of the world (the "days to come," 2:28; see "things to come," 2:29).

Daniel explained to the king that in the dream's image the head made of gold represented Babylon; the upper part of the body made of silver represented the next empire after Babylon; the lower part of the body made of bronze represented a third kingdom; and the legs of iron and the feet of iron and clay represent the fourth empire. Later, in Daniel 8:20–21, two of the empires are named: Medo-Persia and Greece. Nebuchadnezzar was so impressed by this revelation that he immediately appointed Daniel ruler over the province of Babylon (2:48)—the extensive area around the city of Babylon, not other countries conquered by Nebuchadnezzar— even though Daniel was still a young man and a foreigner. This began their long relationship.

After reigning forty-three years, Nebuchadnezzar died in 562 B.C. and a series of rulers followed until 539 B.C., when the Medes and Persians (the "kingdom of silver," according to Dan. 2:32) conquered Babylon in 539, the night of Belshazzar's feast (Dan. 5).

### Daniel's Vision of the Four Empires

Fourteen years before the events of Daniel 5, however, in Belshazzar's first year as king (553 B.C.), Daniel had a vision of four beasts. This vision, recorded in Daniel 7, corresponds to the four empires in chapter 2, but gives additional information.

The first beast was a lion, representing Babylon. "Daniel said: 'In my vision at night I looked, and there before me were the four winds of heaven churning up the great sea. Four great beasts, each different from the others, came up out of the sea. The first was like a lion, and it had the wings of an eagle. I watched until its wings were torn off and it was lifted from the ground so that it stood on two feet like a man, and the heart of a man was given to it'" (7:2–4).

The second beast, a bear, represented Medo-Persia. "And there before me was a second beast, which looked like a bear. It was raised up on one of its sides, and it had three ribs in its mouth between its teeth. It was told, 'Get up and eat your fill of flesh!'" (7:5).

The third, a leopard, represented Greece. "After that, I looked, and there before me was another beast, one that looked like a leopard. And on its back it had four wings like those of a bird. This beast had four heads, and it was given authority to rule" (7:6). The fourth empire was a great terrifying beast with large iron teeth; it crushed and devoured its victims (7:7). These four beasts are apt illustrations of the kingdoms they represented. The prophecy of the first three empires has been fulfilled in history.

*The first beast: Babylon.* In Daniel 2, four great gentile empires of the future were prophetically revealed by Nebuchadnezzar's gigantic image, which Daniel interpreted. These four empires are viewed from the standpoint of the world.

But in Daniel's vision in chapter 7 the empires are seen from the divine perspective as great beasts, powerful but wicked. Unlike the previous revelations given to Nebuchadnezzar and interpreted by Daniel (Dan. 2; 4), this is the first of four visions given to Daniel himself. They are recorded in Daniel 7; 8; 9:20–27; and 10:1–12:5. The first of these visions came to Daniel in a dream (7:1).

In Daniel's vision "the four winds of heaven churning up the great sea" (7:2) represent God's dealings with the world. In Scripture the sea often represents the world (Matt. 13:47; Rev. 13:1; 17:1, 15). The stormy seas themselves are also symbolic of conflicts in the gentile world (Isa. 17:12–13; 57:20; Jer. 6:23). The symbolism of winds striving with the sea may represent God's power as He deals with sinful man to attain divine ends.[1]

The whole point of revealing the four gentile powers in Daniel 7 is to show that God is in control of world events. The Old Testament often refers to the Mediterranean Sea as the Great Sea,[2] and these four nations surrounded it.

While Babylon is not identified by name as the first beast, the lion no doubt is Babylon for several reasons. First, the four beasts of Daniel 7 correspond to the four metals of the dream image in Daniel 2, in which gold, the first metal, is identified as Babylon. Second, the general recognition of the lion as king of the beasts corresponds with Babylon as the first of these great empires. The lion symbolizes royal power, as illustrated in Solomon's use of twelve carved lions on the six steps leading to his throne (1 Kings 10:20; 2 Chron. 9:19). Third, in Babylon lions with wings were portrayed as guarding the gates of the palaces of Babylon.

The lion is depicted as having eagle's wings. As the lion is the king of beasts on earth, so the eagle is the king of the birds of the air. The eagle symbolizes both Babylon (Ezek. 17:3–7) and Egypt (17:7–8, 15).

In his vision Daniel saw the wings being plucked out and the lion lifted from the earth and given a human heart. This is often related to Daniel 4, which records Nebuchadnezzar's being humbled by insanity and eventually recognizing the greatness of God.

The vision of the beast that follows the lion obviously builds on the fall of Babylon, which is not detailed here by Daniel (although the fall of Babylon is prominent in other Scriptures, including Isa. 13:1–22; 21:1–10; 47:1–15; Jer. 50:1–51:58; Eze. 17:11–24; and 30:10–20). While some of these passages refer to Babylon's fall to the Medes and Persians in 539 B.C., others refer to a future fall of Babylon prior to the Second Coming.

*The second beast: Medo-Persia.* The second beast looked like a bear raised up on one side and with three ribs in its mouth. It was told, "Get up and eat your fill of flesh!" (Dan. 7:5). Though Russia in the modern world is often compared to a bear, the beast here is obviously Medo-Persia, since that empire followed Babylon. This empire was referred to by name in 8:20.

While liberal scholars have generally accepted the view that the first beast is Babylon, they have challenged the idea that the second kingdom is Medo-Persia. They want to divide this empire into two empires, with the Medes being the second kingdom in the vision and the Persians the third. By doing this they identify the Greek Empire, represented by the third beast, as the fourth empire. This is an effort on their part to eliminate the prophetic character of the vision, building on the false premise that the Book of Daniel is a forgery written in the second century B.C. and thus is not prophecy about the Greek and Roman empires.

The traditional view, held by most conservatives, is that the Medes and the Persians were one kingdom. They had at one point been separate kingdoms (with Media northeast and Persia east of Babylon respectively), but in 550 B.C. Cyrus the Persian conquered the Medes, bringing them under his rule. Together they conquered Babylon (Dan. 5:28). This means that the Greek Empire is represented by the third beast, not the fourth.

The meaning of the three ribs is not specified in Scripture, and various explanations have been given. One of the most plausible is that in the conquest of Babylon the three ribs refer to its major components, namely, Media, Persia, and Babylon. An alternative view is that the kings who were conquered by Persia are Lydia, Babylon, and Egypt. These were conquered in 546, 539, and 525 B.C. respectively.

A bear, though not as majestic as a lion, is equally powerful. The fact that the bear raised itself on one side seems to indicate that though there are three entities in the empire, the Persians were more powerful than either the Medes or the Babylonians, whom they conquered. Persia's dominance over Media is suggested in Daniel 8:3, in which the prophet in a vision saw a ram (Media and Persia, 8:20) with two horns, one of which was longer than the other.

The Medo-Persian kingdom dominated the Middle East from 539 B.C. until the rise of Alexander the Great in Greece, slightly more than two hundred years later. Though Daniel lived to see the Medes and the Persians take over Babylon, he was writing prophetically, not historically, when he described the second kingdom as a bear.

It is significant that under the Medo-Persians, the Jews were treated kindly and allowed to go back and rebuild their temple (Ezra 1:1–4:5; 5:1–6:18), completing it in 516 B.C. Then in 444 Nehemiah built the walls of Jerusalem in less than two months (Neh. 1:1–6:15), and in the next half-century the city of Jerusalem was built on top of the ruins of the ancient city. By enabling the Jews to return to Jerusalem, the center of their life and government, the Medo-Persians unknowingly paved the way for the fulfillment of Micah's prophecy that Christ would be born in the nearby Judean town of Bethlehem (Mic. 5:2).

*The third beast: Greece.* The third beast dramatically presents the rapid conquest of Alexander the Great and the rise of the Grecian Empire. Greece is appropriately represented as a leopard, a swift beast, which is even speedier than normal because of its four wings (Dan. 7:6). It is also represented by the goat of Daniel 8:5, 21. In only a few years Alexander conquered the entire Middle East, including Israel, Egypt, and Persia, and even present-day Pakistan, Afghanistan, and India. After these conquests, Alexander died in a drunken feast in Babylon. He had conquered the world but could not conquer himself. A few years later his empire was divided among his four generals, represented by the four heads (see 8:8, 22).

These four kings were Ptolemy, Seleucus, Philip, and Antigonus. However, power switched to other leaders and the subsequent political entities were headed by Lysimachus, who controlled Thrace and Bithynia; Cassander, who controlled Macedonia and Greece; Seleucus, who had power over Syria, Babylon, and territories to the east as far as India; and Ptolemy, who had control of Egypt, Palestine, and Arabia. These prophecies have been literally fulfilled, just as predicted, even though the prophecies were given many years before the events.

*The Syrian leader.* A notable prophecy was recorded in Daniel 8:9–14, 23–27 and 11:21–35 concerning one of these four divisions. One of the horns of the goat depicted a king named Antiochus Epiphanes, who ruled over Syria from 175 to 164 B.C. God told Daniel that this "goat" would defile the Jewish temple, cause the daily sacrifices to be taken away (8:11;

see 11:21–35), and cause many to die (8:24–25). This was precisely fulfilled in 167 B.C., but even before Antichos died in 164 B.C. the temple and Jewish worship had been restored.

In many respects Antiochus illustrates the Antichrist, who at the end of the age will also stop Israel's sacrificial system and cause many to die (9:27; 12:11; Matt. 24:15).

*The fourth beast: Rome.* As previously noted, liberal scholars do their best to make the fourth beast Greece in an effort to destroy the prophetic character of the Book of Daniel, which, they say, was a forgery written in the second century B.C. This wrong view of Daniel must be abandoned because of the discovery of copies of the Book of Daniel among the Dead Sea Scrolls near Qumran, which were transcribed two hundred years before Christ. Since these are copies, the original composition of Daniel had to be earlier than that of the Qumram community. This makes it impossible for Daniel to have written at the same time (second century B.C.) since some time would have elapsed between its composition in Babylon and its being copied in Qumran. Thus, the book had to have been written *earlier* than two hundred years before Christ.

The fourth beast, though not named in the Book of Daniel, is obviously the Roman Empire, which in its prime conquered the whole Mediterranean world and Europe, and became the greatest empire up to that time. The Roman Empire was formed gradually, beginning in the Italian peninsula. The empire began to expand geographically as early as 241 B.C., when Rome conquered Carthage less than one hundred years after the Grecian Empire was formed. A few decades later Rome conquered Asia Minor, Macedonia, and Greece. As Daniel had predicted, Rome was like a powerful, terrifying beast with large iron teeth, devouring its victims (Dan. 7:7, 23). Under the Roman expansion Jerusalem fell to the Roman army in A.D. 70, and for several hundred years thereafter Rome controlled the nations around the Mediterranean Sea. Again prophecy was fulfilled exactly as God predicted, even though the fulfillment occurred hundreds of years after the prophecy was originally given. According to Daniel, however, Rome will eventually be destroyed by the kingdom from heaven (7:23–27).

Actually the Roman Empire disintegrated slowly over many centuries, and though it existed much longer than any of the preceding empires and embraced more territory than the others, it eventually lost its power because of both internal decay and external invasions. Today the Roman Empire no longer exists. Yet the destruction of the empire as prophesied in the Bible has not taken place.

*The revival of Rome.* About the time of the Rapture, the Roman Empire, according to Scripture, will be revived in the form of ten countries described in Daniel 7:7 as ten horns of the fourth beast, Rome. "After that, in my vision at night I looked, and there before me was a fourth beast—terrifying and frightening and very powerful. It had large iron teeth; it crushed and devoured its victims and trampled underfoot whatever was left. It was different from all the former beasts, and it had ten horns."

These ten horns depict ten kings or their kingdoms. "The ten horns are ten kings who will come from this [fourth] kingdom: After them another king will arise, different from the earlier ones; he will subdue three kings" (7:24). In other words the final stage of the Roman Empire will occur when ten kingdoms are banded together. Then a leader will conquer three countries and eventually all ten. This requires a revival of the ancient Roman Empire in the form of a political union of ten nations. So far this has not taken place. This revived empire, according to Scripture, will eventually become a worldwide empire, something the world so far has never seen. "He gave me this explanation: 'The fourth beast is a fourth kingdom that will appear on earth. It will be different from all the other kingdoms and will devour the whole earth, trampling it down and crushing it' " (7:23). The world empire will be brought to ruin by the second coming of Christ and the judgments that will occur at that time (7:26–27). These prophecies will be considered at length later.

A number of interpreters have attempted to find fulfillment of this prophecy of the fourth beast in ways other than as described in Scripture. A popular theory advanced by some prophecy teachers is that the ten nations are ten economic components throughout the world. This, however, does not satisfy the prophecy, because in Daniel's vision the ten horns come out of the Roman Empire and the ten are kingdoms, not economic unions. The Roman Empire has not yet been revived, even though there is common talk of a "United States of Europe" now that Europe is relatively at peace. Such a united kingdom would be possible.

The Old Testament provides a broad outline of world history, beginning with Creation, followed by the Flood and the call of Abraham, and then continuing in the gentile world in the kingdoms of Egypt, Assyria, Babylon, Medo-Persia, Greece, and Rome. The final kingdom will be Christ's millennial kingdom, established after His second coming.

## GOD'S SOVEREIGNTY OVER THE NATIONS

It should be evident from Scripture that our God knows the future and is sovereign over it. He has ordained that the nations will ultimately reflect His power over them, even though at times they seem to be allowed to display great power and evil. For Christians, this is greatly reassuring because our world is not what it should be, and we are surrounded by wickedness and unbelief almost without parallel in the history of the world, especially given the fact that the gospel and the Bible have been made accessible to the world as a whole. Though the final episodes of prophetic history have not yet been fulfilled, believers in Christ are reminded that God is on the throne, that things will turn out exactly as He has predicted, and that the great prophecies related to Israel and the church will be fulfilled.

## THE CHALLENGE OF PROPHECY

All this points to the fact that life continues after death, and the greatest challenge that faces individuals is the question of whether they are ready to meet God either in the Rapture or in death. The only way is through faith in Jesus Christ as the Savior who died on the cross for our sins and rose again. Only through faith in Him can our sins be forgiven and can we be assured of eternal life and of receiving God's grace throughout all eternity. Along with this challenge is the appeal to Christians to live for Christ every day, and to honor, worship, and love Him, as the Scriptures command. Any reasonable understanding of the prophetic Word, its fulfillment in history, and its anticipation of the future leads to these important conclusions that give meaning to life and promise for the future.

# 9

# Israel's 490
# Prophetic Years

---

THE PROPHET DANIEL had the unusual responsibility of recording not only the outline of prophecy for the gentile world, as in Daniel 2 and Daniel 7–8, but also Israel's 490 prophetic years, as recorded in 9:24–27. An amazing amount of prophetic detail is furnished in these four verses.

The ninth chapter of the Book of Daniel begins with the record of Daniel's discovery of Jeremiah's prophecy concerning the seventy years in which Jerusalem would lie desolate. Daniel wrote, "In the first year of Darius son of Xerxes (a Mede by descent), who was made ruler over the Babylonian kingdom—in the first year of his reign, I, Daniel, understood from the Scriptures, according to the word of the LORD given to Jeremiah the prophet, that the desolation of Jerusalem would last seventy years" (9:1–2).

Belshazzar's feast and the fall of the Babylonian Empire, recorded in Daniel 5, occurred chronologically between chapters 8 and 9. After Daniel's earlier prophecies about the second kingdom of the Medes and the Persians (2:39a; 7:5; 8:3–4, 20) were fulfilled, he learned of Jeremiah's prophecy apparently for the first time. Somehow there fell into Daniel's hands the very manuscript Jeremiah wrote. Believing in the literal fulfillment of prophecy, Daniel was immediately prompted to pray the great prayer recorded in chapter 9, in which he pleaded with God to fulfill His promise to restore Jerusalem and the people of Israel (9:4–19).

When the Babylonians entered Jerusalem and killed the royal family, Jeremiah was taken to Egypt by Jews who were rebelling against Nebuchadnezzar (Jer. 43:1–6). The prophet apparently ended up in a nameless grave in Egypt. How his prophecies ever reached Daniel is not recorded. But reading Jeremiah led him to understand the prophecy of the seventy-year captivity and to realize that most of that period, probably sixty-seven years, had already been fulfilled. The first year of Darius (Dan. 9:1) was 538 B.C., sixty-seven years after Daniel himself was taken to Babylon in 605. Jeremiah's prophecy says: "This whole country will become a desolate wasteland, and these nations will serve the king of Babylon seventy years. But when the seventy years are fulfilled, I will punish the king of Babylon and his nation, the land of the Babylonians, for their guilt. . . . and will make it desolate forever" (Jer. 25:11–12).

Jeremiah 29:10–14 records a more specific prophecy concerning these seventy years.

> This is what the LORD says: "When seventy years are completed for Babylon, I will come to you and fulfill my gracious promise to bring you back to this place. For I know the plans I have for you," declares the LORD, "plans to prosper you and not to harm you, plans to give you hope and a future. Then you will call upon me and come and pray to me, and I will listen to you. You will seek me and find me when you seek me with all your heart. I will be found by you," declares the LORD, "and will bring you back from captivity. I will gather you from all the nations and places where I have banished you," declares the LORD, "and will bring you back to the place from which I carried you into exile."

As discussed previously, there is a distinction between the seventy-year period following the captivity, which began in 605 B.C. and ended when the exiles returned to Jerusalem in 536 B.C., and the desolation of Jerusalem, which began with its fall in 586 B.C. and ended in 516 B.C. with the rebuilding of the temple.

## THE BACKGROUND OF THE 490 YEARS

The important background of these seventy years is obvious. Daniel's eloquent prayer (9:4–19) is based on God's promises and his belief that God's prophecies would be literally fulfilled. Daniel repeatedly acknowledged that the captivity and the desolation of Jerusalem occurred because of Judah's sins and that confession of sin was necessary for their restoration.

Most significant for Israel's future, however, was the message by the angel Gabriel (9:20–23), which followed Daniel's prayer. The prophecy of the "seventy sevens" of Israel is one of the most significant prophetic passages in the Old Testament.

As with other prophecies, major rules of interpretation help clarify the situation. First, the prophecy is literal and should be interpreted that way; and second, the details of the prophecy should be closely observed. Any interpretation that departs from these rules misses the main thrust of the passage. Information about the "seventy sevens" pertaining to Israel is given in Daniel 9:24–27:

Seventy "sevens" are decreed for your people and your holy city to finish transgression, to put an end to sin, to atone for wickedness, to bring in everlasting righteousness, to seal up vision and prophecy and to anoint the most holy. Know and understand this: From the issuing of the decree to restore and rebuild Jerusalem until the Anointed One, the ruler, comes, there will be seven "sevens," and sixty-two "sevens." It will be rebuilt with streets and a trench, but in times of trouble. After the sixty-two "sevens," the Anointed One will be cut off and will have nothing. The people of the ruler who will come will destroy the city and the sanctuary. The end will come like a flood: War will continue until the end, and desolations have been decreed. He will confirm a covenant with many for one "seven." In the middle of the "seven" he will put an end to sacrifice and offering. And one who causes desolation will place abominations on a wing of the temple he will set up an abomination that causes desolation, until the end that is decreed is poured out on him.

## THE 490 YEARS OF ISRAEL'S FUTURE

The translation "seventy sevens" in the New International Version is more accurate than the King James Version and other versions that have "seventy weeks." Obviously the events that are prophesied in this passage could not possibly be fulfilled in seventy weeks of days—that is, 490 days or about sixteen months. Daniel 10:2 refers to "three sevens of days" (literal translation), making clear that his fasting then lasted for twenty-one days of twenty-four hours each. But the seventy sevens in 9:24 refer not to "sevens" of days, a literal "week," but to "sevens" of years. Had he meant seventy "sevens" of days (i.e., 490 weeks or 3,430 days or a little more than nine years), he would no doubt have added "of days." That the "sevens" were heptads of years, totaling 490 years (not 490 days or weeks), is suggested by the fact that Daniel was already thinking in terms of years (9:1; see Jer. 25:11–12). Also in Israel heptads pertained not only to days (a week) but also to years (Lev. 25:1–9).

### Three Major Time Periods

The prophecy of the 490 years is divided into three time periods: (a) seven "sevens," or forty-nine years, (b) sixty-two "sevens" or 434 years, and (c) the last seven years (Dan. 9:25, 27). The first two sections of these prophecies totaling 483 years have already been fulfilled.

### Problems of Interpretation

This passage, which obviously is so structural in Israel's prophetic future, has unfortunately been the source of many confusing interpretations. Two major divisions can be considered. Some of the interpretations can be labeled Christological or literal, and some non-Christological. The non-Christological perspective may again be divided between the liberal view, which is critical of the text and does not accept the inspiration of the Bible, and the conservative amillennial view, which recognizes the passage as genuine prophecy but interprets it in a nonliteral sense.

## Is the Book of Daniel a Forgery?

The Book of Daniel has been subjected to misrepresentations by liberal scholars who claim, as discussed earlier, that Daniel was a forgery written about two hundred years before Christ. They also say Daniel himself was confused on the relationship of the seventy years of Israel's captivity and the "seventy sevens" of Daniel's vision. As a matter of fact, Daniel was not confused and the two are separate prophecies. As a result of this, critics not only deny that this is genuine Scripture but also claim that it is impossible to provide any logical interpretation. Thus they have seldom agreed on how this passage should be interpreted.

## Amillennial Views

Among amillennial scholars no satisfactory explanation of Daniel 9:24–27 has emerged. Amillenarians take the Tribulation in a nonliteral sense, and this does not fit with Daniel's prophecy. While most conservative thinkers accept the time units as representing years, others disagree because they do not interpret the passage literally. The fact that years are intended in this prophecy is confirmed by the fact that the seventy years of Israel's captivity were literal. There is no uniformity in the amillennial view, and it is confusing to an interpreter who wants to find out what this passage actually means.

The Jewish view, another non-Christological approach to the passage, says the seventy "sevens" concluded with the destruction of Jerusalem in A.D. 70. This also does not agree with the text.

## Christological Interpretation

The Christological interpretation on the whole attempts to be more literal, though in view of the many other interpretations care must be exercised when we attempt to determine the exact meaning of the text. Those who interpret this passage Christologically and literally generally agree that a prophetic year is 360 days, in keeping with the tradition of the Jewish nation that each year has 360 days. (This would occasionally require an additional month in order to correct the calendar for the five days each year that are missing under this arrangement.)

## THE SIX MAJOR PROPHETIC ACCOMPLISHMENTS

Daniel 9:24 states that in 490 years six important accomplishments will be completed. At the outset it should be understood that the phrase "your people and your holy city" (9:24; see 10:14; 11:14) clearly refers to Israel, and not to the church or world history. One of the most destructive ideas in interpreting prophecy has been the thought that the church is the new Israel and that the church fulfills Israel's promises. Nowhere is this stated in the Bible, and the hundreds of verses that mention Israel clearly refer to the twelve tribes descended from Jacob's twelve sons.

The six major accomplishments mentioned in 9:24 are divided into two groups of three each. The first three pertain to sin and redemption ("to finish transgression, to put an end to sin, to atone for wickedness"), and the last three relate to the kingdom ("to bring in everlasting right-eousness, to seal up vision and prophecy, and to anoint the most holy"). The prophecy that transgression will be finished refers to the fact that at the second coming of Christ Israel's wandering will end. She will be brought back to the land, the rebels will be purged, and the godly rem-nant will be brought into the millennial kingdom. This will "put an end to sin" (see Ezek. 37:23; Rom. 11:20–27). Jeremiah had prophesied that after seventy years of captivity in Babylon Israel would be restored to her land. Daniel's prophecy of 490 years, however, addresses the final restora-tion of Israel. This will be the complete answer to Daniel's prayer for Israel's restoration.

In the Old Testament, every year, on the Day of Atonement, the high priest offered sacrifices for the sins of Israel, applying blood to the mercy seat, the cover on the ark of the covenant in the Most Holy Place of the tabernacle (Lev. 16). But this was a temporary provision. It was necessary for Christ to come and die on the cross, "to atone for wickedness" for the sins of Israel as well as the whole world before sin could be ended. Though atonement was provided, however, Israel's rebellion has continued in the present age. At the Second Coming, the atonement will be applied to Israel and she will be restored spiritually.

The final three accomplishments pertain to the return of Christ and the establishment of His kingdom on earth. When He comes, He will bring in what is called "everlasting righteousness," that is, He will reign in righteous judgment over the earth, and Israel will be restored to walking righteously with the Lord. That age will be characterized most of all by righteousness (Isa. 60:21; Jer. 23:5–6).

Another accomplishment is that vision and prophecy will be sealed up—that is, all that God predicted through visions and oral and written prophecies for Israel will be fulfilled at Jesus' second coming, when the full truth of God will be revealed in the person of His Son. Until these prophecies are fulfilled, they are "unsealed."

The phrase "to anoint the most holy" could refer to the millennial temple described in Ezekiel 41–46, which will be set apart to God. Or it may refer to Christ Himself, the Holy One, who will be enthroned as "the Anointed One" (Dan. 9:25–26). These six prophecies clearly pertain to Israel, though they will also have an impact on the rest of the world. They summarize God's promises to Israel in the Abrahamic, Davidic, and New Covenants (Gen. 15:18–21; 2 Sam. 7:16; Jer. 31:31–34).

## THE BEGINNING OF THE 490 YEARS

After the overall program for Israel is stated in verse 24, the beginning of the 490 years is discussed in Daniel 9:25. The 490 years will begin, Daniel was told, at "the issuing of the decree to restore and rebuild Jerusalem." There has been much discussion on which decree is indicated.

Actually, four decrees by Persian rulers pertained to the return of Israel from captivity to the Promised Land. The first decree, concerning the building of the temple, was made by Cyrus the Great in 538 B.C.; it began the process of Israel's return (2 Chron. 36:22–23; Ezra 1:1–4; 5:13). The second decree confirmed the first decree and was issued by Darius I (522–486 B.C.) in the year 520 B.C. (Ezra 6:1, 6–12). The third decree was issued by Artaxerxes Longimanus (464–424 B.C.) in 457 B.C. (7:11–26). The first two decrees dealt with the temple, and the third offered financial backing for animal sacrifices in the temple. Actually the city of Jerusalem was not rebuilt in response to these first three decrees. Rebuilding Jerusalem was the subject of only the fourth decree, one issued by Artaxerxes Longimanus on March 5, 444 B.C. (Neh. 2:1-8). This generous decree, given in response to Nehemiah's concern, made it possible for Nehemiah to go to Jerusalem and rebuild the wall.

The first segment of the fulfillment of the 490 years, forty-nine years (seven "sevens"), was the period in which the city was rebuilt (444–395 B.C.). Nehemiah was able to encourage the people to reconstruct the city's wall in fifty-two days (6:15). After the wall was completed, one of every ten families in Judah was required to live in the city (11:1), and during the next forty-nine years the city's debris was removed, houses were built, and "the streets and a trench" (Dan. 9:25) were rebuilt.

## THE SECOND PERIOD OF 434 YEARS

The second segment in the seventy "sevens" was 434 years (sixty-two "sevens," 9:25). Adding the first forty-nine years, these two segments total 483 years, after which the Messiah, the "Anointed One, the Ruler," was to come.

The period of 483 years extends from March 5, 444 B.C., when Artaxerxes issued the decree for Nehemiah to rebuild Jerusalem's wall, to March 30, A.D. 33, the date of Christ's triumphal entry into Jerusalem, which was followed in a few days by His death on the cross. At first glance the period of time from 444 B.C. to A.D. 33 does not seem to equal 483 years (the sixty-nine "sevens"). But in biblical times a prophetic year was 360 days (twelve months of thirty days). For example, forty-two months in Revelation 11:2 are said to have 1,260 days (12:6; 13:5). Thus when the 483 years are multiplied by 360 days, the total number of days is 173,880, which corresponds exactly to the time from 444 B.C. to A.D. 33, when leap years are added. This total of 173,880 days ended shortly before Christ was crucified, or as Daniel's prediction states, before He was "cut off and will have nothing."

## EVENTS AFTER THE 483 YEARS

To understand this prophecy properly, it is most important to note that verse 26 says Christ would be cut off *after* the sixty-ninth "seven" (i.e., after 483 years), not *in* the seventieth. This indicates that there would be a time interval between the end of the 483 years (A.D. 33) and the beginning of the last seven years. Christ's crucifixion was in that interval, right after His Triumphal Entry. Also in this interval "the city and the sanctuary" would be destroyed. This occurred in A.D. 70, about thirty-seven years after the death of Christ. This too, according to verse 26, occurred *after* the sixty-ninth "seven," not *in* the last seven years. This interval will continue throughout the present church age until the end times.

Most amillenarians argue that the decree to restore and rebuild Jerusalem was Cyrus's decree in 538 and that the seventieth "seven" has already been fulfilled in Jesus' ministry on earth. They say He was "cut off" (crucified) in the seventieth week. Thus there is no future fulfillment of a seventieth "seven"; all seventy "sevens" are past. However, this presents several serious problems. First, this requires a nonliteral approach to the numbers. The length of time from Cyrus's decree to Jesus' death is far more than 490 years. Amillenarians respond that the numbers are to be "spiritualized" to mean simply a "long period of time." Second, Jesus' ministry was not seven years long. Third, the decree of Cyrus, as already noted, pertained only to the temple, not to Jerusalem.

Also amillenarians suggest the six accomplishments in Daniel 9:24 are being fulfilled today in the church. But this overlooks the fact that these six actions pertain to Daniel's people (Israel) and the holy city, Jerusalem. Nothing in Daniel 9:24 suggests the church is fulfilling these promises.

The events following the sixty-ninth "seven," including the death of Christ and the destruction of Jerusalem, have been fulfilled. But the Rapture and the time of trouble including the Great Tribulation leading up to the Second Coming did not immediately follow the sixty-nine "sevens"; they are yet future. This is confirmed by the fact that the Second Coming has not occurred.

## EVENTS IN THE SEVENTIETH "SEVEN"

Daniel 9:27 discusses events that relate to the last seven years, years that are yet to come. The verse begins, "He will confirm a covenant with many for one 'seven,' " that is, the final seven of the 490 years. Some amillenarians insist this refers to the New Covenant Christ inaugurated by His death on the cross, but this was not a seven-year covenant. Further, as already noted, the destruction of Jerusalem did not occur until thirty-seven years after His crucifixion. Therefore one cannot say these prophecies were fulfilled during Jesus' life on earth. Also the pronoun "he" does not refer to Christ. Instead it points back to the previous person mentioned, who is the "ruler" whose "people," the Romans, "will destroy the city" (9:26).

The people of the ruler, not the ruler himself, destroyed the city. That ruler, the Antichrist—not Christ—is the one who will "confirm a covenant" with Israel in the last seven of the 490 years.

## DESECRATION OF THE TEMPLE

This future ruler will stop the Jewish sacrifices and the grain offerings and will desecrate the temple. This refers to a temple yet to be built and the sacrifices that will be offered in it. After making a seven-year peace agreement with Israel, this ruler, the Antichrist, will discontinue these sacrifices in the middle of the last seven years leading up to the second coming of Christ, as stated in verse 27 (see 12:11). Other Scripture verses confirm the point that the Great Tribulation will occur in the last three and a-half years before the Second Coming (12:1; Matt. 24:21; Rev. 7:14). The length of the Great Tribulation will be forty-two months, or 1,260 days (Rev. 12:11; 13:5). This coincides with the last half of the seven years of Daniel 9:27, which indicates that persecution of Israel by the Antichrist will begin in the middle of the last seven years, when he will break his covenant with her. When Christ returns to earth, He will deliver Israel from her persecutors, and the Antichrist and the forces of wickedness will be destroyed (Rev. 19:17–21).

These facts together demonstrate that the last seven years of Daniel's prophecy of seventy "sevens" have not been fulfilled, but will be fulfilled just prior to the second coming of Christ.

The entire present age from Pentecost until the time of the Rapture—the lengthy interval between the sixty-ninth and the seventh "sevens"—must run its course before the events in these last seven years will occur. The seven years (Daniel's seventieth "seven") leading up to the Second Coming will be a time of terrible judgments from God, as recorded in Revelation 6–18.

### Israel's Glorious Future to Begin after the 490 Years

Inherent in this revelation in Daniel 9:24–27 is the assurance that Israel has a glorious future, which will begin at the second coming of Christ, but that before that time she will suffer terrible persecution as a people who have not come to Christ. This judgment will fall in the seven years leading up to Christ's return.

# 10

# The Road to
# Armageddon

A$_S$ $_{WE}$ $_{SAW}$ $_{IN}$ $_{THE}$ $_{PREVIOUS}$ $_{CHAPTER}$, the last seven years of
Israel's prophetic program, climaxing in the second coming of Christ, are
unfolded in Daniel 9:27. While many have attempted to find the fulfillment of these seven years in the past, no historical event corresponds to
this prophecy of a great political leader who will make a covenant with
the people of Israel. Nor have the events of the Great Tribulation in the
last half of those seven years been fulfilled. An initial question, of course,
is, Who is this ruler who will enter into this covenant with Israel?

## THE TEN-NATION CONFEDERACY

In the Old Testament the present age from Pentecost to the Rapture of
the church is not dealt with, and often the prophecies of the first and
second comings of Christ are considered together as if there were no time
lapse between them (e.g., Isa. 61:1–2; Mic. 5:2–5a). Since the present age
is not indicated, no discontinuity is recognized between the Roman Empire of the past and the revived Roman Empire of the future.

Daniel 7 indicates that the last stage of the Roman Empire, which was
never fulfilled, will be a ten-nation confederacy. The fourth beast, which
depicts the Roman Empire, is described in verse 7. "After that, in my vision at night I looked, and there before me was a fourth beast—terrifying

and frightening and very powerful. It had large iron teeth; it crushed and devoured its victims and trampled underfoot whatever was left. It was different from all the former beasts, and it had ten horns."

History has already recorded the fulfillment of the first part of this verse. The Roman Empire was indeed like a terrible beast with iron teeth that tore apart country after country as its soldiers advanced. But the last stage, in which the beast has ten horns, has never been fulfilled. A number of expositors have tried to point to a time in Rome's history when ten kings ruled, but nothing actually corresponds. At no time were ten kings ruling over the empire at once. Though presented in symbolic terms as horns, there is no need for speculation as to what this means because Daniel 7:24 states, "The ten horns are ten kings who will come from this kingdom."

Opinions differ as to the nature of these ten countries. A popular theory advanced by some is that the ten nations are not political entities but are economic centers, and they attempt to divide up the world into ten economic centers of power. While it is true that the Roman Empire had its own economic impact on the then-known world, the context of this passage is political, not economic. The ten nations are referred to as "kingdoms," which does not properly describe an economic situation. Furthermore, the Roman Empire does not correlate with the Western Hemisphere, Russia, China, or other major areas of the world. So the suggestion of economic centers rather than kings imposes something on the text that it does not say or even imply. While there will undoubtedly be economic divisions of the world in the end time, the main point is that there will be a world government that is political in character and that will be behind whatever economic system emerges. The four great empires of Daniel's time were political entities, not economic divisions. Many people today wonder if the Common Market of Europe, with its several member nations, will fulfill this future Roman Empire. These nations, however, are united by economic, not political, concerns.

## THE COMING RULER

The ten-nation kingdom, having been established presumably in a peaceful way, will be overtaken by a ruler who will conquer three of the nations and then apparently all ten. "While I was thinking about the horns, there before me was another horn, a little one, which came up among them; and three of the first horns were uprooted before it. This horn had eyes like the eyes of a man and a mouth that spoke boastfully" (Dan. 7:8). "After them another king will arise, different from the earlier ones; he will subdue three kings" (7:24).

No mention is made of how this eleventh "horn" will become the leader of the other seven nations, but perhaps they will simply capitulate to him. Daniel 7:23 states that after the ten-kingdom stage arises, this fourth kingdom will become a world empire, something the world will have never seen before that time: "The fourth beast is a fourth kingdom that will appear on earth. It will be different from all the other kingdoms and will devour the whole earth, trampling it down and crushing it." Verse 25 describes the reign of this eleventh horn and his persecution of the people of Israel. "He will speak against the Most High and oppress his saints and try to change the set times and the laws. The saints will be handed over to him for a time, times and half a time." The reference to time, times, and half a time is normally understood as the three and a-half years leading up to the second coming of Christ.

## PEACE TREATY BROKEN BEFORE THE GREAT TRIBULATION

After this ruler conquers three and then all ten nations, he will impose a peace treaty on Israel for seven years (9:27). Then he will break this covenant after three and a-half years and will become a persecutor of Israel. This period of time is called the Great Tribulation, a time of unparalleled trouble (Dan. 12:1; Matt. 24:21; Rev. 7:14). When the Antichrist becomes ruler over the entire world, his rule will be Satan's attempt to imitate the worldwide millennial reign of Christ.

The first half of the seven years will be a relatively peaceful time. Many Bible expositors feel that Ezekiel 38–39 will be fulfilled at that time, because when the battle of Gog and Magog begins, Israel will be in her land in peace and safety (Ezek. 38:8, 11, 14). Six countries will then attack Israel. Five of them are mentioned by name (Persia, Cush, Put, Gomer, and Beth

Togarmah; 38:5–6), and the sixth, "the land of Magog," undoubtedly relates to a portion of the former Soviet Union, for it will go against Israel from "the far north" (38:15; 39:2). Perhaps only some of the states of the former Soviet Union will participate in this war.

When these countries attack Israel, God will intervene, and a series of catastrophes will wipe out the armies (38:18–23). Addressing Gog, God said, "On the mountains of Israel you will fall, you and all your troops and the nations with you. I will give you as food to all kinds of carrion birds and to the wild animals" (39:4). Then Ezekiel's prophecy indicates that seven months will be needed to bury the dead bodies (39:12).

Some writers place this battle at the beginning of Daniel's seventieth seven years, while others put it at or near the end of that period. Some say it will occur at the second coming of Christ, and still others put it at the end of the Millennium. However, it seems preferable to place the invasion in the first half of those seven years or at the middle. Besides being an attack on Israel, this invasion will be a challenge to the ten-nation ruler, who supposedly will be protecting Israel. So when the invading armies are defeated, the ruler of the ten nations will elevate himself and proclaim himself ruler of the entire world.

## THE WORLD RULER

Daniel 11:36–45 casts further light on this coming world ruler. As an absolute ruler he "will do as he pleases," claiming to be God and blaspheming the true God (11:36). As Paul wrote, this world ruler, the Antichrist, will oppose God and exalt himself, even setting himself up in God's temple, proclaiming to be God (2 Thess. 2:4). "He will be successful until the time of wrath [the Great Tribulation] is completed, for what has been determined must take place" (Dan. 11:36).

Also he will disregard "the God of his fathers" (11:37, NKJV). Here the word for God is *Elohim*, a general word for God, and not *Yahweh*, the God of Israel. This suggests that this world ruler will be a Gentile. The only god he will recognize, according to verse 38, is the "god of fortresses"; that is, he will engage in warfare, financed by his material wealth ("gold and silver, with precious stones and costly gifts"). Verses 40–45 describe the war that will characterize the last part of that seven-year period leading up to the second coming of Christ. While that period will begin with a world government in place, the judgments of God will be poured out on this blasphemer. Various armies of the world, dissatisfied with his rule, will congregate in Israel to fight it out for power. Reports of these armies approaching from the east and the north will alarm him, and he will seek to destroy them. He will pitch his tents in Israel, but eventually he will be defeated at the Second Coming.

## THE FINAL WORLD WAR

According to Revelation 16:16, armies will be marshaled at Armageddon, "the hill of Megiddo," in northern Israel. The gigantic world war that follows will rage right up to the day of the second coming of Christ (Zech. 14:1–3), when armies will gather also at Jerusalem. Most of the facts relating to these world events just before the Second Coming are found in the Book of Revelation.

## THE PROPHECIES OF THE BOOK OF REVELATION

Unfortunately many scholars write off the Book of Revelation as if it were uninterpretable and useless in determining future events. While it is true that parts of the Book of Revelation are written in symbolic terms, it is also true that many of these symbols are interpreted in the text and that alongside these symbols are plain literal statements of prophetic events.

The Book of Revelation begins in chapter 1 with the revelation of Christ in glory, in sharp contrast to the Christ in the Gospels, where His glory is hidden. John was instructed to send a message to seven churches (1:11), represented in 1:20 and 2:1 as "lampstands." These messages addressed to the churches illustrate the fact that even in the first century all was not well within the local church. The seven churches, contemporary to Revelation, illustrate that the problems in the church through the ages were anticipated in these messages.

The church in Ephesus was accused of having forsaken its "first love" (2:4). As the Ephesian church probably included second-generation

Christians, it lacked the zeal of the earlier church. However, it was commended for its doctrinal convictions and its opposition to false practices. The second church, Smyrna, was in terrible persecution and no fault was found with it. It was exhorted to "be faithful, even to the point of death" (2:10). The third church, Pergamum, was guilty of worldliness and compromise and was exhorted to repent (2:16). The church at Thyatira was worse than the church in Pergamum. Its members were criticized for allowing a woman called "Jezebel" to encourage them to engage in sexual immorality and to eat sacrifices offered to idols (2:20). Judgment was promised them if they did not repent and return to the Lord. In Revelation 3 a message was addressed to the church in Sardis, which was accused of being dead but which included some who were standing true.

Most interesting is the message to the church in Philadelphia, a church with spiritual strength that kept the commandments of God. To the Philadelphians Christ gave a special promise, "I will also keep you from the hour of trial that is going to come upon the whole world to test those who live on the earth" (3:10). This command harmonizes with the expectation of the church that the Rapture will occur before the troubles of the end time. The church will be kept *from* the coming worldwide Tribulation, not kept *through* it. To "keep from" differs significantly from "keep through." This verse thus serves to reinforce the expectation of a pretribulational Rapture.

The seventh message, to the church in Laodicea, records a severe criticism because the believers there were neither cold nor hot. In other words, they were lacking zeal for the things of God and were concerned instead for material things.

These seven messages applied first to the local churches of the first century that are specifically named in Revelation 2–3. Also these messages apply throughout the present church age to any church that is similar to any of these seven. Each of the messages is also addressed to individuals to take heed that the sins mentioned do not become part of their own Christian profession. Some feel that the order of the churches beginning with Ephesus and climaxing with Laodicea is a historical pattern followed by the professing church through the centuries, with Ephesus depicting the early church and Laodicea representing the church in the last days just before the Rapture. While this may have some substance to it, it should be borne in mind that the Bible does not authorize this historical application.

After the opening three chapters of Revelation, including the messages to the seven churches with their contemporary exhortations, John was introduced to a vision of heaven in chapters 4–5. Then in chapter 6 he saw a scroll rolled up with seven seals attached to its edges in such a way that as the scroll was unrolled these seals were broken one by one.

## The Seven-Sealed Scroll

The scroll is a record of the major events in this future time of trouble. Some writers say these events depicted in the scroll will occur in the first half of Daniel's seventieth "seven" of years, and others say they pertain to all seven years. It seems preferable, however, to see them as focusing on the last three and a-half years. When the first seal is broken in Revelation 6, it is interpreted as a step toward world government. As seen in Daniel, the Antichrist will establish himself as world ruler at the middle of the seven-year period before the Second Coming.

A conqueror is seen riding on a white horse, a symbol of victory. "Its rider held a bow, and he was given a crown, and he rode out as a conqueror bent on conquest" (Rev. 6:2). It is significant that he has a bow but no arrow, which indicates that his conquest will be accomplished at the beginning without war. As noted in Daniel 11:36–39 he will declare himself world ruler, and no one will be strong enough to stand against him (see Rev. 13:4).

The other seals describe the terrible catastrophes and judgments God will bring on the earth. The second seal deals with war, which eventually breaks out (6:3–4); the third seal depicts a devastatingly widespread famine (6:5–6). The fourth seal describes the death of a fourth of the world. "When the Lamb opened the fourth seal, I heard the voice of the fourth living creature say, 'Come!' I looked, and there before me was a pale horse! Its rider was named Death, and Hades was following close behind him. They were given power over a fourth of the earth to kill by sword, famine and plague, and by the wild beasts of the earth" (6:7–8). It should be obvious that these catastrophes will be part of the Great Tribulation.

Though contained in only two verses, this prophecy of the fourth seal judgment is overwhelming. One fourth of the world's population will be destroyed by sword, hunger, disease, and wild animals. We should remember that these same four elements were involved when Judah was taken captive by Babylon (Jer. 16:4; Ezek. 14:21). If the global population at that time is six billion, it means that 1.5 billion people will perish. Some writers recoil against the idea that this is literally true, but there is no scriptural basis for taking it in other than its plain ordinary meaning. Clearly this period of destruction and devastation on earth, as noted in these four seals, will be terrible. This makes understandable what Christ said in Matthew 24:21–22: "For then there will be great distress, unequaled from the beginning of the world until now—and never to be equaled again. If those days had not been cut short, no one would survive, but for the sake of the elect those days will be shortened."

The destruction of human life, Jesus said, will exceed anything the world has ever seen. This leads to Jesus' statement that if He did not intervene by His second coming and end the terrible time of destruction, no one would be left alive on the earth. Obviously, Jesus' words harmonize with the statements in Revelation 6:7–8, when understood in their literal meaning. Jeremiah also wrote of this terrible time: "How awful that day will be! None will be like it. It will be a time of trouble for Jacob, but he will be saved out if it" (Jer. 30:7).

The fifth seal has to do with martyrs who will die for their faith (Rev. 6:9–11). They will be innumerable, for they are described in 7:9–17 as "a great multitude that no one could count" coming out of the Great Tribulation and standing before God's throne in heaven. This clearly contradicts the false notion that believers will be protected from death in the Great Tribulation.

The sixth seal refers to the cosmic disturbances and earthquakes that will characterize this period when "the wrath of the Lamb" (6:16), that is, of Christ, will be poured out on the unbelieving world. "For the great day of their wrath has come, and who can stand?" (6:17).

### The Trumpet Judgments

When the seventh seal is broken, a new series of seven judgments will be introduced by trumpets blown by angels (Rev. 8). As these trumpets sound, each will signal a catastrophe over a portion of the earth, usually involving a third of the world or its people. When the first trumpet sounds, a third of the trees of the earth and all the green grass will be burned up (8:7). With the second trumpet a third of the sea will become blood, a third of the living creatures in the sea will die, and a third of the ships will be destroyed (8:8–9). This will disrupt the shipping of food and other necessities and may explain why there will be widespread famine. With the third trumpet a third of the rivers and springs of water will become terribly bitter, and many people will die from drinking the water (8:10–11). In the fourth trumpet a third of the sun, a third of the moon, and a third of the stars will be darkened (8:12), resulting in disturbances of the earth's climate. The fifth trumpet, though given symbolically, apparently will reveal the work of demons (pictured as locusts from hell, "the Abyss"), who will torment unbelievers for five months (9:1–11).

The sixth trumpet has to do with the great battle at the end of the Great Tribulation, when a third of the earth's population will be killed (Rev. 9:13–16). Since a fourth of the world's population will have been destroyed in the opening of the fourth seal (6:7–8), deaths resulting from the sixth trumpet will reduce the population by 50 percent total (or possibly more, as the other judgments no doubt will also result in loss of life).

After the sounding of the seventh trumpet is recorded in Revelation 11:15, a parenthetic section follows in 11:16–14:13, which does not advance the elapsed time. The seventh trumpet introduces what is portrayed in Revelation 15–16 as the bowl judgments.

### The Bowl Judgments

The seven bowl judgments introduced in Revelation 15 and described in chapter 16 are devastating judgments similar to the trumpet judgments, but they are unlike them in that they will affect the whole earth rather than being restricted to one third of the earth. They will be the final judgments of "God's wrath" (16:1), apparently given in rapid succession just before the second coming of Christ. These catastrophic judgments are seen as bowls that angels will overturn and pour out on the earth.

In the first bowl judgment the unsaved will be afflicted with loathsome sores (16:2). In the second the sea (i.e., the oceans) will be turned into blood, and every living thing in it will die (16:3). The third bowl judgment will turn the rivers and springs into blood (16:4). The fourth has to do with changes in the climate, resulting in people being scorched with great heat from the sun (16:8–9). The fifth bowl judgment will bring darkness on the earth and intense pain (16:10). The sixth refers to the drying of the Euphrates River. The fact that dams have been built on the Euphrates River even now causes it to dry up at certain times of the year. This is a further development of what will happen to the Euphrates in the sixth trumpet judgment (9:13–16). The drying up of this great river will enable kings and their armies to march from the East against the world ruler in Israel (see Dan. 11:44). They will be gathered by demonic persuasion to this battle "on the great day of God Almighty" (Rev. 16:14), that is, the Battle of Armageddon.

The seventh bowl will introduce a cataclysmic judgment of a great thunderstorm and a severe earthquake which will destroy civilization as we know it: "Then there came flashes of lightning, rumblings, peals of thunder and a severe earthquake. No earthquake like it has ever occurred since man has been on earth, so tremendous was the quake" (Rev. 16:18). The dramatic statement is made that in the earthquake "the cities of the nations" will collapse (16:19), including Babylon (see Rev. 18). Though the structures of the entire world will be shaken to pieces, apparently the nation Israel will escape, for the Greek word rendered "the nations" often refers to Gentiles. In this terrible catastrophe "every island fled away and the mountains could not be found" (16:20). Apparently the configuration of the entire globe will be changed, with terrible loss of life and property. Also great hailstones weighing about one hundred pounds each will fall on people (16:21). So terrible will be this hailstorm that unbelievers will curse God, but they will not repent. The same will be true earlier in the sixth trumpet judgment (9:20–21). The wickedness of the unsaved, in spite of God's display of judgment against them, is almost unbelievable.

## The Judgment on Babylon

The destruction of Babylon, predicted in the Old Testament in Isaiah 14:22–27 and in Jeremiah 50–51, is depicted in Revelation 18. Attempts have been made to write off this future destruction of Babylon as something already fulfilled or as something relating to the United States. A careful reading of these prophecies, however, indicates plainly that these passages refer to an actual city, Babylon, that will be destroyed suddenly and completely and never again inhabited (see Jer. 50:39–40; 51:8, 29, 37). However, this has never happened. Babylon has continued to be partially inhabited ever since the days of Nebuchadnezzar, as it is even today. Babylon's future destruction will immediately precede the second coming of Christ, described in Revelation 19.

Taking prophecies in their natural or literal sense means that the world is destined for an awful time of divine judgment because of its rejection of Christ and the Scriptures. Sadly, unbelief leads to judgment whether in time or eternity.

## THE CHURCH IN RELATION TO END-TIME PROPHECIES

One of the major issues pertaining to the course of events in the end times is the question of whether the church—the body of Christ composed of believers in the present age—will go through the Tribulation and be raptured at the second coming of Christ to earth or whether she will be raptured before these end-time events. These two points of view are often described as the posttribulational and the pretribulational Rapture positions. This is more than a minor theological issue for it deals with the central question concerning our hope for the Rapture. (See the lengthy discussion in chap. 3, "The Blessed Hope of the Lord's Return.") It is most important to observe that the Rapture is never mentioned in connection with any event relating to the Second Coming. A posttribulational Rapture is not mentioned in the Scriptures and in fact is contradicted by many Scripture verses.

## THE WARNING OF JUDGMENT REJECTED

The Book of Revelation graphically describes unbelievers who will continue to be unrepentant in spite of all the evidence of God's power and judgment on them for their sin (Rev. 9:20–21; 16:21). This casts light on why hell will continue forever; it is not redemptive and people do not improve under judgment, but continue to blaspheme God and blame Him for their troubles. Even after the three great series of judgments climaxing in the seventh bowl judgment, the unrepentant "cursed God on account of the plague of hail, because the plague was so terrible" (16:21).

## THE ROLE OF SATAN IN END-TIME EVENTS

As the Scriptures reveal, throughout history Satan has had access to heaven, where he makes accusation of believers' sins and shortcomings. Satan challenged God to permit Job to undergo a number of trials and troubles (Job 1:6–12; 2:1–7). Of course, Satan is limited in what he can do; he can attack Christians only to the extent God permits. For this reason it is possible for Christians to have relatively peaceful lives; this would be impossible if Satan had his full way.

A dramatic change, however, will take place in the future. Satan and his demons, who now have access to heaven, will be thrown down to the earth at the beginning of the last three and a-half years of the Great Tribulation (Rev. 12:9–10). They will lose "their place in heaven" (12:8). John heard a loud voice in heaven say, "But woe to the earth and the sea, because the devil has gone down to you!" (12:12).

Interestingly, while Satan understands that Christ is coming and knows that his doom is certain and that his time will be short (12:12), he will act according to his nature, which is to rebel against God. In the Great Tribulation Satan will have his supreme hour of seeming triumph and power as innumerable saints will be killed. However, at the Second Coming Satan will be captured and bound for a thousand years (20:1–3), and then at the end of Christ's millennial kingdom he will be cast into the lake of burning sulfur (20:7–10).

Demons, Satan's "angels" (12:7, 9)—some who have been bound since their rebellion against God (2 Pet. 2:4; Jude 6) and others who have been free to serve Satan—also will end up in the lake of burning sulfur. Matthew 25:41 declares that this place of eternal fire was "prepared for the devil and his angels." The Antichrist, whom Paul called "the man of lawlessness" (2 Thess. 2:3) and "the lawless one" (2:8–9), is "doomed to destruction" (2:3). He will be destroyed "by the splendor of [Jesus'] coming" (2:8). But this does not mean he will be annihilated. As John wrote, this world ruler (also known as the first beast of Revelation 13), will be thrown "into the fiery lake of burning sulfur" (19:20) at Jesus' second coming, to be tormented there forever (20:10). The world ruler and the false prophet who will be cast into the lake of fire at the beginning of the Millennium will still be there at the end of the Millennium, when Satan will join them. Though evil may seem to be triumphing in the world, in God's time and way every evil thing will be brought into judgment and His righteousness and sovereignty will be fully vindicated.

## THE FUTURE WORLD GOVERNMENT

Another major feature of the end times is the world government that will dominate the earth during the last three and a-half years leading up to Christ's second coming. The power of the Antichrist, the world ruler who is depicted as a beast coming out of the sea (13:1), will continue for forty-two months (13:5), or three and a-half years, which will be terminated by the second coming of Christ. The false world ruler will blaspheme God (13:6; see Dan. 11:36). He will fight against the saints and overcome them, and will rule "over every tribe, people, language and nation" (Rev. 13:7). He will be universally worshiped as God, except by those who are Christians (13:8).

This world dictator will be assisted by another individual described as a beast "coming out of the earth" (13:11). His role will be to cause people to worship the world ruler. He will be able to perform miracles by the power of Satan, which will deceive many. He will have power to require everyone to receive the mark of the Beast as a permit to buy or sell anything (13:17). This will put individuals around the world under terrible pressure to submit to the Beast in order to be able to buy the necessities to sustain their lives.

Prophetically it is most significant that we already have on earth the United Nations, a weak form of a single worldwide government. This or something similar to it may be Satan's instrument for preparing the world to accept a world government under the Antichrist.

Maintaining a government that controls the entire globe will require certain features. One of these is rapid transportation, such as is provided by giant airplanes. This was graphically brought out in the Gulf War in 1991 when President George Bush ordered airborne troops to be deployed to Saudi Arabia when Iraq invaded Kuwait, thus deterring the armies of Iraq from attacking Saudi Arabia. Before World War II, weeks would have been needed for armed forces and supplies to get to the Persian Gulf, and by that time much of the entire Middle East could have been conquered. This shows how rapid transportation is needed to deploy armies and equipment all over the world in relatively few hours and how it can change the course of a war.

Also to maintain a world government it will be necessary to have immediate communication, such as we have with telephones, radios, televisions, facsimile machines, and the Internet. Computer technology may be necessary to control worldwide buying and selling, and missile warfare with its capacity to destroy distant objects will give the coming world ruler tremendous power to punish any nation that rebels against him. In spite of all this, the Great Tribulation will end in rebellion, and as has been pointed out, a gigantic war at Armaggedon will occur just before the second coming of Christ.

## THE WORLD-CHURCH MOVEMENT

In the early apostolic days local churches sprang up in response to missionary efforts, and gradually they were grouped into one large organized church. Later this church movement was recognized as legal and grew into a great political power, which it maintained for many centuries.

Though the church was united for centuries, eventually Eastern and Western divisions of the church occurred, resulting in the Roman Church in the West and the Greek Orthodox Church in the East. Further divisions occurred during the Protestant Reformation of the sixteenth century when believers rebelled against the Roman Catholic Church and formed independent churches or groups of churches. As a result hundreds of separate churches were formed, and the church divided in many ways.

In the twentieth century a movement back to unity has begun, and we have today a worldwide ecumenical church movement, which was formally inaugurated in 1948 as the World Council of Churches. One of its major goals is to bring all churches—Protestant, Roman Catholic, Greek Orthodox, and others—into one superchurch controlled by one hierarchy. So far this has not been achieved, but after the Rapture occurs, when every true believer will be taken out of the world, the world-church movement will come to its climax.

This world church after the Rapture is described as a prostitute astride a scarlet-colored beast (Rev. 17:1–3). The beast will be a representation of the ten-nation group (17:12; Dan. 7:24) that will attempt to gain world domination. The harlot's sitting on the beast indicates that this world church and the Antichrist will support each other and have common goals. However, this woman, representing the world church, will eventually be killed by the ten nations (Rev. 17:16–17). Apparently this will occur at the beginning of the last three and a-half years when the world ruler will take over, demanding that everyone worship him as God.

## SIGNS OF THE END: THE NATIONS, ISRAEL, AND THE CHURCH

The world-church movement today, in which many churches and denominations participate, is setting the stage for world events to come. When this is coupled with the fact of a single world government and the return of many Israelites to their land, the present world situation brings into prominence the three major areas of prophecy in the Bible: the nations, Israel, and the church. This leads to the strong possibility that the consummation of the believers' hope, the Rapture, could occur very soon. Apostate world religion, symbolized by Babylon, will be destroyed at the time of the second coming of Christ.

These facts reveal that the world today is standing on the threshold of this awful time of future judgment. The major event in Bible prophecy to occur before the seven-year period known as Daniel's seventieth "week" is the Rapture of the church, the removal of the body of Christ to heaven. Once this occurs, events will follow rapidly and will move on to their great conclusion, the second coming of Christ. The following charts depicting these tremendous prophetic events help bring them into focus.

## CHART A

## FACTS AND PROPHECIES RELATING TO THE CHURCH

1. The spread of worldwide atheism is aided by communism and materialism.
2. Liberalism and apostasy sap the power of the church, first in Europe and then in America.
3. The present-day ecumenical movement with its superchurch sets the stage for the apostate church in Revelation 17.
4. Departure from Christianity in both morality and doctrine has increased.
5. The increase in demonology and spiritism prepares the world for Satan's final religion.
6. The presence of Jews in Israel becomes the focus of religious controversy and military conflict with Palestinians.
7. The Rapture and the disappearance of the church on earth will occur.
8. The restraint of the Holy Spirit will be lifted, and evil will be allowed to manifest itself.
9. The ecumenical movement after the departure of all evangelical Christians will pave the way for the end-time superchurch, which will dominate the first three and a-half years of the last seven years before the Second Coming.
10. The superchurch will be destroyed by the ten nations at the middle of the three-and-a-half-year Great Tribulation to make way for the worship of the Antichrist and Satan.
11. Prophecies of the Great Tribulation as an unparalleled time of suffering and martyrdom will be fulfilled in the last three and a-half years before the Second Coming in the absence of the church.
12. World war and world chaos will disrupt the rule of the world ruler before the Second Coming.
13. The second coming of Christ, accompanied by those in heaven including the church and His angels, will bring judgment on the unsaved world and rescue Tribulation saints on earth.

## CHART B—FACTS AND PROPHECIES RELATING TO THE GENTILE NATIONS

1. Beginning in 1945 the United Nations has paved the way for acceptance of the concept of a world government.
2. In 1948 Israel was recognized as an independent nation.
3. The Soviet Union rose as a world power, and even after its breakup it has continued to support Arab countries.
4. The Common Market of Europe and the World Bank have paved the way for the Antichrist and his domination of the world economy.
5. The rise of communist China as a world power forms a basis for the fulfillment of the prophecy of an army of two hundred million in the end time (Rev. 9:16).
6. The oil crisis of 1974 and subsequent events make the Middle East strategic in the political power struggle of the world.
7. The prominence of oil in the Middle East has increased the political and economic power of that part of the world.
8. Just before or just after the Rapture ten European nations will be united, reviving the ancient Roman Empire as the basis for the final world government.
9. The ten-nation group will be dominated by a dictator, the Antichrist, who will control first three nations and then all ten.
10. The Antichrist will make peace with Israel and will impose peace on the world seven years before the Second Coming.
11. In the first three and a-half years of the last seven years before the Second Coming, some of the nations of the former Soviet Union, along with five other countries, will invade Israel but will be miraculously destroyed by God.
12. The fall of those six nations will enhance the power of the ruler of the revived Roman Empire. Three and a-half years before the Second Coming he will proclaim himself a world dictator, claiming to be God and breaking his peace settlement with Israel.
13. The temple built by Israel to revive ancient Levitical worship will be desecrated and occupied by the world dictator.

14. The judgments of God as well as the persecutions of the world ruler will dominate the three and a-half years before the Second Coming, justifying the term "the Great Tribulation."

15. The world, reeling from the catastrophes of the Great Tribulation, will break out in world war just before the second coming of Christ, with the land of Israel as the battlefield.

16. Christ will return to earth, and He will judge the wicked and rescue those who have become believers and have lived through the Great Tribulation.

## CHART C
## FACTS AND PROPHECIES RELATING TO ISRAEL

1. After World War II Israel was established in the Promised Land.

2. Following the political establishment of the nation in 1948, millions of Jews returned to their homeland.

3. With the help of the United States, Israel was able to survive attacks by its Arab enemies in 1948 and in subsequent wars.

4. The present-day presence of Israel in the Holy Land harmonizes with prophetic pictures of the end time, which predict that Israel will be in the land after centuries of wandering over the entire earth, even though they will not be believers in Christ.

5. Following the Rapture, Israel's military power will be weakened by dependence on the ruler of the ten nations who will make a peace treaty with her.

6. Worldwide anti-Semitism will undermine the safety of Israel and will pave the way for her persecution in the three and a-half years before the Second Coming.

7. The temporary peace provided for Israel by the coming world ruler will delay the persecution of Israel but also will set the stage for the Great Tribulation.

8. Israel will escape the invasion from several countries, including those from the far north, which will occur in the middle of the last seven years before the Second Coming.

9. Beginning with the Great Tribulation Israel will be under terrible persecution, and two out of three people in Israel will perish.

10. In the midst of Israel's persecution many Jews will turn to Christ and be saved.

11. Israelites, twelve thousand from each of the twelve tribes, will be miraculously preserved through the Great Tribulation, but many others will perish.

12. At the second coming of Christ believing Israelites will be delivered from judgment but unbelieving Israelites will be purged out.

13. Believing Israel will be regathered to the Promised Land following the Second Coming.

# 11

# The Second Coming
of Christ

---

CHRISTIANS ARE AWARE of the first coming of Christ because of their acquaintance with the four Gospels and other parts of the New Testament. Because this is a matter of history it is easy to understand.

But the Second Coming is also a major revelation of the Bible. Though the exact expression "the second coming of Christ" is not found in the Bible, Hebrews 9:27–28 refers to that event. "Just as man is destined to die once, and after that to face judgment, so Christ was sacrificed once to take away the sins of many people; and he will appear a second time, not to bear sin, but to bring salvation to those who are waiting for him."

## THE SECOND COMING OF CHRIST
## IN THE OLD TESTAMENT

In the Old Testament the first and second advents of Christ were so mingled that people did not understand they were separate events. Jesus' followers expected Him to fulfill the glorious promises relating to His second coming and His reign on the earth. They did not understand the concept of two comings until Christ actually ascended to heaven. Only then did they realize they were living in the time period between His two appearances.

There is a similar confusion today regarding His coming at the Rapture and His second coming to judge the world. While apparently no one in the Old Testament times understood the difference between the first and second comings, many today recognize major differences between the Rapture and the Second Coming, which will be separated by an extended period of time.

From the present-day vantage point, however, since the first coming is history and the Second Coming is prophecy, it is comparatively easy to go back into the Old Testament and separate the doctrine of Jesus' two comings. In His first coming He came as a man, lived among people, performed miracles, ministered as a prophet as the Old Testament predicted, and died on the cross and rose again. All these events clearly relate to His first coming. On the other hand, the passages that speak of His coming to reign, judging the earth, rescuing the righteous from the wicked, and installing His kingdom on earth relate to His second coming. They are prophecy, not history.

Frequent statements about God's reign over the world are found in the Old Testament. In general, the concept of God's kingdom can be divided into three major facets. The first is the universal, eternal kingdom of God in which He has always reigned over the nations, is now reigning, and will continue to do so (Pss. 47:8; 93:1–2; 97:1; 99:1; 146:10). The second is His kingdom rule over Israel, referred to as the kingdom of David. God revealed to David that his descendants would sit on his throne forever (2 Sam. 7:10–16). This is combined with prophecies of Christ's messianic rule in the Millennium over Israel and the whole world. A third concept of God's kingdom involves those who are born again; this is a spiritual kingdom (John 3:3, 5; Col. 1:13). It is important to distinguish these forms of God's rule in the world. The second coming of Christ is linked to God's purpose in ruling the world.

The Old Testament includes many references to God's sovereignty over the world. His sovereign rule will be consummated in His ultimate judgment on Satan, anticipated in Genesis 3:15, where God promised that Satan's head will be crushed, that is, he will be utterly defeated.

Christ's return is also related to God's plans to bless Israel. At the time of the Second Coming, He will regather Israel to her land. This is anticipated in Deuteronomy 30:3: "Then the LORD your God will restore your fortunes and have compassion on you and gather you again from all the nations where he scattered you." In the verses that follow, God promised the ultimate spiritual revival of Israel (30:6), judgment on her enemies (30:7), and her exaltation and prosperity (30:9). This is the basis of God's exhortation to the children of Israel to obey the Lord in anticipation of His ultimate victory.

Psalm 2 speaks of the Second Coming in relation to Jesus' ultimate exaltation over the entire world. Though nations rebel against God, He ridicules them. "The One enthroned in heaven laughs; the Lord scoffs at them. Then he rebukes them in his anger and terrifies them in his wrath, saying, 'I have installed my King on Zion, my holy hill' " (2:4–6). God's installing His King (the Messiah, Jesus Christ) in Jerusalem in the Millennium is part of His eternal purposes, what the psalmist called "the decree of the LORD" (2:7). In view of the fact that the Messiah will rule over the nations with an iron scepter (2:9, i.e., with firmness and justice), Israel is exhorted to serve the Lord and to kiss the Son (i.e., love and worship Him) before His wrath descends on the world (2:11–12). The millennial kingdom, distinguished from present forms of the kingdom, will follow the Second Coming and will confirm the promises of God's sovereignty over the world as well as over Israel.

In Daniel's dream of four great empires God gave him a dramatic revelation of the Second Coming: "In my vision at night I looked, and there before me was one like a son of man, coming with the clouds of heaven. He approached the Ancient of Days and was led into his presence. He was given authority, glory and sovereign power; all peoples, nations and men of every language worshiped him. His dominion is an everlasting dominion that will not pass away, and his kingdom is one that will never be destroyed" (Dan. 7:13–14).

We have seen that Old Testament prophecies of the Second Coming are sometimes mingled with prophecies of the first coming. An example is Isaiah 61:1-2. Reading from this passage in the Nazareth synagogue (Luke 4:18–19), Jesus stopped in the middle of Isaiah 61:2 after the words "the year of the Lord's favor." The second part of verse 2 refers to the yet-future "day of vengeance of our God" and His comfort for those who mourn, which refers to the Second Coming.

One of the outstanding prophecies of the Second Coming is in Zechariah 14:2–3: "I will gather all the nations to Jerusalem to fight against it; the city will be captured, the houses ransacked, and the women raped. Half of the city will go into exile, but the rest of the people will not be taken from the city. Then the LORD will go out and fight against those nations, as he fights in the day of battle." These verses point to the fact that on the very day of Jesus' return the Battle of Armageddon will include house-to-house fighting in Jerusalem.

Zechariah then described how the Mount of Olives will be divided and other supernatural changes will occur in the area when the Lord returns:

> On that day his feet will stand on the Mount of Olives, east of Jerusalem, and the Mount of Olives will be split in two from east to west, forming a great valley, with half of the mountain moving north and half moving south. You will flee by my mountain valley, for it will extend to Azel. You will flee as you fled from the earthquake in the days of Uzziah king of Judah. Then the LORD my God will come, and all the holy ones with him. On that day there will be no light, no cold or frost. It will be a unique day, without daytime or nighttime—a day known to the LORD. When evening comes, there will be light. On that day living water will flow out from Jerusalem, half to the eastern sea and half to the western sea, in summer and in winter. The LORD will be king over the whole earth. On that day there will be one LORD, and his name the only name. (14:4–9)

The rest of Zechariah 14 discusses other great dramatic changes that will follow the second coming of Christ. From these passages it is obvious that the Second Coming is a major doctrine of the Old Testament.

In many respects the Second Coming will be the consummation of God's plan for mankind and the universe. A number of important events relate to it. In the Second Coming Christ will rescue the world from the terrible events of the Great Tribulation that will have threatened to destroy the human race. In the Second Coming He will come to judge the wicked and reward the righteous. When Jesus returns, He will establish His kingdom on the earth and rule as King of kings and Lord of lords

(Rev. 19:16). In His second coming He will fulfill the role of the Son of David, ruling over the house of Israel while seated on David's throne in Jerusalem. Jesus' second coming will reveal God's power and majesty as well as His grace and salvation.

Many of the prophecies concerning the Second Coming relate to Christ's establishment on earth as the sovereign Ruler, in which He will reign over the world. This theme is frequently presented in the Psalms. Daniel testified to the sovereignty of God over the nations in His relation to Nebuchadnezzar (Dan. 4:17, 25b). When Nebuchadnezzar came to faith in the God of Israel, he spoke of God's eternal rule over the earth (4:34b–35). Nebuchadnezzar's conviction was far-reaching. "His dominion is an eternal dominion; his kingdom endures from generation to generation. All the peoples of the earth are regarded as nothing. He does as he pleases with the powers of heaven and the peoples of the earth. No one can hold back his hand or say to him: 'What have you done?' "

Some Bible interpreters, especially amillenarians, tend to ignore the political reign of Christ after the Second Coming and relate it instead to His spiritual kingdom. The concept of a spiritual kingdom, however, is embedded in that of the political kingdom. The spiritual kingdom of God extends not only over all the earth and over those who willingly submit to Him; it also includes the holy angels who worship God. Those who come to Christ as their Savior become members of this spiritual kingdom. Entrance into the kingdom and family of God in its present spiritual form is actualized by faith in Christ (John 3:3, 5; Col. 1:13–14). God's political rule over the earth, however, is related to Christ's second coming, not His first.

The promise of God to David that a Descendant of His would rule over the earth forever will be fulfilled in Christ when, following His second coming, He will occupy David's throne and reign as the Messiah.

## THE SECOND COMING OF CHRIST
## IN THE NEW TESTAMENT

The New Testament records the Second Coming in more graphic terms and distinguishes it from the first coming more sharply than does the

Old Testament. Though Christ recognized that the disciples were under the mistaken notion that the glorious kingdom was immediately ahead, only toward the end of His public ministry did He begin to talk about the rejection He would experience. At least three times He predicted His crucifixion and resurrection (Matt. 16:21; 17:22–23; 20:17–19). In the midst of all this Christ predicted that the disciples would judge Israel. "Jesus said to them, 'I tell you the truth, at the renewal of all things, when the Son of Man sits on his glorious throne, you who have followed me will also sit on twelve thrones, judging the twelve tribes of Israel' " (19:28). The disciples did not understand that this "renewal," the Millennium, would follow the Second Coming.

The Olivet Discourse, delivered shortly before Jesus' death, gave the disciples much more information about His glorious second coming. The entire passage of Matthew 24:3–25:46 deals with the Second Coming and events related to it. Jesus spoke in detail about His second coming. "Immediately after the distress of those days [the Great Tribulation] 'the sun will be darkened, and the moon will not give its light; the stars will fall from the sky, and the heavenly bodies will be shaken.' At that time the sign of the Son of Man will appear in the sky, and all the nations of the earth will mourn. They will see the Son of Man coming on the clouds of the sky, with power and great glory" (24:29–30).

The distinction between the two comings was noted in the Council of Jerusalem. James said the present age is largely a time of gentile blessing, whereas the future age following the Second Coming will usher in a time of blessing for Israel (Acts 15:13–18).

The teaching of some today that Israel has been cast off forever is not supported by the New Testament. In Romans 11:11–16 Paul stated that Israel's failure to respond to God's challenge resulted in blessing on the Gentiles in the present age. Then, using the figure of an olive tree, he referred to Israel's branches as being broken off because of her unbelief so that gentile branches could be grafted in (11:17–21). But it will be natural for Israel to be grafted back into the place of blessing. "And if they [the people of Israel] do not persist in unbelief, they will be grafted in, for God is able to graft them in again. After all, if you [Gentiles] were cut out of an olive tree that is wild by nature, and contrary to nature were grafted into a cultivated olive tree, how much more readily will these, the natural branches, be grafted into their own olive tree!" (11:23–24).

In the present age, however, "Israel has experienced a hardening in part against Jesus Christ, and this will continue until the full number of the Gentiles has come in. And so all Israel will be saved, as it is written: 'The deliverer will come from Zion; he will turn godlessness away from Jacob. And this is my covenant with them when I take away their sins' " (11:25–27).

The New Testament confirms what the Old Testament predicted in Psalm 2:4–6 regarding Christ's coming to rule as King over the earth. It also confirms Psalm 24, which describes Christ's ruling over the earth as "the King of glory," and Isaiah 59:20, which refers to Christ's return as the Redeemer coming to Zion. While much of Psalm 72 referred initially to Solomon's reign, it also refers to the millennial reign of the Messiah, which, along with Isaiah 11:1–12:6, is confirmed in the New Testament.

In the Book of Acts Jesus' second coming stands in sharp contrast to His first coming. At the time of the Ascension the promise was given that Christ would come back in the same way He went, that is, bodily, visibly, suddenly, and in the clouds (Acts 1:11). (This does not refer to the Rapture, though He will come in a similar way at the Rapture. At the Rapture His coming will probably not be visible to the world.) The present age is described in Acts 15:14 as the time of largely gentile blessing, but this will be followed by the restoration of Israel at the Second Coming (15:16–18). As previously noted, the "branches" of the Gentiles are now being grafted in to God's place of blessing, but Israel, "the natural branches," will be grafted back in at the Second Coming (Rom. 11:17–24). Paul added that when Christ comes Israel will be delivered (11:26–27).

Jude 14–15 presents a dramatic picture of the Second Coming. "Enoch, the seventh from Adam, prophesied about these men: 'See, the Lord is coming with thousands upon thousands of his holy ones to judge everyone, and to convict all the ungodly of all the ungodly acts they have done in the ungodly way, and of all the harsh words ungodly sinners have spoken against him.' "

The most comprehensive picture of the Second Coming is found in the Book of Revelation. Several verses refer to the Rapture (Rev. 3:3, 10–11), but the Second Coming is also anticipated all through the Book of Revelation, beginning in 1:7, which declares, "Look, he is coming with the clouds, and every eye will see him, even those who pierced him; and all the peoples of the earth will mourn because of him. So shall it be! Amen."

Jesus' second coming will probably be the most dramatic event of history and prophecy. John described it in these words:

> I saw heaven standing open and there before me was a white horse, whose rider is called Faithful and True. With justice he judges and makes war. His eyes are like blazing fire, and on his head are many crowns. He has a name written on him that no one knows but he himself. He is dressed in a robe dipped in blood, and his name is the Word of God. The armies of heaven were following him, riding on white horses and dressed in fine linen, white and clean. Out of his mouth comes a sharp sword with which to strike down the nations. "He will rule them with an iron scepter." He treads the winepress of the fury of the wrath of God Almighty. On his robe and on his thigh he has this name written: KING OF KINGS AND LORD OF LORDS." (19:11–16)

In John's vision of Christ's return he saw Him as One riding on a white horse (19:11). A white horse was symbolic of victory, for Roman generals would ride white horses in victory parades. Jesus is described as "Faithful and True," and He will come with justice to judge and make war. The purpose as well as the description of the Second Coming is completely different from that of the Rapture. In the Rapture the church is taken from earth to heaven. But the Second Coming is a movement of saints and angels from heaven to earth, and its primary purpose is to condemn evil and to bring in Christ's righteous judgment.

Christ is described in 19:12 as having eyes "like blazing fire." This is a picture of a judge executing perfect righteousness on the wicked. His many crowns signify His supreme right to rule. The fact that His robe is dipped in blood signifies that He will come as both Savior and Judge. As in John 1:1 ("In the beginning was the Word, and the Word was with God, and the Word was God"), Christ is declared to be the Word (Rev. 19:13)—that is, the expression of what God is.

The Bible makes no mention of angels or others accompanying Christ to take the church out of the world. But in the Second Coming He will be accompanied by the armies of heaven (19:14), who, clothed in white and clean linen, will ride white horses, symbols of victory. This is the angelic host. Also accompanying them will be all the saints of all ages; they will come with Christ from heaven to reign with Him on earth.

## THE REIGN OF CHRIST ON EARTH

Christ is pictured as having a sharp sword issuing out of His mouth, which will be used in judgment on rebellious nations (Rev. 19:15). In keeping with the prediction of Psalm 2:9, He will "rule them with an iron scepter," signifying an absolute monarchy with complete justice and righteousness. Because the world is so wicked, His coming is compared to treading the winepress in which grapes spurt out their juice, and the earth is regarded as "the winepress of the fury of the wrath of God Almighty" (Rev. 19:15). There can be no mistake as to the identity of the Person riding on the horse, for He is described in verse 16 as having on His robe and His thigh the title "KING OF KINGS AND LORD OF LORDS."

It would be difficult to paint a more awesome picture. Earlier in Revelation the effect of God's judgments on the world caused the wicked to say, "Fall on us and hide us from the face of him who sits on the throne and from the wrath of the Lamb! For the great day of their wrath has come, and who can stand?" (6:16–17). If the judgments anticipating the Second Coming have this fearful effect, how much more stupendous will be the visual return of Jesus Christ.

"The Day of the Lord," a term used frequently in the Old and New Testaments (along with the similar terms "that day" or "the day"), refers to an event or events in which God will bring judgment on His enemies and/or blessing on His people in a dramatic way. It may refer to a past event, such as the Lord's destruction of the Babylonians (Isa. 13:6, 9, 13; Jer. 46:10; Ezek. 7:19; 13:5) or Egypt (Ezek. 30:3). The future Great Tribulation is called "the Day of the Lord," for in it Israel will experience anguish and mourning (Isa. 2:10–21; Amos 8:10; Zeph. 1:7–18). The Lord's anger will be demonstrated in "the Day of the Lord" when Christ returns and destroys enemy nations (Isa. 24:21)—including Edom (Isa. 34:8–9; Obad.)—at the Battle of Armageddon (Zech. 14:1–5). It will be a time of darkness (Isa. 24:23; Amos 5:18, 20; 8:9). "The Day of the Lord" also includes the blessings of the Millennium, as seen in Zechariah 3 and Zehariah 14, in which Israel will be restored, cleansed, and comforted (Isa. 61:2; Amos 9:11; Mic. 4:6–7; 5:10–14).

Peter also used the term "the Day of the Lord" in referring to the time at the end of the Millennium when new heavens and a new earth will be created. The Thessalonians wondered if they were already experiencing "the Day of the Lord." Paul assured them, however, that this could not be because "the rebellion" (unusual worldwide apostasy, 2 Thess. 2:3) had not yet occurred nor had "the man of lawlessness" (2:3; also called "the lawless one," 2:8–9) been "revealed," as he will be in the Great Tribulation. The future "Day of the Lord," then, will include the Tribulation, Christ's second coming, and the Millennium.

## THE SECOND COMING CONTRASTED WITH THE RAPTURE

The Scriptures make no mention of a rapture in connection with the second coming of Christ. The picture of the Second Coming is totally different from that of the Rapture, and most certainly does not represent any event of the past. It is understandable that unbelievers try to persuade themselves there will be no future judgment and no Second Coming (2 Pet. 3:3–4). As Peter pointed out, they willfully ignore the judgments of God in the past, such as the Flood in Noah's day, a forerunner of these future events (3:5–7). Though the earth will not be destroyed immediately, that is, until after the millennial kingdom, it nevertheless is doomed once Christ returns and installs His righteous kingdom.

Two main lines of revelation are given as the result of the Second Coming. First, judgment will come on the world at the time of Christ's return, along with the many other judgments mentioned in Scripture; and second, a resurrection will occur, which will be one of many resurrections mentioned in Scripture. These two lines of truth will be studied in the following two chapters.

Since the world today is experiencing the grace of God and the withholding of divine judgment on wickedness, it is perhaps difficult to comprehend such a graphic and terrible event as the Tribulation. On the other hand, the Second Coming provides hope for those who in the Great Tribulation will come to Christ, suffer, and be persecuted, but who will be rescued by the return of Christ. What we must keep in mind is that prophecy is just as certain as history. It will be fulfilled in God's time and way—and perhaps relatively soon.

# 12

# The Order of
# Resurrections

From Genesis through Revelation the testimony of Scripture is that physical death does not end human existence, but that in one form or another life will go on. After death the soul of every human being continues its existence. Accountability for what has happened in life becomes a major issue in existence after death. In addition to teaching that life goes on after death, the Scriptures teach that at one time or another all will receive bodies suited for eternal existence. This is a standard biblical doctrine.

Because of the influence of amillennial theology, there is a widespread theory that at the end of human history every dead person will be raised in one general resurrection and be given new bodies suited for eternity. In this theory there is no future Millennium, and at the Second Coming the world will pass immediately into its eternal state.

However, the idea of a single resurrection for all does not harmonize with Scripture. Instead there will be a number of resurrections. All will be raised but not at the same time, nor will all receive the same kind of bodies. This doctrine of various resurrections helps establish a chronological order of future events in relation to the human race. Some resurrections are past, but most of them are still to come.

## OLD TESTAMENT REFERENCES TO RESURRECTION

It is obvious that the prophecies stating that Christ would be raised from the dead have been literally fulfilled. In the Old Testament the doctrine of resurrection seems to be taught in Job 19:25–26. Anticipating resurrection, Job said, "I know that my Redeemer lives, and that in the end he will stand upon the earth. And after my skin has been destroyed, yet in my flesh I will see God." Job's claim that he would see the Lord in his flesh refers to his resurrected state after his death, for, as he said, this will occur after his skin has been destroyed. The Book of Job, probably written several hundred years before the rest of the Old Testament, presents substantial proof that the doctrine of resurrection was part of God's original revelation to the human race, carried forth by tradition and embodied here in the Scriptures. In Psalm 17:15 David declared his belief in resurrection. "And I—in righteousness I will see your face; when I awake, I will be satisfied with seeing your likeness." And in Psalm 11:7 he wrote, "Upright men will see his face."

The resurrection of saints in the Old Testament is mentioned more specifically in two other passages. Isaiah wrote of the resurrection of the people of Judah: "But your dead will live; their bodies will rise. You who dwell in the dust, wake up and shout for joy. Your dew is like the dew of the morning; the earth will give birth to her dead" (Isa. 26:19). This states specifically that the bodies of Old Testament saints will rise from the earth. In Daniel 12:1–2, the resurrection of the Old Testament saints, and ultimately of everyone, is again predicted: "At that time Michael, the great prince who protects your people, will arise. There will be a time of distress such as has not happened from the beginning of nations until then. But at that time your people—everyone whose name is found written in the book—will be delivered. Multitudes who sleep in the dust of the earth will awake: some to everlasting life, others to shame and everlasting contempt." These verses in Isaiah and Daniel will be considered later when we discuss the chronology of the resurrections.

In Ezekiel 37 the future restoration of Israel to her land is described as a resurrection of "dead bones." While this chapter as a whole is not speaking of physical resurrection, verse 24 implies that David will be resurrected bodily, for he will reign over Israel as her prince (37:25; 34:23–24), under Christ the Messiah. David, as well as resurrected Israelites, will live forever. In Psalm 24:7–10 Jesus Christ is pictured entering Jerusalem. This will be fulfilled in the millennial kingdom, but it assumes the resurrection of Christ. Other Old Testament passages that predict Jesus' reign (e.g., Isa. 11:3–5) build on the fact that He will be raised from the dead.

## NEW TESTAMENT REFERENCES TO RESURRECTION

In His ministry on earth Christ proclaimed the doctrine of the resurrection. He stated in Matthew 22:31–32, "But about the resurrection of the dead—have you not read what God said to you, 'I am the God of Abraham, the God of Isaac, and the God of Jacob'? He is not the God of the dead but of the living." In Luke 14:13–14 Christ said that good works will be repaid when the righteous are resurrected: "But when you give a banquet, invite the poor, the crippled, the lame, the blind, and you will be blessed. Although they cannot repay you, you will be repaid at the resurrection of the righteous." Christ predicted the resurrection of everyone in John 5:28–29: "Do not be amazed at this, for a time is coming when all who are in their graves will hear his voice and come out—those who have done good will rise to live, and those who have done evil will rise to be condemned."

In conversation with Martha about the death of Lazarus, Jesus gave additional information about the resurrection. "Lord," Martha said to Jesus, "if you had been here, my brother would not have died. But I know that even now God will give you whatever you ask." Jesus said to her, 'Your brother will rise again.' Martha answered, 'I know he will rise again in the resurrection at the last day.' Jesus said to her, 'I am the resurrection and the life. He who believes in me will live, even though he dies; and whoever lives and believes in me will never die. Do you believe this?' 'Yes, Lord,' she told him, 'I believe that you are the Christ, the Son of God, who was to come into the world'" (11:21–27).

Frequent references to resurrection are found throughout the rest of the New Testament, all of which fit the view that there will be a sequence of resurrections in which everyone will be raised though not at the same time.[1] Of course, as discussed in chapter 3, believers who are alive at the

Rapture will be given new bodies, but they will not have died (1 Cor. 15:51; 1 Thess. 4:17).

As Jesus approached the latter days of His public ministry, on three occasions He predicted His death and resurrection (Matt. 16:21; 17:22–23; 20:17–19). These predictions of His resurrection were fulfilled as recorded in the Gospels and as the rest of the New Testament also testifies. Jesus Christ probably was resurrected at sundown on Saturday, the beginning of the first day of the week in Israel. The stone was rolled away so the disciples could see the evidence of His resurrection in the grave clothes left behind. The postresurrection appearances of Christ to His disciples gave them ample proof that His resurrection was real. He appeared first to Mary Magdalene, then to the women who made their second trip to the tomb, then to Peter, then to the disciples on the road to Emmaus, and finally to the faithful Eleven gathered in an upper room. These and subsequent appearances all substantiated the fact that Christ was raised with the same body in which He died—but it was marvelously transformed. As such He is the pattern of all the righteous who will be raised from the dead. The apostles' preaching and teaching often mentioned the fact of Jesus' resurrection.[2]

### The Token Resurrection of Matthew 27:51–53

Matthew wrote that at the time of Christ's death some tombs were opened in Jerusalem, and that after His resurrection some of those who had been buried in these tombs came to life and appeared to others in the city of Jerusalem. "Then behold, the veil of the temple was torn in two from top to bottom; the earth quaked and the rocks were split and the graves were opened; and many bodies of the saints who had fallen asleep were raised; and coming out of the graves after His resurrection, they went into the holy city and appeared to many" (Matt. 27:51–53, NKJV).

Nowhere does the Bible explain this event; naturally we wonder about its significance. The explanation may lie in Israel's Feast of Firstfruits. According to Leviticus 23:9–14 Israelites were to bring a sheaf of grain at the beginning of harvest to the priest, who would wave it before the Lord. The one making the offering would also bring a lamb, a grain offering of flour and oil, and a drink offering of wine. The priest's waving the sheaf of grain before the Lord was a token of the harvest that was yet to come.

It may be that the resurrection of the saints in Jerusalem on the day of Christ's resurrection was, like the firstfruits offering, a token of the "harvest" to come when other saints will be raised. Since a sheaf consisted of more than one stalk of grain, so in Jesus' resurrection others needed to be raised with Him, who is the "firstfruits" (1 Cor. 15:20, 23). Probably they were given resurrection bodies like that of Christ and then were later taken to heaven, though Scripture does not give us details.

This token resurrection needs to be distinguished from restorations to life. The Bible records seven such miraculous restorations: a boy raised by Elijah; a boy raised by Elisha; three raised by Jesus (Jairus' daughter, the son of a widow of Nain, and Lazarus); Dorcas raised by Peter; and Eutychus raised by Paul. However, these individuals were not given resurrection bodies, so they died a second time. The first ones to be given resurrected bodies were those referred to in Matthew 27:51–53. They were a foretaste of the harvest of souls that will occur in the various resurrections of the righteous.

This token resurrection of some saints in Jerusalem shows that there is not a one-time resurrection of everyone, as some have maintained. Instead there will be a series of resurrections, with two (these token saints and that of Jesus) already having taken place.

## The Resurrection at the Rapture

As discussed previously, in the Rapture the church will be taken out of the world. This will include the resurrection of those who have died and the immediate translation into new bodies of those who are living (1 Cor. 15:51–53). As described in 1 Thessalonians 4:13–18, the church will rise from the earth to meet the Lord in the air. According to John 14:1–3, Christ will come to take His followers to heaven. After meeting Him in the air they will proceed into the presence of God the Father (2 Cor. 4:14). Christ's own resurrection guarantees the resurrection of believers (1 Cor. 6:14; 15:12, 20; 1 Thess. 4:14).

Bible interpreters have debated the question of who will be included in this resurrection and translation. The answer is given in 1 Thessalonians 4:16, which refers to "the dead in Christ" who "will rise first." The expression "in Christ" is a technical theological description of Christians, who are baptized by the Holy Spirit at the moment of salvation. This "baptism" places Christians into Christ and into His "body," the church. "The body is a unit, though it is made up of many parts; and though all its parts are many, they form one body. So it is with Christ. For we were all baptized by one Spirit into one body—whether Jews or Greeks, slave or free—and we were all given the one Spirit to drink" (1 Cor. 12:12–13).

There is no record of such a baptism of the Spirit occurring before the Day of Pentecost. In the Gospels the baptism of the Spirit is predicted as a future event (Matt. 3:11; Mark 1:8; Luke 3:16; John 1:33). Based on these Scriptures, the baptism of the Spirit is an unusual and innovative work of the Spirit that did not occur until the Day of Pentecost and is limited to the present age. It is never mentioned as occurring in the period after the Rapture or in the millennial kingdom. Therefore it should be distinguished from the indwelling of the Holy Spirit, which is recorded in some instances in the Old Testament and will occur in the future millennial kingdom as well as the present age.

The baptism of the Holy Spirit should also be distinguished from regeneration, though it occurs in the present church age at the same time. The regenerating work of the Spirit is the giving of spiritual life—the new birth—which probably is true of all who are saved regardless of the dispensation in which they live.

The Spirit's baptism should also be distinguished from the filling of the Spirit, which can be a repeated experience. The baptism of the Spirit is related to the special work of God in calling out a people, both Jews and Gentiles, to form a new entity, the body of Christ, consisting of those born again in this present age. It is a work of God at the time of salvation, not a human experience following conversion. No similar situation is said to have occurred in the Old Testament, nor will it occur after the Rapture. Both Jews and Gentiles will be saved and born again in later dispensations, but they will not be baptized by the Holy Spirit into the church.

Because the baptism of the Spirit distinguishes saints of the present church age, 1 Thessalonians 4:16 points to the conclusion that only church-age believers will be taken up at the time of the Rapture; other believers will be resurrected later. This is confirmed by biblical revelation about later resurrections, as will be noted in this discussion. The Rapture is the next major event in God's program, an event that can be anticipated at any time. It will be a marvelous experience for living saints to be raptured, for it will (a) give them freedom from the burden of this life and the wonder of a resurrection body (1 Cor. 15:53; 2 Cor. 5:6; Phil. 1:23; 3:21); (b) enable them to join loved ones who have preceded them in death; and (c) give them the transcending experience of seeing Christ in His glory and being the objects of His love and care throughout eternity.

## The Resurrection of the Two Witnesses

In the final days before the second coming of Christ there will be various forms of witness to the power of God and to the gospel. Among them will be the unique and unparalleled work of the two witnesses whose work is described in Revelation 11:1–6. They will prophesy for 1,260 days, that is, forty-two months of thirty days each. They are compared to two olive trees and two lampstands.

The comparison to olive trees is apparently based on Zechariah 4:3, which refers to two olive trees standing beside a gold lampstand in the temple. The two olive trees there possibly represent Joshua and Zerubbabel, who, Zechariah was told, "are anointed to serve the Lord" (4:14). In Revelation 11, as in Zechariah 4, the power for an effective witness comes from God. This is summarized in the Lord's words to Zerubbabel, " 'Not by might nor by power, but by my Spirit,' says the LORD Almighty" (Zech. 4:6). The two olive trees in Revelation 11 are placed beside the two lampstands, which speak of God's revelation to the world, similar to the golden lampstand in Zechariah 4:2, 11–12. The two witnesses will minister during the Great Tribulation, when thousands will be killed as martyrs. But God will protect the two and will give them supernatural power, enabling them to destroy any who would try to harm them (Rev. 11:5). They also will have the ability to withhold rain, to turn water into blood, and to bring about plagues (11:6).

At the end of 1,260 days, or forty-two months, apparently just before the second coming of Christ, the Antichrist will be allowed to kill them and their bodies will lie in Jerusalem for three and a-half days as symbols of the victory over them. Gloating over this victory, people will celebrate by sending each other gifts (11:7–10). After three and a-half days, however, God will resurrect them and transport them to heaven. Having seen this future event in a vision, John wrote that "they went up to heaven in a cloud, while their enemies looked on. [This raises the question of whether this event will be captured on television.] At that very hour there was a severe earthquake and a tenth of the city collapsed. Seven thousand people were killed in the earthquake, and the survivors were terrified and gave glory to the God of heaven" (11:12–13).

Numerous ideas have been suggested as to the identity of these two witnesses. Many interpreters believe the witnesses will be Moses and Elijah, whereas others say they will be Enoch and Elijah. It seems preferable, however, to view them as two now-unknown individuals whose ministry will be similar to that of Moses and Elijah.

The resurrection of the two witnesses and their being taken up to heaven does not depict the Rapture, as some writers suggest. This is because, taken literally, their resurrection is not a Rapture of living believers but specifically refers to only two individuals who had already died. Further, it will occur near the end of the Great Tribulation after they have prophesied for three and a-half years, which is not true of the church. Nor does this event refer to an alleged general resurrection of all mankind. The severe earthquake, which will kill seven thousand people in Jerusalem, gives evidence of the awesome power of God, to be seen in its fullness almost immediately afterward in the second coming of Christ.

### The Resurrection of the Martyred Dead

According to the Book of Revelation many believers in the Great Tribulation will die for their faith. Contrary to the sanguine predictions of posttribulationists, who say the church will go through the Great Tribulation unharmed, Revelation 7:9–17 makes clear that countless individuals will come to Christ after the Rapture but will be martyred because of their refusal to worship the world ruler (13:15). As pointed out previously, the role of believers in the Great Tribulation will be more difficult than that of the unsaved. While both will be subject to the same catastrophic judgments—such as earthquakes, famine, pestilence, war, and others—believers will have the additional problem of being the objects of hatred by Satan and by the Antichrist, the world ruler. When Satan, depicted as a dragon, is cast out of heaven at the beginning of the three-and-a-half-year Great Tribulation, he will express unusual rage and power toward those who trust Christ in the Great Tribulation. He will be enraged against Israel and all "those who obey God's commandments and hold to the testimony of Jesus" (12:17).

Revelation 20:4–6 refers to the resurrection of those who were beheaded by the world ruler in the Great Tribulation:

> I saw thrones on which were seated those who had been given authority to judge. And I saw the souls of those who had been beheaded because of their testimony for Jesus and because of the word of God. They had not worshiped the beast or his image and had not received his mark on their foreheads or their hands. They came to life and reigned with Christ a thousand years. (The rest of the dead did not come to life until the thousand years were ended.) This is the first resurrection. Blessed and holy are those who have part in the first resurrection. The second death has no power over them, but they will be priests of God and of Christ and will reign with him for a thousand years.

A number of facts stand out in this passage. First, this is not a general resurrection of all saints, but rather of a particular group, namely, the saved of the Tribulation who will die as martyrs in that period. Second, they will be resurrected so they can reign with Christ for a thousand years. This indicates their resurrection will occur before the Millennium, not during or after it. Third, their resurrection will occur after the Second Coming (Rev. 20:4–6 follows Christ's return in 19:11–21), probably several days after it—not before or at the time of His second coming. This is another reason for rejecting the posttribulational view that the Rapture will occur just before or at the Second Coming. The fact that this special resurrection will occur several days after the Second Coming makes clear that no rapture of living saints will occur at the Second Coming. Fourth, the timing of this resurrection of Tribulation martyrs provides convincing proof for premillennialism, the view that Christ will come to earth *before* His thousand-year reign.

Amillenarians say Revelation 20:4–6 depicts the new birth of believers, but this has no correspondence to what the biblical text says. The people spoken of here will be believing martyrs, not the unsaved. Also their resurrection is to physical life, not to a spiritual rebirth. This is made clear in verse 5, which speaks of "the rest of the dead." In addition, to say this refers to people being born again throughout the ages overlooks the sequence of events in Revelation 19–20: (a) the return of Christ, (b) the binding of Satan for a thousand years, (c) the resurrection of Tribulation martyrs, (d) the one-thousand-year reign of Christ, and (e) the resurrection of the wicked dead to the Great White Throne judgment.

Some confusion has arisen because this event is referred to as "the first resurrection" (20:5). Again amillenarians and posttribulationists ignore what the passage says. This resurrection is "first" in the sense of being "before" the resurrection of the wicked dead that will occur "later," that is, at the end of the Millennium. In ordinary conversation we often say we will do something "first," not because it is the first time we will have ever done it, but because it will precede a later event. The first resurrection, which has several phases, is of one group of people, the saved, and the second resurrection (20:11–15) is of another group, the unsaved. The first resurrection includes Christ the Firstfruits, some Jerusalem saints at His resurrection, two witnesses in the Great Tribulation, martyrs in the Tribulation, and also Old Testament saints, who will be raised about the same time as Tribulation martyrs (Dan. 12:1–2). Revelation 20:4–6 is another example of how normal, literal interpretation helps avoid confusion in biblical interpretation.

## The Resurrection of Old Testament Saints

The Old Testament does not often mention the resurrection of saints, but a significant passage, as mentioned earlier in this chapter, is Isaiah 26:19. When Old Testament saints died, their bodies were placed in the grave. But for them, as well as for the saints of other dispensations, there is the promise of resurrection, as Isaiah wrote. The time of this resurrection is given in the second major passage, Daniel 12:1–2. After Israel's "time of distress," the Tribulation, believing Israelites "will be delivered. Multitudes who sleep in the dust of the earth will awake: some to everlasting life, others to shame and everlasting contempt." This shows that the resurrection of Old Testament saints will occur after the Great Tribulation, the "time of [Israel's] distress" (see Jer. 30:7; Matt. 24:21). The exact time is not given, but it will either precede or immediately follow the resurrection of Tribulation martyrs, mentioned in Revelation 20:4–6.

Daniel 12:2 says some will be raised "to everlasting life, others to shame and everlasting contempt," that is, both the righteous and the wicked dead will be subject to future resurrections. Daniel did not distinguish between the resurrection before the Millennium and the resurrection after the Millennium, because such time differentials were not common in the Old Testament. This is illustrated, as we have said, by the fact that the first and second comings of Christ are placed side by side in the Old Testament text. The Book of Revelation, however, shows that the millennial kingdom will come between this resurrection of Old Testament saints (which will come right after the Great Tribulation) and the resurrection of the wicked (which will occur just after the Millennium). John 5:28–29 also refers to the resurrection of believers ("who have done good") and of unbelievers ("those who have done evil"), without mentioning the Millennium in between.

These descriptions of the resurrections show that before the Millennium all the righteous dead will have been raised in one resurrection or another and will enter the millennial kingdom in their resurrection bodies. Only the wicked will remain in their graves to be subject to resurrection at the end of the millennial kingdom.

## The Resurrection of the Wicked

After Satan has been bound for a thousand years (Rev. 20:3, 7–8), he will be loosed for a brief time and then cast into the lake of fire. "And the devil, who deceived them, was thrown into the lake of burning sulfur, where the beast and the false prophet had been thrown. They will be tormented day and night for ever and ever" (20:10). The Beast and the False Prophet, who were cast into the lake of burning sulfur a thousand years earlier (19:20–21), will still be in existence and will still be suffering.

Immediately after Satan is thrown into the lake of burning sulfur, the wicked dead will be resurrected and judged. This is the seventh and final resurrection. John described it this way:

> Then I saw a great white throne and him who was seated on it. Earth and sky fled from his presence, and there was no place for them. And I saw the dead, great and small, standing before the throne, and books were opened. Another book was opened, which is the book of life. The dead were judged according to what they had done as recorded in the books. The sea gave up the dead that were in it, and death and hades gave up the dead that were in them, and each person was judged according to what he had done. Then death and hades were thrown into the lake of fire. The lake of fire is the second death. If anyone's name was not found written in the book of life, he was thrown into the lake of fire. (20:11–15)

This resurrection and judgment clearly will differ from any of the previous ones. We should carefully note the details of this passage. The book of life, which includes the names of all who are saved, will be opened to show that the wicked dead are not listed in it. Then the dead will be judged according to their works. The resurrection of the dead includes all the unsaved, regardless of where they are. Hades will be abolished and combined with the lake of fire, which is called the second death, that is, eternal separation from God. All those whose names are not found written in the book of life will be thrown into the lake of fire to share the punishment of the Beast, the False Prophet, and Satan. According to Matthew 25:41, this place of torment was prepared especially for the devil and his angels (demons), but those who refuse Christ will be sharing this eternal punishment. Further details about this Scripture will be considered in the next chapter, "The Judgments."

## CONCLUSION

Seen in their chronological order, the seven resurrections are proof that there will be not just one final resurrection and judgment in the future, but rather a series of judgments and resurrections. The great drama at the end of human history will play out according to God's schedule. Ultimately His sovereignty, righteousness, and grace will be amply demonstrated in the unending ages of the future. We know that the hope that characterizes the Christian faith is not fulfilled entirely in this life. It extends beyond earth's temporal existence into eternal glory, the place prepared by Christ for his followers for all eternity.

# 13

# The
# Judgments

---

$T$HE SECOND COMING OF CHRIST will bring judgment of catastrophic proportions on the earth's unsaved population. This judgment, however, will be only one in a series of final judgments.

In interpreting prophecy many scholars have made a major error in merging all the final judgments into one grand event that they correlate with the second coming of Christ. But to do this, they must ignore significant details given about each judgment. The Bible pictures a series of judgments, beginning with the judgment of Christ on the cross and ending with the judgment of the wicked dead at the end of the Millennium.

According to Hebrews 9:27 judgment is appointed for everyone, and the normal order is for each person to die once and then after death to face judgment. But even the judgments of the wicked do not occur all at the same time.

Many temporal judgments are cited in the Old Testament. When Israel strayed from the Lord, God judged her in the captivities by Assyria and Babylon, and by the destruction of Jerusalem in A.D. 70. Other judgments have fallen on various generations throughout the history of the world. The first such judgment fell on Adam and Eve when they sinned and incurred spiritual death; then the judgment on Cain followed. Cain was said to be a fugitive and a wanderer on the earth even though he was protected from death (Gen. 4:12–15). In contrast to these and other temporal judgments by God, the Bible mentions several more judgments of a more specific nature, beginning with the death of Christ on the cross.

## THE JUDGMENT OF CHRIST ON THE CROSS

Christ's death on the cross was a divine judgment on the sin of the whole world. He was the Redeemer available to the entire human race. Though some interpreters question whether Christ died for everyone, the Bible in numerous passages supports His universal substitutionary death. Christ died in response to God's love for the entire world, according to John 3:16. Even though the whole world was not and will not be saved, the death of Christ made salvation available to all persons. His death as a substitute for our sins changed our situation from hopeless condemnation to freely offered salvation. Salvation is possible because Christ bore our condemnation. According to 1 Peter 3:18, "For Christ died for sins once for all, the righteous for the unrighteous, to bring you to God." His substitutionary death, in which He was judged for our sins, is well expressed in 1 Peter 2:24 ("He himself bore our sins in his body on the tree") and Romans 5:8 ("while we were still sinners, Christ died for us").

According to 2 Corinthians 5:19, "God was reconciling the world to himself in Christ, not counting men's sins against them. And he has committed to us the message of reconciliation." While Christ reconciled the whole world, that reconciliation does not take effect until a person receives Christ as his or her Savior. That is why 2 Corinthians 5:20 reads, "We implore you on Christ's behalf: Be reconciled to God." The basis for this is stated in verse 21: "God made him who had no sin to be sin for us, so that in him we might become the righteousness of God."

The second coming of Christ has seemingly been delayed because, according to 2 Peter 3:9, "The Lord is not slow in keeping his promise, as some understand slowness. He is patient with you, not wanting anyone to perish, but everyone to come to repentance." He "wants all men to be saved" (1 Tim. 2:4). This expresses God's desire, but not His sovereign plan. The death of Christ makes it possible for anyone to be saved who is willing to put his trust in Christ. He "gave himself as a ransom for all"

(2:6). Peter prophesied that "there will be false teachers among you. They will secretly introduce destructive heresies, even denying the sovereign Lord who bought them—bringing swift destruction on themselves" (2 Pet. 2:1). In this passage even the unsaved false teachers, who probably never would be saved, are said to have been "bought." This word signifies redemption, that is, that Christ died for them. They can be saved if they accept God's pardon and redemption in Christ which is completely paid for by the infinite value of His death on the cross. His death is one of the significant judgments mentioned in Scripture.

## THE END-TIME JUDGMENTS

### The Judgment Seat of Christ

Soon after the church is raptured and taken to heaven, the "judgment seat" of Christ will occur. In this judgment Christians will be evaluated as to the quality of their lives and their suitability for rewards. (This was discussed previously in connection with the Rapture in chap. 3.) As stated in 2 Corinthians 5:10, "For we must all appear before the judgment seat of Christ, that each one may receive what is due him for the things done while in the body, whether good or bad." This verse shows that the issue then will not be salvation, because everyone in heaven is saved. This will not be a judgment pertaining to sin, because believers are justified by faith and stand in the perfect righteousness of Christ. Rather, the question will be: What have we done for God and how have we used the opportunities for service He has given us?

As previously pointed out, the apostle Paul used three illustrations of the judgment seat of Christ. In 1 Corinthians 3:10–15 the Christian life is pictured as building on the foundation of salvation in Christ and then being subject to searching judgment, much as a building is "tested" by fire. Gold, silver, and costly stones speak of deeds in one's Christian life that are eternal in value, and the wood, hay, and straw consumed by fire and reduced to ashes speak of deeds that are not counted worthy of eternal recognition. Believers will receive rewards for those deeds in the Christian life that are of lasting value, but not for other deeds. Also, in 1 Corinthians 9:24–27 the Christian life is compared to the running of a race in which the winner gets a prize. In contrast to the winners of a race at Corinth, who received a crown of leaves that would soon decay, Christians are promised a crown that will not fade away. In contrast to human races in which only one person wins, every Christian can win. Each believer is not running against someone else but only against the possibilities of his or her own life. The rules of running a successful race are here brought to bear on the Christian life.

Christians are reminded in Romans 14:10–12 not to judge the quality of others' works, because we will all appear before the judgment seat of Christ. On that occasion we will each give an account to God of what we have done with what He has committed to us, much as stewards or trustees are accountable for what has been entrusted to them. Obviously Christians differ greatly in abilities and opportunities. Therefore no one will be judged on the basis of what God has given others, but only on the basis of what God has given him or her. These three passages graphically emphasize the need for Christians to invest their lives in the things that will count for eternity.

While the Bible is not specific about the rewards believers will receive in heaven, those rewards may be in the form of privileged service. Throughout eternity those who have served God well in this life will be given tasks for further service in keeping with what they have achieved on earth. The judgment seat of Christ is a an important event for Christians to consider as they seek to serve the Lord.

### Temporal Judgments in the Great Tribulation

As brought out dramatically in the Book of Revelation, God will pour out judgments in the Great Tribulation, which Scripture calls part of "the Day of the Lord." While many expositors attempt to tone down or eliminate entirely the reality of the judgments described in Revelation 6–18, these prophecies, when taken literally, indicate that in the three and a-half years leading up to the second coming of Christ much of the earth will be devastated and billions of people will be killed. As previously shown, this will reduce the world's population to a fraction of what it is now. The seventh "bowl" judgment with its earthquake will level the world's buildings and undoubtedly kill millions more (16:17–21). In this final judgment, which will occur immediately before the Second Coming, mountains and islands will disappear; the configuration of the whole world will change (except for, presumably, the land of Israel). This catastrophic situation will be God's righteous judgment on unbelievers who have followed Satan rather than Jesus Christ. The judgments in the coming Great Tribulation are a reminder of how important it is to be saved before the Rapture and thus to be caught up to heaven before this terrible time of trouble overtakes the world.

## The Judgment of World Armies at the Second Coming

On the very day of the Second Coming the armies that for some time have been fighting each other for power will have invaded the city of Jerusalem and will have been engaged in house-to-house fighting. When the glory of the second coming of Christ appears in the heavens, however, these soldiers will forget their contest for power on earth and will turn to fight the army from heaven (16:16; 19:19). Yet their best efforts will be futile because Christ will smite them with the sword in His mouth (19:15, 21), and they will all be killed, along with their horses. An angel will then invite vultures to "eat the flesh of kings, generals, and mighty men, of horses and their riders, and the flesh of all people, free and slave, small and great" (19:18). This "great supper of God" (19:17) contrasts with the marriage supper of the Lamb, to which the righteous will be invited (19:7–9). The destruction of millions of soldiers in the Battle of Armageddon is the first of a series of judgments in preparation for the millennial kingdom.

## The Judgment of the World Dictator and the False Prophet

When Christ returns, the armies gathered in Israel to fight against each other will join forces, as noted above, to fight against Christ when His glory appears in the heavens. They will be killed by Christ, and the Beast (the Antichrist) and his companion, the False Prophet, will be cast alive into the lake of burning sulfur (Rev. 19:20).

When the unsaved die, they go to hades, the place of punishment and torment (Luke 16:19–31). At present the lake of fire is uninhabited. The world ruler and the False Prophet will be the first to be cast alive into this "fiery lake of burning sulfur" (Rev. 19:20), the place of final judgment of the wicked. A thousand years later, all unbelieving dead will be cast into this lake, their final place of eternal judgment (20:11–15). It is foolish for people to rebel against God, Psalm 2:1–3 tells us. God holds them in ridicule (2:4–5) because He knows every evil person will be judged and because His Son, the Messiah, will return and establish His rule in Jerusalem (2:6).

### The Judgment of Satan

When Christ returns to earth, Satan, who will be given great power and freedom in the three and a-half years of the Great Tribulation, will be captured by an angel, chained, cast into the Abyss, and rendered inactive for a thousand years. In Revelation 20:1–3 a distinction must be made between what John saw and what he heard. "And I saw an angel coming down out of heaven, having the key to the Abyss and holding in his hand a great chain. He seized the dragon, that ancient serpent, who is the devil, or Satan, and bound him for a thousand years. He threw him into the Abyss, and locked and sealed it over him, to keep him from deceiving the nations anymore until the thousand years were ended. After that, he must be set free for a short time."

John visually saw the angel coming down from heaven with a key to the Abyss or bottomless pit, the home of the demon world. He also saw the angel bind Satan—the "dragon, that ancient serpent, who is the devil, or Satan"—with a great chain and throw him into the Abyss. John could visualize the angel binding and rendering the devil inactive, but the fact that Satan would be bound for a thousand years had to be *told* to him. Therefore the thousand years should be considered a literal number. Satan will be unable to deceive the world for a thousand years, and apparently this will also be true of the demon world. At the end of the thousand years he will be let loose again for a short time (20:3), then in his final judgment he will be cast into the lake of fire, where the Beast (the Antichrist) and the False Prophet will already have been suffering for a thousand years (20:10).

## The Judgment of the Tribulation Martyrs

In the Tribulation many people will be saved and many of them will be killed, either because of their refusal to worship the Beast or because of the worldwide catastrophes. At Christ's second coming the saved martyrs will be raised from the dead so they can reign with Christ throughout His millennial kingdom. John wrote, "I saw thrones on which were seated those who had been given authority to judge. And I saw the souls of those who had been beheaded because of their testimony for Jesus and because of the word of God. They had not worshiped the beast or his image and had not received his mark on their foreheads or their hands. They came to life and reigned with Christ for a thousand years" (20:4).

This is clearly a specific judgment of a certain portion of those who have died, that is, believers who were beheaded by the world ruler. This does not mean all saints of all ages, nor is this a group of church saints, for they will have been raptured seven years earlier (and of course not all church saints are martyred). The individuals seated on thrones with "authority to judge" are not identified. Possibly they will be the apostles, who, Jesus said, will "eat and drink at my table in my kingdom and sit on thrones, judging the twelve tribes of Israel" (Luke 22:30). These judges will evaluate the Tribulation martyrs and determine that they should "come to life," that is, be given resurrection bodies (see the previous chapter) and reign with Christ for a thousand years as His priests. "Blessed and holy," they will have a special relationship to Christ in the millennial kingdom, sharing in His reign (Rev. 20:6).

This fact has confused some because church saints are also promised they will reign with Christ (2 Tim. 2:12). There is no reason, however, why both groups, though different, cannot experience this same reward from God for their faithful service.

## The Judgment of Living Israel at the Second Coming

Jews living in Israel now, though they have been regathered to their land, are not its ultimate residents. The fact that some Israelites now reside in the Holy Land, however, is prophetically significant because Israel's existence as a political state is necessary for the fulfillment of the seven-year covenant the

Antichrist will make with them (Dan. 9:27). At the beginning of the Great Tribulation many Israelites will flee from the land of Israel (Matt. 24:15–22). Then when Christ returns, Israelites who are alive at that time will be regathered and judged. Isaiah wrote that God will "gather the exiles of Israel" and "assemble the scattered people of Judah from the four quarters of the earth" (Isa. 11:12). As Jeremiah prophesied, "'So then, the days are coming,' declares the LORD, 'when people will no longer say, "As surely as the LORD lives, who brought the Israelites up out of Egypt," but they will say, "As surely as the LORD lives, who brought the descendants of Israel up out of the land of the north and out of all the countries where he had banished them." Then they will live in their own land'" (Jer. 23:7–8).

At this regathering those Jews who are not believers in Christ will be separated out, and only the righteous or godly remnant of Israel will be allowed to enter the Millennium. Ezekiel wrote of this judgment in Ezekiel 20:33–38:

> As surely as I live, declares the Sovereign LORD, I will rule over you with a mighty hand and an outstretched arm and with outpoured wrath. I will bring you from the nations and gather you from the countries where you have been scattered—with a mighty hand and an outstretched arm and with outpoured wrath. I will bring you into the desert of the nations and there, face to face, I will execute judgment upon you. As I judged your fathers in the desert of the land of Egypt, so I will judge you, declares the Sovereign LORD. I will take note of you as you pass under my rod, and I will bring you into the bond of the covenant. I will purge you of those who revolt and rebel against me. Although I will bring them out of the land where they are living, yet they will not enter the land of Israel. Then you will know that I am the LORD.

This prophecy indicates that at the time of the second coming of Christ, God will gather Israelites from all over the world and bring them back to their home country. But the ungodly remnant, the rebels, will be purged out and not allowed to enter the Millennium. Only the righteous of Israel will be delivered from judgment. Apparently in the Great Tribulation many Jews will turn to Christ in spite of the persecutions and martyrdoms that await some of them.

When Paul wrote that "all Israel will be saved" (Rom. 11:26), he meant that at the Second Coming all Jews who then believe in Christ will be saved and will enter the Millennium\. Since many Jews who will return to their land at the Second Coming will be rebels, they will be purged out in this judgment of living Israelites. The Deliverer, Paul wrote, "will turn godlessness away from Jacob" (11:26), so that only believing Jews will enter the Millennium. And as Jeremiah wrote, when Christ reigns "Judah will be saved" (Jer. 23:5–6).

Ezekiel 39:25–28 also speaks of the regathering of Israel:

> Therefore this is what the Sovereign LORD says: I will now bring Jacob back from captivity and will have compassion on all the people of Israel, and I will be zealous for my holy name. They will forget their shame and all the unfaithfulness they showed toward me when they lived in safety in their land with no one to make them afraid. When I have brought them back from the nations and have gathered them from the countries of their enemies, I will show myself holy through them in the sight of many nations. Then they will know that I am the LORD their God, for though I sent them into exile among the nations, I will gather them to their own land, not leaving any behind.

Also at the time of the Second Coming, Ezekiel tells us the Promised Land will be divided into twelve sections, one for each of the tribes of Israel. "You are to distribute this land among yourselves according to the tribes of Israel" (47:21). There follows in Ezekiel 48 the description of each of these twelve sections of the Holy Land. In this way God will fulfill the promise to Abraham that his posterity will inherit the land, and as long as the earth lasts Israel will possess the portion of the Holy Land promised to them.

### The Judgment of Living Gentiles at the Second Coming

Some Gentiles who have turned to Christ in the Great Tribulation will survive that awful time and will be on the earth when Christ returns. Other

Gentiles who reject Christ in the Great Tribulation (Rev. 16:9, 11, 21) will be alive at Christ's second coming. The judgment of these believing and unbelieving Gentiles is recorded in Matthew 25:31–46. Believing Gentiles are likened to sheep, and unsaved Gentiles are called goats. In this judgment, which will occur several days after the Second Coming, the righteous will be separated from the unrighteous. The saved will be ushered into the millennial kingdom, but the unsaved will be put to death. This is summarized in verse 46: "Then they [the goats] will go away to eternal punishment, but the righteous [the sheep] to eternal life." While this judgment is sometimes called the judgment of the nations, it is preferable to understand it as a judgment of individual Gentiles (the Greek word *ethme* can be translated either way, but most often it is rendered "Gentiles").

This judgment will be of individuals whose conduct toward Jesus in the Great Tribulation will reflect whether they were trusting Christ. According to Joel 3:2, this judgment will occur in the Valley of Jehoshaphat, possibly located near Jerusalem.

This judgment tends to confirm the fact that the Rapture will not occur on the day of the second coming of Christ. As previously discussed, the Tribulation martyrs and Old Testament saints will be resurrected then. However, if the Rapture were to occur at the second coming of Christ, the sheep and the goats after the Second Coming would no longer be mingled; no separation of them would be needed. This is another proof that the Rapture is not posttribulational.

This series of judgments sets the stage for the millennial kingdom, in which all the adults who enter it will have been saved by faith in Christ. He will reign over the earth with Jerusalem as His capital, sitting on the throne of David and ruling over Israel and over the whole world in universal judgment. The details given in Scripture show that a series of judgments will occur at the second coming of Christ. To teach one final judgment for the entire human race, as many do, is not scriptural. These judgments indicate that individuals are fully accountable to God, and that in His own time He will judge every sin that is not forgiven through faith in Christ based on the grace of God and Jesus' substitutionary death.

*The Judgment of the Wicked at the Great White Throne*

The final judgment of the human race is recorded in Revelation 20:11–
15. This judgment will occur when the present earth and heavens have
fled away (20:11; 21:1). Before the Great White Throne, on which Christ
will be seated, will be gathered the remaining dead, the unsaved of all
ages, who will be resurrected for this judgment, a judgment that will result in all being cast into the lake of fire.

Earlier I memtioned that, every unsaved person who has died or will
die goes at the moment of death to a place called *sheol* in the Old Testament and *hades* in the New Testament. There they suffer punishment in
conscious existence. This has been going on for thousands of years since
the human race began.

Insight into this situation is given in Luke 16:19–31, which records
Jesus' discussion of life after death in the story of a rich man and Lazarus,
a beggar. Though some say this is only a parable and therefore not to be
understood literally, the fact that Jesus gave the name of the beggar indicates this is probably an actual situation, not a parable. In no other parable
did Jesus name any individuals, as He did here.

As the passage tells us, the rich man enjoyed all the blessings of wealth
and abundant luxury in his lifetime. In contrast, Lazarus, a beggar covered with sores, tried to survive by eating crumbs falling from the rich
man's table. When both men died, the rich man went into torment while
Lazarus went to be with Abraham.

After his death the rich man conversed with Abraham and Lazarus, even
though there was a chasm between them that was impossible to cross. The
rich man begged Abraham to ask Lazarus to dip his finger in water to cool
the rich man's tongue, "because," he said, "I am in agony in this fire" (Luke
16:24). In response Abraham told the rich man that he had enjoyed the
blessings of life while on earth, but that Lazarus, who had suffered, was
now being comforted. Besides, there was no way to bridge the chasm between them. Hearing this, the wealthy man begged Abraham to send Lazarus
to his five brothers to warn them not to come to that "place of torment"
(16:27–28). Abraham replied, "They have Moses and the Prophets; let them

listen to them" (16:29). When the rich man said his brothers would believe someone risen from the dead, Abraham answered, "If they do not listen to Moses and the Prophets, they will not be convinced even if someone rises from the dead" (16:31).

This passage shows that the wicked go at the moment of death to *hades*, a place of immediate torment, and that life continues after life on earth. The passage also points out the difference between those who are saved and those who are unsaved, with Lazarus enjoying the blessing of being with Abraham in what Christ called paradise (Luke 23:43), and the unsaved experiencing conscious torment. Scholars debate whether paradise in Old Testament times and in the time of the Gospels is the same as heaven or whether it is distinguished from it. All agree, however, that after the resurrection of Christ, paradise and heaven became synonymous (2 Cor. 12:4) and saints who have died since then go immediately into the presence of God (5:8). Also some suggest that before Jesus' crucifixion hades had two compartments, one for the saved and one for the unsaved.

### The Final Judgment of Millennial Saints

The Scriptures are silent on how God will deal with saints living on earth at the end of the Millennium or saints who have died in the Millennium. Like many other questions the Bible leaves unanswered, people living today do not need to know the answer because they themselves are not involved. It is probable that the righteous who die in the Millennium will be resurrected, much as the church will be at the Rapture, and that living saints will be given bodies suited for eternity like those living church saints will receive. It is clear that the millennial saints will not be involved in the judgment of the Great White Throne, however, because this judgment relates to the wicked dead.

## THE DOCTRINE OF ETERNAL PUNISHMENT

Naturally some Christians tend to shy away from the doctrine of eternal punishment hoping there may be some way out for people who are not saved. Many preachers seldom mention the fact that apart from the grace of God and faith in Jesus there is no forgiveness, and that the unsaved, because of their sin, merit eternal punishment. The idea of a loving God requiring eternal punishment of those who are unsaved naturally raises questions.

What about those who never hear the gospel and who die without learning of the grace of God? Are they doomed to eternal punishment? Is a pious Jew or a religious Muslim who carefully follows his doctrines also doomed to punishment because he has not accepted Christ as his Savior?

The idea of eternal punishment in hell has long been caricatured by those who do not believe it. In fact, some writers say that even if the Bible does teach eternal punishment, still it could not be true. However, for those who believe the Bible is inspired by God and is therefore inerrant, there is no option except to believe what the Bible teaches about hell.

The basic problem is that it is difficult for sinful human beings to contemplate the inexorable righteousness of God that demands infinite punishment for infinite sin and provides no grace or forgiveness for those who have not trusted in Christ. After all, the Bible is our only source of proving that God loves us and has provided grace through Jesus Christ in His death on the cross. The Bible, however, also teaches eternal punishment. We are not free to accept one doctrine and reject the other simply because the latter is contrary to our way of thinking or is difficult to understand.

### Various Approaches to the Doctrine of Eternal Punishment

Some may attempt to soften the Bible's description of hell as a place of fire and sulfur (Rev. 19:20; 20:10; 21:8; "fire and brimstone" in the KJV) by saying the description of it is metaphorical and not literal. Some who hold this position, however, agree that it is eternal even though they hold that it is not literal fire. However, since Christ Himself repeatedly emphasized that the punishment involves fire (Matt. 5:22; 18:8–9; 25:41; Mark 9:43, 48), it is difficult to find any other meaning.

In Roman Catholic theology the doctrine of purgatory emerged. (It was defined in the Council of Trent in the sixteenth century.) This doctrine states that while Christians can be forgiven for sins confessed, sins not confessed require a purging experience of suffering in order to prepare them for heaven. For support of this view Roman Catholics appeal to 2 Maccabees 12:43–46, but this is one of several apocryphal books not found in the Old and New Testaments. Even Roman Catholics admit that the Bible itself apart from the Apocrypha does not teach the doctrine of purgatory. But they say the doctrine is true because it was adopted by a decree of the Church of Rome. They recognize, however, that punishment can be eternal for those who are not believers in Christ.

A popular contemporary view is that of conditional immortality— the idea that only the righteous will be resurrected and at death the wicked are annihilated. While annihilationism has been taught for some time by Seventh-Day Adventists and Jehovah Witnesses, some evangelicals, such as John R. W. Stott, are now teaching it. In a sense immortality is conditional on whether people are righteous in this life. Some take a more moderate view that the wicked may be resurrected and punished for a short time and then annihilated. The problem with the view of annihilationism is that it is not supported in the Bible; it does not mesh with statements on eternal punishment, such as those in Matthew 25:46 and Revelation 20:10, 14–15.

These verses also show that universalism, the popular view that every human being will eventually be in heaven, is false. A number of evangelicals are now teaching universalism. (Others are proposing related views, namely, that individuals who have never heard of Christ can be saved or that people will have opportunity after death to receive or reject Christ.) People holding universalism attempt to base it on Jesus' statement in John 12:32 that He will "draw all men" to Himself, and Paul's words in 1 Timothy 2:4 that God "wants all men to be saved." But in John 12:32 Jesus was saying that the Cross (His being "lifted up") makes it possible for both Jews and Gentiles to be saved, and 1 Timothy 2:4 says that God desires everyone to be saved but does not affirm that all will be. The Bible repeatedly speaks of those who without Christ are perishing (John 3:16, 18, 36; Rom. 5:8; 1 Cor. 1:18; Eph. 2:12; 2 Thess. 1:8–9). Universalism, while appealing to God's love, overlooks the biblical teaching on future judgments and on hell.

*Biblical Terms for Hell*

The principal New Testament word for hell is *hades*, which is equivalent to the Old Testament word *sheol*. These terms refer sometimes to the grave where bodies are buried, and sometimes to life after the grave, that is, to the soul's existence after death.

A New Testament word that clearly refers to eternal punishment is *gehenna* ("hell"), occurring twelve times.[1] One additional word, *tartarus* ("hell"), occurs only in 2 Peter 2:4, and is either another name for *gehenna* or is a separate abode of bound fallen angels who are awaiting final judgment. More than any other person in the New Testament Jesus taught the doctrine of eternal punishment.

The term *gehenna* is related to a place called "the Valley of Hinnom" or "the Valley of Ben Hinnom." It is mentioned in Joshua 15:8; 18:16; and Nehemiah 11:30. This valley immediately southwest of Jerusalem was where garbage was burned and the bodies of criminals were buried. In Jeremiah's day human sacrifices were offered to the false gods Baal and Molech in this valley (Jer. 19:6; 32:35), so that he called it "the Valley of Slaughter" (7:30–33; 19:6). The Jews therefore associated this terrible place with the everlasting punishment of the wicked, which is the way Jesus used it every time He mentioned it. He said, "If your hand or your foot causes you to sin, cut if off and throw it away. It is better for you to enter life maimed or crippled than to have two hands or two feet and be thrown into eternal fire. And if your eye causes you to sin, gouge it out and throw it away. It is better for you to enter life with one eye than to have two eyes and be thrown into the fire of hell" (Matt. 18:8–9). And in Mark 9:47–48 Jesus said, "And if your eye causes you to sin, pluck it out. It is better for you to enter the kingdom of God with one eye than to have two eyes and be thrown into hell, where 'their worm does not die, and the fire is not quenched.' " The expression "their worm does not die, and the fire is not quenched" is a quotation from the last verse of Isaiah (66:24). It supports the idea that Christ's use of the word *gehenna* refers to eternal punishment.

In the judgment of the Gentiles, when Christ will pronounce judgment on the "goats," He will say to them, "Depart from me, you who are cursed, into the eternal fire prepared for the devil and his angels" (Matt. 25:41). This passage affirms that the eternal punishment is one of fire and that it lasts forever, a concept mentioned again in verse 46. "Then they will go away to eternal punishment, but the righteous to eternal life."

Though He did not explain it, Christ indicated that some would be punished more than others, depending on how well they understood the will of their master (Luke 12:47–48). Hypocrites are said to be punished more severely than others (Mark 12:40). And inhabitants of Korazin, Bethsaida, and Capernaum will suffer more than those of Tyre and Sidon (Matt. 11:21–24). "The day of judgment" in 11:22, 24 may refer to the day of their death.

Conscious punishment in hell is also indicated by Jesus' seven references to the fact that after death the wicked will experience "weeping and gnashing of teeth."[2] Hell is also described as a place of darkness (Matt. 8:12; 22:13; 25:30).

### The Doctrine of Eternal Punishment in the Epistles

Though Christ was the principal teacher of eternal punishment, this doctrine is also clearly taught in the Epistles. Sudden destruction is predicted for those whom the Day of the Lord will overtake (1 Thess. 5:3). They are said to be recipients of divine wrath (5:9), and "they will be punished with everlasting destruction and shut out from the presence of the Lord and from the majesty of his power" (2 Thess. 1:9).

Hebrews 6:2 refers to "the resurrection of the dead, and eternal judgment," and Hebrews 10:26–27 speaks of "a fearful expectation of judgment and of raging fire that will consume the enemies of God." Hell is a place of "blackest darkness" (2 Pet. 2:17).

The present judgment of angels who are confined after their original sin will end in judgment: "For . . . God did not spare angels when they sinned, but sent them to hell, putting them into gloomy dungeons to be held for judgment" (2 Pet. 2:4). The Book of Jude refers to the same concept, that bound fallen angels, presently confined in darkness, are awaiting judgment (Jude 6).

### The Doctrine of Eternal Punishment in the Book of Revelation

In describing those who worship the Beast in the Great Tribulation, a word of warning is given by an angel: "If anyone worships the beast and his image and receives his mark on the forehead or on the hand, he, too, will drink of the wine of God's fury, which has been poured full strength into the cup of his wrath. He will be tormented with burning sulfur in the presence of the holy angels and of the Lamb. And the smoke of their torment rises for ever and ever. There is no rest day or night for those who worship the beast and his image, or for anyone who receives the mark of his name." (Rev. 14:9–11)

Though the word *gehenna* is not found in the Book of Revelation, it is clear that the Book of Revelation continues the New Testament teaching about eternal, conscious punishment.

The most comprehensive statement on eternal punishment is found in connection with the judgment of the Great White Throne. "The sea gave up the dead that were in it, and death and hades gave up the dead that were in them, and each person was judged according to what he had done. Then death and hades were thrown into the lake of fire. The lake of fire is the second death" (20:13–14).

Physical death separates an individual from his or her body; the second death separates the individual from the grace and mercy of God. The lake of fire will not annihilate the unsaved, for Revelation 20:10 states that the devil will be "thrown into the lake of burning sulfur, where the beast and the false prophet had been thrown. They will be tormented day and night for ever and ever." Along with the fallen angels, they will suffer punishment forever. While people may dispute whether the Word of God is true, fulfillment of these prophecies will demonstrate that when God speaks He does so in complete accuracy and literalness.

## Summary

The Bible clearly teaches that eternal punishment will be by fire. This was repeated so often from the lips of Jesus as well as by several New Testament writers that interpreters are not free to arbitrarily say it must mean something else.

The question as to whether eternal fire will annihilate those suffering in it is answered by the experience of the Beast, the False Prophet, and Satan, whose torment will last forever. Also the unsaved, from the moment of their death (which in some cases will be thousands of years before the Great White Throne judgment) will suffer, as described in Luke 16:19–31.

However, the souls of believers who die are instantly transported into the presence of God.

The fact of eternal punishment of the lost should motivate Christians to do all they can to lead people to Christ before it is too late. While heaven will be a wonderful reunion of those who are saved, there will be no such fellowship in hell. No doubt much of this is difficult to understand. But apart from faith in Christ there is no mercy or grace. In His holiness and righteousness God has no alternative but to punish those, whether angels or people, who continue to sin against Him.

# 14

# The Millennial
# Kingdom

F EW PROPHETIC THEMES are more determinative in a system of
theology than the doctrine of the Millennium. At the same time, it is a
doctrine over which the historic church has divided into at least three
major schools of thought. The early church viewed prophecy of a future
reign of Christ on earth for a thousand years in a literal way. Their interpretation has been designated in theology as *premillennialism,* the view
that the second coming of Christ will occur before (hence *pre-*) His reign
on earth for one thousand years.

It is difficult to find any other view in the early church until about A.D.
190. At that time the viewpoint was advanced by the theological school at
Alexandria, Egypt, that the Bible should not be interpreted literally. However, this was denounced as heresy by the early church, and in general
there was a return to the concept that the Bible should be interpreted in
its natural or literal sense. This normal approach to the Bible prevailed
except in the area of prophecy. The result was that a departure from
premillennialism began in the third century.

A second major view is called *amillennialism,* meaning that there will
be no (hence *a-*) literal Millennium. While there are several forms of
amillennialism, in general this view teaches that at the second coming of
Christ the eternal state will begin. Accordingly, fulfillment of prophecies

about a kingdom on earth usually are equated either with believers' enjoyment of heaven following death, or with the spiritual kingdom in which Christ reigns in the hearts of believers or in the church on earth. In this view many major passages must be interpreted nonliterally.

In the post-Reformation period a third view, *postmillennialism*, emerged. According to this view the church will be triumphant in preaching the gospel to the whole world, and at the conclusion of this triumph (equated with the Millennium) Christ will return to receive the world to Himself and to begin the eternal state. Obviously these three views are radically different interpretations of what the Bible refers to as the reign of Christ on earth for a thousand years. Thus the interpretation of the millennial kingdom is a major factor in the way Christians approach many Old and New Testament passages.

Most biblical scholars conclude that these views stem from differing approaches in biblical hermeneutics, or interpretation. Interpreting prophecy literally, including the teaching of the millennial kingdom, leads inevitably to the premillennial view. If the millennial kingdom, however, is not viewed as a literal kingdom, then this opens the way for either amillennialism or postmillennialism. The decision as to which path to follow in interpreting prophecy is obviously a crucial one, affecting more Scripture passages than possibly any other question about prophecy.

## POSTMILLENNIALISM

Postmillennialism is the most recent of the three major millennial views. Although some elements of postmillennialism occurred earlier, Daniel Whitby (1638–1725) is usually considered the one who introduced postmillennialism. It became the predominant view of orthodoxy in the nineteenth century.

Postmillennialism, like amillennialism, adopts a nonliteral or figurative interpretation of prophecy. Postmillennialism has as its background the history of amillennialism, beginning in the third century, which established for many the concept that prophecy cannot be interpreted literally. Postmillennialism was influenced partly by the fact that the predictions of some amillenarians that Christ would come relatively soon did not materialize. Though it is not entirely clear, it seems that August-ine (354–430) believed that Christ would return in A.D. 650, and that the Millennium had already begun before Christ was born. When Christ did not return in 650, some believed He would come in the year 1000, some-what similar to the modern-day interest in the year 2000.

Forerunners of Daniel Whitby included Joachim of Fiore (1132–1202), who thought Christ would return shortly after a new age was established in 1260. However, as stated, Whitby gave the first comprehensive presen-tation of postmillennialism. Like amillenarians, he taught that Revelation 20:1–6 does not portray events following the Second Coming, but that the passage refers back to Jesus' death in which He defeated Satan. The binding of Satan (Rev. 20:1–3), then, occurred at the first coming of Christ, and verse 4 refers not to the resurrection of Tribulation martyrs but to the salvation of individuals in the present age.

A major factor in postmillennialism, however, was the rise of evolu-tion and optimism that the world would get increasingly better. Actually, two types of postmillennialism arose. One held that the gospel would be the cause of world improvement, and the other, the view of liberals, was that the world would improve by means of social progress.

Postmillennialism was very popular in the last quarter of the nineteenth century. But World War I, with its millions of casualties, destroyed the illu-sion that the world was improving. As a result many postmillennialists switched to the amillennial point of view, which gave them more freedom in interpreting current history in the light of prophecy.

Charles Hodge, a famous nineteenth-century professor at Princeton Seminary, was an exponent of postmillennialism. He felt that as the gospel was preached the whole world would become Christianized. In this way the Millennium would be established before Christ's return. Postmillennialism regarded the Second Advent as the climax of history, which would be fol-lowed by a general resurrection and judgment and the beginning of the eternal state. In the aftermath of two World Wars in the twentieth century, relatively few individuals have continued to follow the postmillennial view. In recent years, however, a new form of postmillennialism has arisen. Called "dominion theology" or "theonomy," this view is that the Millennium will be ushered in as believers "Christianize" various aspects of society.

## AMILLENNIALISM

As stated earlier, it is difficult to find any substantial evidence of a view other than premillennialism in the first two centuries. However, amillennial scholars often insist that it did exist, and they may interpret the silence of some early church fathers on the subject as evidence they were amillennial.

With the rise of the Alexandrian school of theology and its principle of interpreting prophecy and other portions of Scripture nonliterally, amillennialism established a firm hold in the church and to a large extent superseded the premillennial view in the third century A.D. The leaders of the Alexandrian school, including Clement (155–216) and Origen (ca. 185–254), taught that the Bible is to be understood as an extended allegory. Since the Bible has many difficult passages and many supposed moral problems, they said that its meaning was to be found on a deeper level, in hidden allegorical teachings. The church as a whole discarded the Alexandrian position and in fact labeled it as a heresy. For about two hundred years church leaders in Antioch of Syria opposed the Alexandrian school and emphasized the normal, literal interpretation of Scripture. But the allegorical point of view prevailed in the interpretation of prophecy and to a large extent destroyed the premillennial element in the early church.

The amillennial view, however, was not standardized until the time of Augustine. Some advocates of amillennialism before Augustine held other questionable doctrines that hindered their being widely recognized as amillennial spokesmen. But Augustine became the leading theologian of his day.

Following Augustine the Roman Catholic Church adopted amillennialism as its major eschatological point of view, and this was followed by the Protestant Reformers, who also based their eschatology on Augustine.

Curiously, while Augustine denied that there was a literal Millennium, he accepted other areas of prophecy literally, such as the second coming of Christ, heaven, and hell. Why was the millennial kingdom singled out for nonliteral interpretation? As mentioned in an earlier chapter, one possible reason is that the millennial kingdom, according to the Bible, will have a large Jewish element—that is, Christ will reign in Jerusalem over the nation Israel (as well as over the entire world). In the early church, in which Jews were prominent, this was not a problem. But as the church became more and more gentile, some may have opposed the idea that the Jews have a future in prophecy, and in fact that is the position of some amillenarians today.

According to Augustine, there will be no literal reign of Christ on earth for a thousand years. Though some early adherents of amillennialism said the church would rule for a literal thousand years, this view has now been broadened to an indefinite period of time. Amillenarians say that Revelation 20:1–6 applies to Jesus' first coming, not His second coming. So, as mentioned earlier, they hold that Satan is bound now and that those who "come to life" (20:5) refer not to resurrected Tribulation martyrs but, nonliterally, to people in this age who are saved.

However, seeing Revelation 20:1–6 as a reference to Jesus' first advent carries inherent difficulties. First, this ignores the sequence of events in Revelation 19 and 20. Beginning in 19:11 a series of prophecies is given beginning with the Greek conjunction *kai,* meaning "and." This word occurs more than two dozen times in 19:11–20:15. (In these verses the NIV sometimes translates *kai* as "then," but often it leaves the word untranslated.) It is rather obvious that the events prophesied in these verses are consecutive. The armies that will gather in Jerusalem to fight each other will then turn against Christ when He comes. Then the Beast and the False Prophet, that is, the world ruler and his assistant, will be cast into the lake of fire. After that, Satan will be bound, and then Christ will reign for one thousand years. The word *kai* introduces each of these events in chronological order.

Second, nothing should be clearer than the fact that Satan is now very active—he is not presently bound and unable to deceive the nations. In fact the New Testament teaches just the opposite. Peter wrote, "Be self-controlled and alert. Your enemy the devil prowls around like a roaring lion looking for someone to devour" (1 Pet. 5:8). The next verse states that believers should resist the devil, who is one of the causes of believers suffering throughout the world. This is certainly not a picture of Satan being bound and inactive.

In view of demonic activity today and obvious satanic influence that has deceived the nations, the amillennial explanation of Revelation 20:1–3 is not consistent with other biblical texts or with the church's experience throughout history.

Other Scriptures bear out the same idea. Peter told Ananias that Satan had influenced him to lie (Acts 5:3). And Paul referred to "the power of Satan" over unbelievers (26:18). A sinning Christian in Corinth was handed over to Satan for discipline (1 Cor. 5:5). Also Paul said he handed Hymenaeus and Alexander over to Satan (1 Tim. 1:20). Satan tempts Christians (1 Cor. 7:5), and he can gain an advantage over them (2 Cor. 2:11). In the present age Satan can transform himself into an angel (11:14), deceiving, if possible, even believers. Paul claimed, too, that he was sorely tried by a messenger of Satan (12:7).

The coming of "the lawless one," the Antichrist, in the Great Tribulation "will be in accordance with Satan" (2 Thess. 2:9). In 1 Timothy 5:15, Paul referred to some as having followed Satan. Revelation 2:9 and 13 refer to Satan's activity in the persecution of saints in the churches of Smyrna and Pergamum. Presently Satan seeks to lead "the whole world astray" (12:9), deceiving entire nations (20:3). Also he is "the accuser" of Christians (12:10). At the beginning of the last three and a-half years before the Second Coming, Satan will be cast from heaven into the world, no longer having freedom to accuse believers before the Lord (12:9).

Still other passages describe the devil as being very active. His demons troubled many people when Jesus ministered on earth. But, as Peter reported, Jesus healed many "who were under the power of the devil" (Acts 10:38). Believers are exhorted not to give the devil a foothold in their lives (Eph. 4:27). Ephesians 6:11 refers to his "schemes," and 2 Timothy 2:26 refers to the "trap" ("snare," NKJV) of the devil. The devil in some cases has the power of death, but he will ultimately be destroyed (Heb. 2:14). In James 4:7 believers are exhorted to resist the devil and are promised that if they do, "he will flee." According to Revelation 2:10 the devil cast into prison some believers in Smyrna who were standing up for Christ. In Revelation 12:9 and 20:2 the devil is called "that ancient serpent." These many Scriptures all lead to the conclusion that in this present age the devil, though limited in what he can do because of God's power, is nevertheless actively opposing God and His people.

In spite of all these passages, amillenarians appeal to Jesus' statement to His disciples in Luke 10:18, "I saw Satan fall like lightning from heaven." This is a prophetic anticipation of what will happen at the beginning of the Great Tribulation (Rev. 12:9), or it may refer to Satan's defeat at the Cross (see Col. 2:15). Whichever view is taken of Luke 10:18, it does not cancel the many passages that refer to Satan's present activities. The fact that the devil will be bound after the Second Coming and before the thousand-year reign of Christ (Rev. 20:1–6) supports the premillennial view.

The Book of Job makes clear that Satan is always limited by God. Satan was not able to hurt Job physically until God gave him permission (Job 1:12; 2:6). In a sense Satan has always been limited by God's power, but certainly he has not been bound or rendered inactive.

Probably the most blatant violation of the normal interpretation of the Bible is found in the amillennial interpretation of Revelation 20:4–6. Amillenarians want to eliminate this direct statement about people being resurrected in the days following the Second Coming for the purpose of reigning a thousand years. So they do an extraordinary thing here and say this pictures the salvation of souls. However, those who will "come to life" (20:4) will be tribulation saints martyred because of their refusal to worship the image of the Beast or to receive his mark on their right hands or foreheads (13:15–16). When Christ returns, they will be resurrected and will reign with Him a thousand years. To interpret Revelation 20:4–6 in other than its literal meaning is without justification. Amillenarians would be outraged if the same nonliteral interpretive approach were applied to the deity of Christ, His virgin birth, or His death and resurrection.

Though amillenarians follow Augustine in his allegorizing of prophetic Scriptures, many do not follow his view that the present age is a conflict between the "city" of God and the "city" of Satan. The Reformers generally followed Augustine's nonliteral approach to eschatology, seeing the church as God's kingdom on earth.

In the period after the Reformation, when Bible study became more prominent in the church, the premillennial view was revived, and in the twentieth century it has achieved a status of orthodoxy.

Meanwhile, amillennialism has not remained static. Some scholars, namely Friedrich H. C. Duesterdieck (1822–1906) and Theodor F. D.

Kliefoth (1810–1895), believed the Millennium would be fulfilled in the intermediate state. And Benjamin B. Warfield (1851–1921) taught similarly that the Millennium refers to the reign of saints in heaven. In addition to these variations some have advanced the view that the millennial kingdom will be fulfilled in the eternal state, the New Jerusalem. This leaves unexplained, however, how death and sin can exist in that era.

In summary, the amillennial view makes the Millennium itself indefinite as to length and tries to find a nonliteral fulfillment either on the earth or in heaven, in the present or the future. Much more can be said about amillennialism as a method of interpretation, but the ultimate test is, What does the Bible say?

## OLD TESTAMENT PREDICTIONS
## RELATIVE TO THE MILLENNIUM

In the Old Testament and in the time of Jesus' ministry on earth, the people of Israel believed that when the Messiah came He would deliver them from their enemies, bring His righteous judgment to bear on the earth, restore Israel to glory, and establish a kingdom in which prosperity, righteousness, and peace would rule. As mentioned earlier, they tended to disregard the passages concerning the sufferings of Christ in His first coming and related them instead to Israel. So they expected that at His coming the glorious kingdom would be installed. The Old Testament is very clear that this coming will precede the kingdom on earth, which is the view of premillenarians.

Nebuchadnezzar's vision of an image included toes, probably ten, which are identified as kings (Dan. 2:42, 44). These correspond to the ten horns of the fourth beast in Daniel's vision in Daniel 7, for they too are identified as kings (7:24). Daniel 2:44 gives irrefutable support to premillennialism, for it states that Christ will crush those kings and their kingdoms and establish His own millennial rule "in the time of those kings." That is, He will return to set up His reign when the ten nations of the revived Roman Empire are in existence. Since the revived Roman Empire will not be set up until the Great Tribulation, Christ's second coming to reign on the earth will follow the Great Tribulation. His coming, then, is clearly premillennial.

In the dream God gave Nebuchadnezzar, the king saw a great stone cut out of a mountain, a stone that fell on the image, breaking it to pieces (2:34–35, 44–45), and that "became a huge mountain and filled the whole earth" (2:35). Some Bible teachers say this pictures Christ's first advent, with Christianity spreading quickly throughout the world.

This view, however, has several serious flaws. First, in Christ's first coming He did not destroy the Roman Empire and bring all other kingdoms to an end (2:44). Second, Christianity did not suddenly spread over the entire world. Third, the church is never called a mountain. Fourth, in Jesus' life on earth ten kings, represented by the toes, were not ruling at the same time; they are yet to come. Thus only premillennialism properly explains the dream. The stone depicts Christ at His second advent, in which He will destroy the ten-nation confederacy of the revived Roman Empire, resulting in His kingdom immediately being established worldwide.

Daniel's vision of the four great empires includes a future time when the world powers will be destroyed at the time of the second coming of Christ. While it is true that "the saints will be handed over to him [the world ruler] for a time, times and half a time" (Dan. 7:25), the Messiah, Daniel was told, will triumph and bring in His everlasting kingdom. "But the court will sit, and his [the world ruler's] power will be taken away and completely destroyed forever. Then the sovereignty, power and greatness of the kingdoms under the whole heaven will be handed over to the saints, the people of the Most High. His kingdom will be an everlasting kingdom, and all rulers will worship and obey him" (7:26–27). This indicates that at the second coming of Christ He will conquer the wicked world and His reign will follow.

The Old Testament prophecy of Christ returning also implies that He will reign and judge the world in righteousness. In Isaiah 11, for instance, after describing several divine attributes of Christ, the prophet wrote, "And he will delight in the fear of the LORD. He will not judge by what he sees with his eyes, or decide by what he hears with his ears; but with righteousness he will judge the needy, with justice he will give decisions for the poor of the earth. He will strike the earth with the rod of his mouth; with the breath of his lips he will slay the wicked. Righteousness will be his belt and faithfulness the sash around his waist" (11:3–5). Isaiah added that changes in the animal world will occur during His reign. Lambs will be able to live with wolves, goats with leopards, calves with lions, and cows with bears (11:6–7). Tranquillity will be so prevailing that even a small child will play near a poisonous snake and hold it without being harmed (11:8). God said snakes "will neither harm nor destroy on all my holy mountain, for the earth will be full of the knowledge of the LORD as the waters cover the sea" (11:9). Verses 10–16 describe this kingdom on earth when Israel will be restored to her land.

While part of Psalm 72 addresses Solomon and his reign, it also presents a comprehensive picture of the universal reign of Christ. As King, Jesus Christ, God's "royal Son" (72:1), "will judge your people [Israel] in righteousness, your afflicted ones with justice" (72:2). In describing the Messiah's reign, the psalmist wrote, "He will endure as long as the sun, as long as the moon, through all generations. He will be like rain falling on a mown field, like showers watering the earth. In his days the righteous will flourish; prosperity will abound till the moon is no more" (72:5–7). These comprehensive prophecies are followed by the statements, "He will rule from sea to sea and from the River to the ends of the earth," and "All kings will bow down to him and all nations will serve him" (72:8, 11).

Psalm 89 links the second coming of Christ and His reign with the fulfillment of the Davidic Covenant. The psalm states that in spite of the sins of Israel (89:30–32), David's posterity will be established on the throne forever. "I will establish his line forever, his throne as long as the heavens endure. . . . Once for all, I have sworn by my holiness—and I will not lie to David—that his line will continue forever and his throne endure before me like the sun; it will be established forever like the moon, the faithful witness in the sky" (89:29, 35–37).

Jeremiah wrote that when Christ, "the righteous Branch," rules, "Israel will live in safety" (Jer. 23:5–6; 33:16) "in their own land" (23:8). At the second coming of Christ David will rise from the dead and reign with Christ as a prince over the house of Israel, serving his people like a shepherd caring for its sheep. "I will place over them one shepherd, my servant David, and he will tend them; he will tend them and be their shepherd. I the LORD will be their God and my servant David will be prince among them. I the LORD have spoken" (Ezek. 34:23–24). The idea that David is simply another name for Christ is not a satisfactory explanation since several times David is pictured as reigning with Christ (Jer. 30:9; Hos. 3:5). Christ is referred to as the Son of David or the Seed of David but never as David alone. The only explanation that follows any literal understanding of these prophecies is that they picture David in his resurrected state reigning over the house of Israel with Christ on earth.

Part of the prophecies of the Second Coming pertain to the regathering of Israel, as discussed earlier. Ezekiel 37:21–22 records this prophecy: "And say to them, 'This is what the Sovereign LORD says: I will take the Israelites out of the nations where they have gone. I will gather them from all around and bring them back into their own land. I will make them one nation in the land, on the mountains of Israel. There will be one king over all of them and they will never again be two nations or be divided into two kingdoms.'" The prophecy continues, "My servant David will be king over them, and they will all have one shepherd. They will follow my laws and be careful to keep my decrees. They will live in the land I gave to my servant Jacob, the land where your fathers lived. They and their children and their children's children will live there forever, and David my servant will be their prince forever" (37:24–25). The point of these prophecies is that Israel will be restored to her land and David will be resurrected at the Second Coming and will reign with Christ over Israel. When these and other verses (e.g., Ps. 89:36; Dan. 7:27; Ezek. 37:25; Luke 1:33) speak of Christ's kingdom enduring "forever," they suggest that his millennial reign of one thousand years is like a "vestibule," introducing His eternal reign. He will reign forever!

Joel wrote that when Israel is regathered at the Second Coming "Judah will be inhabited forever and Jerusalem through all generations" (Joel 3:20). God said through the prophet Amos, "The days are coming" when "I will bring back my exiled people Israel" and "I will plant Israel in their own land, never again to be uprooted from the land I have given them" (Amos 9:13–15). And Micah wrote that when Messiah rules, Israel "will live securely" (Mic. 5:4). When the Lord is "king over the whole earth," then "the whole land," Zechariah wrote, "will be inhabited; never again will it be destroyed. Jerusalem will be secure" (Zech. 14:9–11).

## NEW TESTAMENT PREDICTIONS
## OF THE MILLENNIUM

While the Old Testament does not indicate the length of Christ's millennial rule, we know that era will not continue forever because the present earth and heavens will ultimately be destroyed. According to Revelation, however, the kingdom will extend for one thousand years—and this is mentioned six times in Revelation 20:1–7. Satan will be bound for a thousand years. The martyred dead who are resurrected are said to reign with Christ a thousand years. Satan will be released after the thousand years, and then the wicked dead will be resurrected.[1] There is no reason for not taking the thousand years as a literal number. And the thousand years clearly will follow the second coming of Christ. Nothing in the passage suggests that the first advent of Christ or the present age is referred to.

The New Testament confirms the premillennial view in various other ways. The angel Gabriel told Mary, "You will be with child and give birth to a son, and you are to give him the name Jesus. He will be great and will be called the Son of the Most High. The Lord God will give him the throne of his father David, and he will reign over the house of Jacob forever; his kingdom will never end" (Luke 1:31–33). Obviously Mary entertained the same hope held by other Jews that when the Messiah came He would redeem Israel and establish the Davidic kingdom on earth. It would have been deceitful for the angel to have told this to Mary if it were not to be literally true.

When the mother of James and John requested that her sons have special privileges in the kingdom (Matt. 20:20–23), Christ did not say her idea of the kingdom was a mistake. Rather He said someone else would have that privilege. Later He promised the disciples that they would sit on thrones judging the twelve tribes of Israel (Matt. 19:28; Luke 22:29–30), thus showing this will be an earthly situation, not a heavenly one.

When the disciples wanted to know when the kingdom would be restored to Israel (Matt. 24:3), Jesus did not say they were mistaken about the kingdom and that it would be a spiritual kingdom. Instead He told them *when* this would occur (24:36, 42), though the exact time is uncertain. And after His resurrection when the disciples asked Jesus whether

He would establish the kingdom then, He gave them a similar answer (Acts 1:6–7) without correcting their anticipation of it.

Though the doctrine of the Millennium is not a major teaching in Paul's epistles, in Romans 11:13–32 he stated clearly that Israel will be restored in the future. There is no evidence of controversy or opposition to this teaching in the early centuries of the church. As noted earlier, he referred to the Rapture in 1 Corinthians 15:51–52 and 1 Thessalonians 4:13–18. In 2 Timothy 2:12 Paul wrote that believers will reign with Christ. In 2 Timothy 4:1 the apostle wrote of Jesus' kingdom. And in 1 Corinthians 15:24 Paul pointed out that Christ, after He has subdued all His enemies, will hand over His kingdom rule to God the Father.

Some premillennialists believe that references in the Book of Acts to the preaching of the kingdom by Paul and others speak of the millennial rule of Christ on earth. These references include Acts 8:12; 14:22; 19:8; 20:25; 28:23, 31. This is also true, it is suggested, of several references to the kingdom in the Epistles.[1]

## THE MILLENNIAL REIGN OF CHRIST

### Geographic Changes during the Millennium

When Christ returns, a number of dramatic things will happen to the earth. The Mount of Olives will split in two from east to west into a great valley. "On that day his feet will stand on the Mount of Olives, east of Jerusalem, and the Mount of Olives will be split in two from east to west, forming a great valley, with half of the mountain moving north and half moving south" (Zech. 14:4). Also, according to verse 8, there will be a dramatic change in Jerusalem, for water will flow from Jerusalem both west to the Mediterranean Sea ("the western sea") and east to the Dead Sea ("the eastern sea"), in both summer and winter (see Joel 3:18). Apparently Jerusalem will be elevated geographically. "The whole land, from Geba to Rimmon, south of Jerusalem, will become like the Arabah. But Jerusalem will be raised up and remain in its place, from the Benjamin Gate to the site of the First Gate, to the Corner Gate, and from the Tower of Hananel to the royal winepresses. It will be inhabited; never again will it be destroyed. Jerusalem will be secure" (Zech. 14:10–11; see Isa. 2:2). Even deserts will blossom with flowers and will be well watered, no longer parched (Isa. 35:1–2, 6–7).

In the Millennium Israel will occupy the land God promised her, as specified in Genesis 15:18–21. This will include all the land from the river of Egypt to the Euphrates River (Ezek. 47:21–22). This extensive territory includes present-day Lebanon and Syria, and parts of Jordan, Iraq, and the Sinai Peninsula, along with present-day Israel and land presently occupied by the Palestinians. The land of Israel will be divided into three parts. Seven tribes will occupy the northern part, consisting of Dan, Asher, Naphtali, Manasseh, Ephraim, Reuben, and Judah (48:1–7). The southern part of Israel will be devoted to the other five tribes, Benjamin, Simeon, Issachar, Zebulun, and Gad (48:23–28). Between these northern and southern parts a large portion of land will be set aside as sacred to God, as described in verses 8–22. Priests will reside there, and the millennial temple ("the sanctuary," 48:8) will be there. In addition, property in Jerusalem will be designated for the prince, presumably David (48:21–22).

## The Government of the Millennium

In contrast to human governments, many of which throughout history have been led by wicked rulers, the millennial government will be a wholly righteous one, with Christ reigning supreme as the absolute King of kings and Lord of lords. This will fulfill God's promises that He will rule the entire world and revive the kingdom of David. As noted earlier, David will rule with Christ as His coregent, with special responsibilities over the house of Israel.

The twelve apostles will have places of authority in their resurrected state and will judge the twelve tribes of Israel (Matt. 19:28; Luke 22:29–30), who will enter the Millennium in their natural bodies. Church-age believers and Tribulation martyrs as well will enjoy the unique privilege of reigning with Christ in the Millennium (2 Tim. 2:12; Rev. 3:21; 5:10; 20:6; 22:5).

When Christ returns, He will come physically to Jerusalem (Zech. 14:4), where He will reign as "King on Zion, [God's] holy hill" (Ps. 2:6; see Isa.

24:23). Isaiah 11:3–5 depicts this righteous government of Christ, in which even formerly ferocious animals will be peaceable. It should be obvious that there has been no fulfillment of this in the past; the kingdom of God in its present spiritual form has not brought about these changes. The rule of Christ on the earth is mentioned so often in the Scriptures that a millennial fulfillment cannot be questioned.[2] Many who try to deny the doctrine of a future millennial reign of Christ ignore these Scriptures or try to interpret them in some nonliteral way.

The subjects of the kingdom will include (a) all those who have been resurrected, that is, all the righteous (Old Testament saints, church-age saints, and martyred Tribulation saints), and (b) those who have survived the Tribulation, whether Jews (believing Israelites restored to their land) or Gentiles, still in their natural bodies. Presumably those in their natural bodies will bear children; then they will die after their normal course of life is complete. There will be sin, though it will be sharply curtailed by the righteous rule of Christ (Isa. 65:20). And He will judge those who disobey Him, the King. He will be "the judge of all men" (Heb. 12:23; see 2 Tim. 4:1). The Scriptures are silent as to the ultimate destiny of believers in the Millennium who will die, but undoubtedly they will be resurrected at some time, perhaps at the end of the Millennium. The Bible is also silent on what will happen to the saved who will still be in their natural bodies at the end of the millennial kingdom. Apparently these, too, will be given resurrected bodies. The Scriptures are silent on these matters probably because they do not affect the hope or destiny of believers today; perhaps further revelation on those issues will be given during the millennial kingdom.

At the beginning of the Millennium all adults will be believers. This is supported by the judgment of the Gentiles (Matt. 25:31–46) in which the unsaved ("goats") will be purged out and the saved ("sheep") will be allowed to enter the kingdom. This is also confirmed by the parable of the wheat and the weeds (13:24–31) and the parable of the good and bad fish (13:47–50).

As children are born in the Millennium and grow up, many of them may not trust in Christ. Those who rebel against Him will be punished (Zech. 14:16–19), and some will be put to death. And unbelievers living at the end of the Millennium who rebel with Satan against Christ will be judged by Him (Rev. 20:7–9). Christ's rule over the earth will fulfill Psalm 2:8–9, in which God the Father addresses God the Son: "Ask of Me, and I will make the nations your inheritance, the ends of the earth your possession. You will rule them with an iron scepter; you will dash them to pieces like pottery." In view of this fact that Christ will reign over the entire earth, the psalmist appealed to people to serve and worship the Lord (Ps. 2:10–12). Unbelievers are urged to turn to Christ before He pours out His wrath on the unbelieving world.

God's government in the millennial kingdom will be complete in its authority and power (Pss. 2:8; 72:9, 11; Isa. 11:4), and His rule will provide complete righteousness and perfect justice (9:7; Jer. 23:5). In view of the deity of Christ and His infinite power no limitation can be put on Him in executing His righteous judgment.

As previously discussed, Ezekiel 20:33–38 indicates that at the time of the Second Coming the people of Israel will be gathered from all over the world, but rebels in the nation will be purged out. As stated in verse 38, "I will purge you of those who revolt and rebel against me. Although I will bring them out of the land where they are living, yet they will not enter the land of Israel. Then you will know that I am the LORD." Israel will have a prominent place in the millennial kingdom. This is emphasized in so many Scriptures that it is amazing that some try to eliminate Israel entirely from the prophetic picture. Many important passages speak of Israel's future existence under the Messiah, her King.[3] Israel once again will be constituted as a nation in her land (Jer. 3:18; 33:14; Ezek. 20:40; 36:24; 37:15–22; 39:25; Hos. 1:11; Zech. 10:8–12). Israel will be the wife of Yahweh restored and related to Him (Isa. 54:1, 5–10; 62:2-5; Hos. 2:14, 23). Settled in her land, Israel will experience great joy and peace and will know no fear.[4] In addition Israel will enjoy prosperity (Ps. 72:7; Jer. 31:14; Ezek. 36:29–30; Amos 9:13); many nations will bring their wealth to her (Isa. 60:5, 11; 66:12). As evidence of her security and prosperity every family in Israel will have its own grapevine and fig tree (Mic. 4:4; Zech. 3:10). Israel's glorious position in the Millennium is likened to her shining like stars (Dan. 12:3) and the sun (Matt. 13:43).

The millennial kingdom will fulfill God's New Covenant with Israel.

The people of Israel will know God's forgiveness (Jer. 31:34), and His Law will be instilled in their hearts (31:33). They will be clean spiritually (Ezek. 36:25–26), the Holy Spirit indwelling each believing Israelite (36:27), and the nation experiencing once again a sense of close fellowship with the Lord (36:28).

In the Messiah's millennial rule He will sit on David's throne. "He will reign on David's throne and over his kingdom" (Isa. 9:7). "The Lord God will give him the throne of his father David" (Luke 1:32). This will fulfill the Davidic Covenant, in which the Lord promised David that He would establish the "throne of his kingdom forever" (2 Sam. 7:13; see 7:14; Ps. 89:28–29). Christ will rule over Israel from Jerusalem as David's Descendant. Since Christ's throne will be a political throne like David's, Christ cannot be seated on it now in heaven, as some writers suggest. He obviously is not now reigning over restored Israel. Instead He is now seated at God's right hand, as the Scriptures repeatedly state.[5] Not once is He said to be on David's throne in the present age.

The universal reign of Christ in the millennial kingdom will also relate to the Gentiles. The Bible is full of references to this.[6] These many Scriptures show plainly that a literal millennial kingdom will follow the second coming of Christ.

*Worship in the Millennial Kingdom*

Opponents of a literal view of the Millennium often try to equate it with a spiritual kingdom of God ruling in the hearts of believers today. It is true that the millennial kingdom will also have its spiritual aspect, just as life in the church in the present age has a spiritual aspect. But this is not adequate to explain all the many Scriptures that teach that the millennial kingdom will be basically a political kingdom.

One of the most important facts relating to the millennial kingdom is Christ in His deity sitting on the throne of David as King of kings and Lord of lords. His royal sovereignty, His personal presence in the world, and His activities in governing righteously reveal a spiritual climate different from anything before it. All this is aided by the fact that Satan and the demonic world will be rendered inactive and the only evil that will remain in the world will be the sin nature of mankind. In fact, the millennial kingdom will demonstrate that even in ideal situations people will still rebel against God.

In the Millennium Christ's glory, deity, omniscience, omnipotence, and righteous government will be evident. The return of Israel to the Promised Land will be proof of His ability to fulfill prophecy, and His reign as the Son of David will consummate the Davidic kingdom.

In the millennial kingdom there will be universal proclamation of the truth of God. "For the earth will be full of the knowledge of the Lord as the waters cover the sea" (Isa. 11:9). Jeremiah added that all Israel, at least at the beginning of the Millennium, will know the Lord (Jer. 31:33–34). Many people, Isaiah wrote, will go to Jerusalem, "the mountain of the Lord," to be taught God's ways and His word (Isa. 2:3).

The Lord's kingdom will be characterized by righteousness and peace. "He will judge between the nations and will settle disputes for many peoples. They will beat their swords into plowshares and their spears into pruning hooks. Nation will not take up sword against nation, nor will they train for war anymore" (2:4). "All [the world's] rulers will worship and obey Him" (Dan. 7:27).

One of the major features of the Millennium will be the temple, which will be the center of worship in the enlarged millennial Jerusalem. God gave Ezekiel the architectural features of the temple in detail (Ezek. 40:1–46:24). This is a future temple, since no such temple has ever been built. It does not correspond to Solomon's, Zerubbabel's, or Herod's temples. Those who say the temple in Ezekiel 40–46 pictures the spiritual blessings of believers presently on earth or in heaven overlook the many physical details of this structure and its functions. A normal, literal reading of these chapters leads to a premillennial interpretation, with this temple to be constructed in the Millennium. Some scholars have challenged the idea that this will be a physical temple because animal sacrifices are mentioned. They say those references present only a general, spiritualized ideal of worship. However, this overlooks the specific mention of sacrifices and even of rooms in the temple for preparing animals for sacrifice (40:38–43) and an altar for offering the sacrifices (43:13–17).

Others have argued that because Christ died, no such sacrificial system will be needed in the millennial kingdom. In fact, amillenarians usually describe these animal sacrifices mentioned in Ezekiel as bloody and pagan rites, apparently overlooking the fact that such sacrifices were not invented by human beings but were demanded by God Himself in the Old Testament system. Of course, since Christ by His death provided the final sacrifice for sins (Heb. 7:27; 9:26, 28), this raises the question of why any animal sacrifices will be necessary.

The answer lies in the fact that the millennial sacrifices will constitute a memorial of Jesus' death, much as observing the Lord's Supper is a reminder of His death (Luke 22:19; 1 Cor. 11:26). Also, just as the Old Testament sacrifices looked forward symbolically, to Christ's death, so sacrifices in the millennial kingdom will look back in remembrance to His sacrifice on the cross. It is almost impossible to deny the literal, physical character of these sacrifices without denying Ezekiel's detailed prophetic descriptions of the temple.

Ezekiel is not the only prophet who spoke of millennial sacrifices. Isaiah, Jeremiah, Zechariah, and Malachi also referred to them.[7] Obviously the animal sacrifices do not provide a sacrifice for sin and are not expiatory any more than were the sacrifices in the Old Testament.

While the sacrificial system of the millennial kingdom will be similar to that of the Levitical system under the Mosaic Law, there will be a number of differences. For example, there will be no evening sacrifices and no observance of three of Israel's annual feasts (the Feast of Pentecost, the Feast of Trumpets, and the Day of Atonement). The Passover and the Feast of Unleavened Bread will apparently celebrate national cleansing, and the Feast of Tabernacles will depict Israel's special place in God's kingdom. In the millennium temple there will be no gold lampstand, no table for the bread of the Presence ("table of showbread," NKJV), and no ark of the covenant.

## Other Major Features of the Millennium

In Christ's rule of justice, for the first time in the history of mankind the world will not experience war. Three prophets prophesied that weaponry will not be needed; swords and spears will be changed by blacksmiths into farm implements (Isa. 2:4; Joel 3:10; Mic. 4:3). While the Scriptures do not state it in so many words, probably the majority of people during the Millennium will be saved, though some will not.

God said to Adam after the Fall that he would have trouble living from the soil of the earth (Gen. 3:17–19) because the earth was now cursed. This curse on the earth will apparently be lifted to some degree during the Millennium, though physical death will still exist.

General health and well-being of individuals may also result from the lifting of the curse. Freedom from sickness seems to be described in a number of Scriptures (Isa. 29:18; 33:24; 35:5–6). People will experience greater longevity of life than now, and infants will not die (65:20). In general, the Millennium will be a golden age, the climax of God's dealings with the human race.

## THE DIVINE PURPOSE IN THE MILLENNIAL KINGDOM

Why is a millennial kingdom necessary in God's plan for the human race? The answer seems to be that the Millennium is the final illustration of the grace of God and man's need of salvation. Throughout history the human race has been tested in various ways, and people have made various attempts to justify the idea that somehow they can conquer sin on their own. However, people have failed under every possible circumstance. As the human race has progressed, God has engaged mankind in different stewardships—or dispensations—with varying requirements. In the Garden of Eden, Adam and Eve were not to partake of the forbidden fruit. After they fell into sin, God gave mankind a conscience that informed them concerning right and wrong. Conscience, however, proved a failure; the sin of the human race led ultimately to the Flood.

Following the Flood God introduced the principle of human government, including the execution of those guilty of murder. "And for your lifeblood I will surely demand an accounting. I will demand an accounting from every animal. And from each man, too, I will demand an accounting for the life of his fellow man. Whoever sheds the blood of man, by man shall his blood be shed; for in the image of God has God made man" (Gen. 9:5–6). The descendants of Noah, however, did no better than their forebears, and the climax of their sin came at the Tower of Babel when God imposed diverse languages on the human race.

Following the Tower of Babel, God selected a new line in Abraham and his descendants, who would be a special people of God. This line extended from Abraham to Isaac and Jacob and the twelve sons of Jacob, who formed the heads of the twelve tribes of Israel. From that point on in the Old Testament, the nation that descended from Jacob's family illustrated God's special purposes in law and grace. More than six hundred regulations were given to guide the Israelites in their worship and in their social and moral life. The nation, however, failed miserably to keep the Law, demonstrating once again that the human will does not respond properly to the will of God. The Law of Israel was never given to the world in general, though it embodied some of the general rules that governed other nations as well as Israel. Central in the Mosaic law were the Ten Commandments, nine of which are repeated in the New Testament for the present age, with only the commandment on the Sabbath being omitted.

With the death of Christ, the Mosaic Law was terminated as a basis for God's judgment of Israel. The present age is an age of grace in which God is not only saving people by His grace (as He has always done), but He is dealing graciously with their social and moral life. In the church age, however, as well as in preceding dispensations, most humans beings have failed to follow God. Today many are failing to trust in Jesus Christ as their Savior and to worship the true God. When the Rapture occurs, it will end the present age and will begin what the Bible refers to as the Day of the Lord. This will be a time of immediate judgment that will extend throughout the Tribulation period, as well as a time of blessing in the millennial kingdom, which will finally reach its climax in the final judgments at the end of the existence of the physical and temporal world.

# 15

# The

# Eternal State

## THE OLD WORLD DESTROYED AND
## THE NEW WORLD CREATED

IMMEDIATELY AFTER the Great White Throne judgment at the end of the Millennium, when all the unsaved will be cast into the lake of fire, the place of eternal torment, God will establish a new world order for the saved. This is introduced by the statement, "Then I saw a new heaven and a new earth, for the first heaven and first earth had passed away, and there was no longer any sea" (Rev. 21:1). Earlier John wrote that the "earth and sky fled from his presence, and there was no place for them" (20:11). The physical universe as we now know it will be destroyed.

In the Flood in Noah's day God destroyed all life on earth except for Noah and those with him in the ark. God's future destruction of the earth and the heavens will be by fire. Peter wrote of this contrast between water and fire. He said that whereas the world in Noah's day "was deluged and destroyed . . . the present heavens and earth are reserved for fire, being kept for the day of judgment and destruction of ungodly men" (2 Pet. 3:6–7).

Peter added, "But the day of the Lord will come like a thief. The heavens will disappear with a roar; the elements will be destroyed by fire, and the earth and everything in it will be laid bare" (3:10). On the basis of this coming catastrophe Peter exhorted his readers to live godly and holy lives (3:11). He then repeated that the earth would be destroyed: "That day will bring about the destruction of the heavens by fire, and the elements will melt in the heat" (3:12). He held out to his readers the prospect of new heavens and a new earth (3:13), which would replace the present heavens and earth. John added that there will be no sea in the future earth (Rev. 21:1).

The entire physical universe—the earth and the whole panorama of the heavens with its trillions of stars and heavenly bodies—will apparently all be dissolved, reduced to nothing as they were before Creation. The Bible gives no reason for this except that the New Jerusalem will be aglow with the glory of God, and there will be no sun and moon (21:23; 22:5). Apparently, with the new earth brilliantly lit by the glory of God, if there were heavenly bodies they could not be seen. These limited statements, remarkable as they are, seem to suggest that further explanation is unnecessary.

Modern science has affirmed that the physical world is composed of atoms with incredible locked-in power. It is power that is released in nuclear explosions, giving off great heat. The final nuclear conflagration of fire and heat will wipe out the entire physical universe. The scriptural description is clearly in keeping with modern scientific analysis of the structure of matter.

## THE NEW JERUSALEM

John was then introduced to the New Jerusalem. He wrote, "I saw the Holy City, the new Jerusalem, coming down out of heaven from God, prepared as a bride beautifully dressed for her husband" (Rev. 21:2). Some expositors have said the New Jerusalem is not a physical city but is an allegorical presentation of the church or of saints in general. However, it is repeatedly called a city (21:2, 10, 14–16, 18–19, 21, 23; 22:2–3, 14, 19) and given specific physical dimensions.

Because the New Jerusalem is said to "come down" from heaven, not created like the new earth and new heavens, some have postulated that it will exist during the millennial kingdom. However, because of its immense size it could not rest on the earth, for there will be an earthly Jerusalem in the Millennium. If it did exist during the Millennium, the only way it could do so would be as a satellite city.

While the Bible makes no direct statement about the New Jerusalem hovering over the earth (this is only an inference), this may solve a problem about the relationship between saints with resurrected bodies and those with natural bodies in the Millennium. The difference between these two is often cited by amillenarians as proving that a Millennium is impossible. However, in Jesus' postresurrection ministry He met with His disciples in His resurrection body while the disciples were still in their natural bodies. In the Millennium people will build houses, plant crops, live, and die (Isa. 65:20–21), but there is no word in Scripture about whether a person in his natural body could live in one place and a person in a resurrection body live nearby. In fact, it has been suggested that the New Jerusalem as a satellite city would be the residence of all who are resurrected. They could come to earth from their residence in the New Jerusalem, much like one who has a home in the country and an office in the city, or like angels coming from heaven to earth.

All this, however, is conjecture and should not be treated as a formal doctrine of the Scriptures. It is only a possibility based on the fact that the New Jerusalem is not said to be created at the time the new heavens and the new earth are created.

On the other hand, the sequence of events in Revelation 19–21 shows that the New Jerusalem will begin in the eternal state. This sequence is as follows: the Second Coming; the binding of Satan; the resurrection of Tribulation saints; the Millennium; the release and final judgment of Satan; the Great White Throne judgment; the creation of new heavens and a new earth; and the appearance of the New Jerusalem and its descent to the new earth.

In Revelation 21 John described the new world, which will include the new earth and the New Jerusalem. The first thing mentioned is that God will dwell intimately in the city with His people (21:3). Because of His presence, grief and pain will pass away. "He will wipe every tear from their eyes. There will be no more death or mourning or crying or pain, for the old order of things has passed away" (21:4) and everything will be new (21:5).

## The Citizens of the New Jerusalem

Jesus was introduced to John in the vision as "the Alpha and Omega, the Beginning and the End" (Rev. 21:6). In other words, He is the eternal One. As *alpha* and *omega* are the first and last letters of the Greek alphabet, so Christ is the beginning of time and the end of time. As the eternal One, He offers eternal life to those who put their trust in Him. "To him who is thirsty I will give to drink without cost from the spring of the water of life" (21:6). Heaven is only for those who have eternal life. This is true also of the New Jerusalem. In addition to receiving eternal life, believers in Christ have an inheritance from God. "He who overcomes will inherit all this, and I will be his God and he will be my son" (21:7). By contrast, the unbelievers are destined for the lake of burning sulfur. "But the cowardly, the unbelieving, the vile, the murderers, the sexually immoral, those who practice magic arts, the idolaters and all liars—their place will be in the fiery lake of burning sulfur. This is the second death" (21:8).

## The Glory of the New Jerusalem

Revelation 21:1–8 introduced the New Jerusalem. Then verse 9 and following give details of its appearance and function. As in verse 2, the New Jerusalem is said to be beautiful like "the bride, the wife of the Lamb" (21:9). Also it is said to be like a gigantic jewel. "It shone with the glory of God, and its brilliance was like that of a very precious jewel, like a jasper, clear as crystal" (21:11). The city's high wall will have twelve gates, three facing each of four directions, with one of the names of Israel's twelve tribes on each gate (21:12–13). The city will also have twelve foundations (21:14). The fact that the gates are named after the twelve tribes of Israel demonstrates that Israel will be in the New Jerusalem, and the fact that the twelve apostles of the Lamb will have their names on the twelve foundations represents the church. These apparently are the two principal bodies of saints who will be present in the New Jerusalem.

According to John's account the city wall measured twelve thousand stadia on each side (21:16), or about fourteen hundred miles. It will be two hundred feet thick (or perhaps "high"). It will be "made of jasper, and the city of pure gold, as pure as glass" (21:18). Apparently the city will be gold in color but this gold, unlike the gold known today, is transparent. In fact, all the gems in the city seem to be transparent; perhaps this is to allow God's glory to be evident everywhere.

The foundations of the walls will have twelve kinds of jewels in them (21:19–20). In the New Jerusalem the number twelve is prominent: there are the twelve tribes of Israel (21:12), twelve foundations (21:14), twelve apostles (21:14), twelve jewels (21:19–20), twelve gates (21:21), twelve pearls (21:21), and twelve kinds of fruit (22:2), 12,000 stadia for the length of the wall (21:16) and 144 cubits (twelve times twelve) in the wall's width or height (21:17).

The first of the twelve jewels in the city's foundations is a jasper. A jasper stone today is opaque and not clear as crystal (see 21:11). Perhaps the stone in John's vision looked more like a diamond. The second foundation gem is a sapphire stone, similar to a diamond but blue in color. The third foundation is a chalcedony, a stone found in Chalcedon in Turkey, thought to be also blue with stripes of other colors in it. The fourth jewel, an emerald, is dark green in color. The fifth, the sardonyx, is a red and white stone. The sixth gem, a carnelian, also known as a sardius, is a reddish stone. It is also mentioned in Revelation 4:3, in connection with the jasper, describing the glory of God. The chrysolite, the seventh stone, is gold colored, different from the modern stone of that name, which is of a green shade. The eighth, beryl, is sea green in color. Topaz, the ninth stone, is a transparent yellow-green gem. The tenth stone, chrysoprase, is also a green jewel. The jacinth, the eleventh gem, is violet in color, and the twelfth jewel, the amethyst, has a purple shade. Together these jewels portray a mass of tremendously brilliant colors, all reflecting the glory of God.

Because the glory of God will be present, the city will not require a sun or moon. "The glory of God gives it light, and the Lamb is its lamp" (21:23). Besides the New Jerusalem reflecting the glory of God, the glory of earthly kingdoms will come into the city (21:26). But nothing impure or wrong will be allowed in the city. Only those whose names are in the Lamb's Book of Life will inhabit the New Jerusalem (21:27).

## The River of Life and the Tree of Life

Besides all these glorious features, a river, called the water of life, will flow from God's throne and down the middle of the city's street (Rev. 22:1). This may suggest that the New Jerusalem will be like a gigantic pyramid rather than a cube. If the throne is at the top, a pyramid will allow the water to come down the side of the city. The Tree of Life, of which Adam and Eve were forbidden to partake, will be on both sides of the river (22:2). But how can a tree be on both sides of a river? Perhaps a group of trees is intended, or, more likely, the river may be narrow enough to allow a tree's branches to reach over both sides.

Most important, however, is the statement, "And the leaves of the trees are for the healing of the nations" (22:2). Some writers say this verse shows that this passage refers to the Millennium, not the eternal state. However, the word "healing" is better translated "health." It is entirely possible that the tree's fruit will have something to do with the well-being of people in the New Jerusalem, even though they do not need healing in the sense of recovering from illness. The verse that follows states emphatically, "No longer will there be any curse" (22:3). In other words, the effects of the Fall on the human race will no longer exist.

## God's Throne in the New Jerusalem

John also saw that "the throne of God and of the Lamb will be in the city, and his servants will serve him. They will see his face, and his name will be on their foreheads" (Rev. 22:3–4). The question is often raised as to what saints will do throughout eternity. The Scriptures state for one thing that they will minister to the Lord as priests (1:6). It is apparent that in raising up a host of people who are saved God intends that they respond to Him by serving Him in love, by being "His servants" (22:6). While the Bible does not exactly indicate how they will do so, perhaps their service for God in the eternal state will be linked in some way to their faithfulness in their present life on earth. Believers will also be with the Lord (John 14:3; 17:24), will reign with Him (2 Tim. 2:12; Rev. 1:6; 3:21; 5:10; 20:6; 22:5), and will worship Him (22:9).

As stated earlier in 21:23, the Lord's glory will provide light in the city, so that the sun, moon, and man-made lights will not be necessary. All this will come to pass "soon" (22:6; see vv. 7, 12) or better "quickly" (NASB, NKJV), that is, the events will occur in sudden succession. The Lord Jesus Himself announced, "Behold, I am coming soon [suddenly]! Blessed is he who keeps the words of the prophecy in this book" (22:7).

## FINAL EXHORTATIONS

When John heard and saw this tremendous revelation, he fell down to worship the angel, who told him not to worship him, the angel, but to worship God (Rev. 22:8–9; see 19:10). The angel also told John not to "seal up the words of the prophecy of this book, because the time is near" (22:10). It is amazing how many neglect this book in view of this exhortation that commands that its contents be communicated.

If the fulfillment of end-time events was near in the apostle John's day, it certainly is near today! Even so, life goes on, with people continuing either in sin or in upright living (22:11). Again the Lord Jesus announced that He is coming soon (22:12; see vv. 7, 20). When He comes in the Rapture, believers will be rewarded at the judgment seat of Christ, and then unbelievers will be judged in the Tribulation judgments and other judgments to follow. Those judgments will be executed by the Lord Jesus, the eternal One—"the Alpha and the Omega, the First and the Last, the Beginning and the End" (22:13; see 1:4, 8, 17; 2:8; 21:6).

Only the redeemed will have access to this city and its Tree of Life (22:14; see 2:7; 22:2); those who are immoral will be excluded. John was to give the testimony of this book to the seven churches mentioned in Revelation 2–3; and of course, the message of Revelation is to be heeded by everyone (1:3; 22:7, 9).

A final invitation is recorded in 22:17: "The Spirit and the bride [the church] say, 'Come!' And let him who hears say, 'Come!' Whoever is thirsty, let him come; and whoever wishes, let him take the free gift of the water of life." A word of warning is then added in verses 18–19. "I warn everyone who hears the words of the prophecy of this book: If anyone adds anything to them, God will add to him the plagues described in this book.

And if anyone takes words away from this book of prophecy, God will take away from him his share in the tree of life and in the holy city, which are described in this book." The Book of Revelation closes with Christ's promise, given for the third time in Revelation 22, "I am coming soon" (22:20; see 22:7, 12), and with a benediction of grace: "The grace of the Lord Jesus be with God's people. Amen" (22:21).

No expositor of the Book of Revelation can find adequate words to describe the wonder of God's revelation of the glorious future which saints of all ages will enjoy in the New Jerusalem for all eternity. We are looking forward, as Abraham did, "to the city with [permanent] foundations, whose architect and builder is God" (Heb. 11:10). This "city that is to come" (13:14) will be part of the new heavens and new earth, "the home of righteousness" to which believers are "looking forward" (2 Pet. 3:13). The Book of Revelation calls attention to the temporary nature of this present life, the accountability of every person to God, and above all to the marvelous grace of God, which offers salvation to all who put their trust in Christ.

# 16

# The Significance of Prophecy in Biblical Theology

---

As a significant part of Christian theology, prophecy plays an important role in Christian faith and life. Since one-fourth of the Bible was predictive prophecy when it was revealed, it is clearly God's intention that facts about the future be believed and understood. Without a future hope Christianity has little to offer, and hope is related to prophetic revelation. The modern tendency to live in the present or past with little or no regard to the future is not a biblical perspective.

## PROPHECY IN RELATION TO BIBLICAL INSPIRATION

A fundamental issue in theology is the question of whether the Bible is a supernatural book inspired by God and therefore an authoritative and accurate record of what God wants us to know about the past, present, and future. The study of prophecy has no significance if the Bible is not accepted for what it is, the very Word of God. In biblical prophecy God has revealed facts far beyond the ability of humans to know or discover for themselves.

While prophecy depends on belief in the Bible as the inspired Word of God, it also constitutes clear evidence that the Bible is the Word of God. The fact that half of the Bible's approximately one thousand prophecies have already been fulfilled is overwhelming evidence that yet-unfulfilled prophecy will also be fulfilled.

## PROPHECY IN RELATION TO
## LITERAL INTERPRETATION

Throughout church history the question has been raised as to whether biblical prophecy should be interpreted literally or nonliterally. This has been previously discussed, but should be restated as part of the large picture. A school of theology in Alexandria, Egypt, which arose about A.D. 190, advanced the view that the Bible is an allegory, which should not be regarded as literal, and so one should search for hidden, symbolic meanings. To regard Scripture as a nonliteral allegory, however, subverts its meaning. The early church denounced this view as heretical.

The normal, grammatical, historical, literal view of Scripture for the most part was regained by church fathers in the second and third centuries, particularly by the school of Antioch in Syria. However, premillennialism, based on the literal interpretation of prophecy, eventually fell by the wayside, especially in North Africa, where the Alexandrian school of thought predominated.

Later, biblical interpretation was somewhat standardized by Augustine, the famous bishop of Hippo in North Africa. He adopted the point of view that Scripture, with the exception of prophecy, should be interpreted naturally and literally. Augustine held a rather inconsistent view of this, however, stating that in Scripture the Millennium pictures excessive feasting, which he regarded as carnal and unworthy of scriptural faith. While he accepted a literal second coming of Christ, as did the church generally, and a literal heaven and hell, he somehow selected the millennial doctrine as not being subject to future fulfillment. In fact, he felt that the church was already living in the Millennium in the sense that the church is part of the spiritual kingdom of God, and he believed Christ is now reigning in the hearts of Christians.

However, this point of view disregards the many passages in both the Old and New Testaments that describe the millennial kingdom in straightforward terms, so that, taken in their normal sense, passages on the

Millennium cannot be interpreted allegorically. Possibly some church leaders were unconsciously anti-Semitic, resulting in their not wanting to give Israel a prominent place in the future as required by premillennialism. Unfortunately Augustine's view became the dominant view of the Roman Catholic Church, and later in the Protestant Reformation Martin Luther, John Calvin, and others based their view of prophecy on Augustine rather than on the early church of the first two centuries, which held to a premillennial view. As a result, many Christians since the Reformation have questioned the principle of interpreting prophecy in its literal, normal sense.

However, it is inconsistent to deny a literal Tribulation and a literal Millennium but to accept a literal Rapture and a literal Second Coming. No scriptural support exists for such an approach, and it is difficult if not impossible to find prophecy that is being fulfilled in a nonliteral way.

## PROPHECY AND CHRISTIAN FAITH AND LIFE

Because of the prominent place given to prophecy from Genesis to Revelation, it seems clear that God intended people to understand His prophetic program. Yet many have misinterpreted biblical prophecy. Even in the Old Testament and during Jesus' life on earth few if any people understood the difference between the first and second comings of Christ. In fact, Jesus' disciples believed He would at that time fulfill the promises related to His second coming, including establishing His glorious kingdom on earth, in which they would sit on thrones judging the twelve tribes of Israel.

If a major doctrine of the Bible such as the first and second comings of Christ could be misunderstood, this serves as a warning to each of us today to beware of misinterpreting prophecy. Why did people in the Old Testament and in Jesus' ministry misunderstand prophecy? The answer is clear: They failed to pay attention to the details of the prophecies concerning Jesus' first coming in contrast to the details of the prophecies about His second coming. Even the Old Testament makes clear that Jesus' first coming involved His sufferings, death, and resurrection, and that His second coming would occur only after a time of great tribulation and trouble in which Israel would be persecuted before being rescued by the return of Christ. This became more evident in the New Testament after Christ ascended into heaven. Only then did the disciples realize, perhaps for the first time, that the First Advent related to His sufferings and death, that the Second Coming relates to His glorious reign, and that they themselves were living in a time period in between those two advents. Nor did they imagine that this period of time would last at least two thousand years, for they expected Christ to come back within their lifetime.

The lessons for interpreting prophecy are clear. A search should be made for what the prophecies say, noting various details. Then an attempt should be made to understand them in their normal sense, while recognizing symbolic or nonliteral terms and the literal meaning they are intended to convey. Finally all the prophecies should be put together to create an overall view of prophecy that is harmonious and noncontradictory.

## PRACTICAL APPLICATION OF PROPHECY

Prophecy is intended not only to inform people about future events. It also has practical implications for present-day living. In fact, most Bible prophecies were written in times of difficulty when a prophetic Word was needed to give hope and assurance of God's ultimate victory. Unfortunately, the practical side of prophecy is often overlooked. But a study of prophecy should impact our lives. As we study biblical prophecy, we can gain insight into how we should live now and what our value system should be.

In light of the Rapture, the next event to occur on God's prophetic calendar, Christians should heed five exhortations given in the New Testament—commands that encourage believers to apply prophetic truth to their lives.

In the Upper Room, just before Jesus' arrest, trial, and crucifixion, His disciples were dismayed that He had said He would leave them. This did not fit with their expectation that He would establish His glorious kingdom on earth and free Israel from her oppressors. John 14:1–3 records Jesus' words in answer to their dismay, even though they were not capable of understanding Him fully. "Do not let your hearts be troubled. Trust in God; trust also in me. In my Father's house are many rooms; if it were not so, I would have told you. I am going there to prepare a place for you. And if I go and prepare a place for you, I will come back and take you to be with me that you also may be where I am."

These verses are the Bible's first revelation of the Rapture, in which Christ will come back to take His own to heaven. He exhorted the disciples not to be troubled. Since they trusted the Father, they also should trust Christ, whose power was demonstrated in His many miracles. Having referred to Himself as the Source of peace, Jesus spoke of His coming to take them to heaven. They need not be anxious about His leaving because later He would return for them.

The disciples were unprepared to accept this truth, however, for they were looking for Him to establish His kingdom on earth at that time. It was not until later, under the ministry of the apostle Paul, that the doctrine of the Rapture was given to the church in more detail.

A second major exhortation is found in 1 Thessalonians 4:18. At the conclusion of the classic passage on the Rapture (1 Thess. 4:13–17) Paul wrote, "Therefore encourage each other with these words." The word *encourage* also means "to exhort or urge on." The Rapture by its very nature should impel believers to make the most of life. In addition, the word means "to comfort," as it is rendered in the King James Version. In the pressures of life we enjoy the wonderful assurance that someday our struggles will be over, including the end to our longing for loved ones who have gone on to heaven before us. Struggles with mortality and aging will end when Christ comes and believers are caught up to be in the presence of the Lord forever.

A third exhortation is recorded in 1 John 3:2–3. "Dear friends, now we are children of God, and what we will be has not yet been made known. But we know that when he appears, we shall be like him, for we shall see him as he is. Everyone who has this hope in him purifies himself, just as he is pure." The hope of the Rapture, when we will meet the Savior, should be a sanctifying force in our lives. We will be made completely like Him then; so we should endeavor with His help to serve Him faithfully now and to lead lives of purity. As Peter wrote, "You ought to live holy and godly lives as you look forward to the day of God" (2 Pet. 3:11–12). He added, "Dear friends, since you are looking forward to this, make every effort to be found spotless, blameless and at peace with him" (3:14). "While we wait for the blessed hope" (Titus 2:13), we are "to say 'No' to ungodliness and worldly passions, and to live self-controlled, upright and godly lives in this present age" (2:12). While salvation is ours by grace apart from works, our works will be evaluated at the judgment seat of Christ.

The fourth and most comprehensive exhortation regarding the Rapture is given toward the end of 1 Corinthians 15. In this chapter Paul discussed the fact that our present bodies need to be exchanged for bodies suited for heaven. Normally that exchange is accomplished in the resurrection of dead bodies, but a grand exception is recorded in verses 51–55. In the Rapture an entire generation of Christians will be caught up to heaven. Without experiencing death they will be instantly changed and presented to the Lord. With this truth in mind, Paul gave a challenging exhortation: "Therefore, my dear brothers, stand firm. Let nothing move you. Always give yourselves fully to the work of the Lord, because you know that your labor in the Lord is not in vain" (15:58).

In view of the Rapture, we should be standing firm in faith regardless of the troubles that may arise in this life. Unmoved, we should be serving the Lord "always" and "fully." The reason for this is that our "labor in the Lord is not in vain." One of the most important facts of life is that we are accountable to God and that He will reward those who serve Him faithfully.

A fifth exhortation in light of the Lord's return is to be patient. Just as a farmer must wait months before his acreage yields its crops, so we must wait patiently for the Lord to come back (James 5:7–8). We are to look forward eagerly to that day, as we are told in Romans 8:25; 1 Corinthians 1:7; Philippians 3:20; and Hebrews 9:28. These five exhortations show us that the truth of the soon-to-come Rapture motivates us to set aside anxiety, to be comforted and encouraged, to be morally pure, to serve the Lord faithfully and diligently, and to be patient.

## THE RELEVANCE OF PROPHECY

Because prophecy reaches beyond this life into the life to come, believers are encouraged to live according to principles that will count for eternity—to reject the world's value system and to live for Christ. This is clearly stated in Romans 12:1–2: "Therefore, I urge you, brothers, in view of God's mercy, to offer your bodies as living sacrifices, holy and pleasing to God—this is your spiritual act of worship. Do not conform any longer to the pattern of this world, but be transformed by the renewing of your mind. Then you will be able to test and approve what God's will is—his good, pleasing and perfect will."

These exhortations point out that Christians are to offer themselves to the Lord in sacrifice and obedience. Because we as Christians have been redeemed and justified by God, we are now in a position to offer ourselves (the word "bodies" probably suggests the entire person) to God for service, which would not have been possible before salvation. In addition, we are urged not to conform to the pattern or value system of the world, but rather to "be transformed by the renewing" of our minds. Spiritual growth comes from viewing life from God's point of view, that is, altering our perspective on life so that it conforms to His will, not to the ways of the world. This underscores the importance of preaching, teaching, and comprehending prophetic truth, which gives us a clear picture of our destiny.

The most important benefit from studying prophecy is the challenge to live in light of our ultimate destiny. God has given us adequate revelation concerning the future, though many questions remain. We can trust God with the unknown, and we need to believe and respond to the truth He has given us concerning the life to come. Prophecy by its very nature reveals a sovereign God who is omniscient, who knows the future as well as the past, and who is able to give us guidance and direction as we seek to live for Him. Biblical prophecy, then, gives hope for the future as well as comfort and zeal for the present. We, like Paul, are to love "His appearing" (2 Tim. 4:8), that is, to wait eagerly for the return of Christ for His bride, the church, anticipating the fulfillment of our "blessed hope" (Titus 2:13).

# Endnotes

---

## CHAPTER 3—THE BLESSED HOPE OF THE LORD'S RETURN

1. Revelation 6:16–19; 11:18; 14:10, 19; 15:1–7; 16:1, 19.

## CHAPTER 8—GOD'S MASTER PLAN FOR THE WORLD

1. Genesis 8:1; Exodus 10:13–19; 14:21; 15:10; Numbers 11:31; 2 Kings 18:45.
2. Numbers 34:6–7; Joshua 1:4; 9:1; 15:12, 47; 23:4; Ezekiel 47:10, 15, 20; 48:28.

## CHAPTER 12—THE ORDER OF RESURRECTIONS

1. Matthew 22:30–31; Luke 14:14; 20:35–36; John 5:21; 6:39–40, 44, 54; 11:24–25; Acts 17:18, 31–32; 23:6; 24:15, 21; 26:8; Romans 6:5; 8:11; 1 Corinthians 6:14; 15:11–58; 2 Corinthians 1:9; 4:14; Philippians 3:11; 1 Thessalonians 4:15; Hebrews 6:2.
2. Acts 1:22; 2:24, 31–32; 3:15, 26; 4:2, 10, 33; 5:30; 10:40; 13:30, 34, 37; 17:31; Romans 1:4; 4:24–25; 6:4–5, 9; 7:4; 8:11, 34: 10:9; 1 Corinthians 6:4, 14; 15:4, 12–20; 2 Corinthians 4:14; 5:15; Galatians 1:1; Ephesians 1:20; 2:6; Philippians 3:10; Colossians 2:12; 1 Thessalonians 1:10; 4:14; 1 Timothy 2:8; 1 Peter 1:3, 21; 3:21.

## CHAPTER 13—THE JUDGMENTS

1. Matthew 5:22, 29–30; 10:28; 18:9; 23:15, 33; Mark 9:43, 45, 47; Luke 12:5; James 3:6.
2. Matthew 8:12; 13:42, 50; 22:13; 24:51; 25:30; Luke 13:28.

## CHAPTER 14—THE MILLENNIAL KINGDOM

1. 1 Corinthians 6:9–10; 15:50; Galatians 5:21; Ephesians 5:5; Colossians 4:11; 1 Thessalonians 2:12; 2 Thessalonians 1:5; James 2:5.
2. Isaiah 2:1–4; 9:6–7; 11:1–10; 16:5; 24:23; 32:1; 40:1–11; 42:1–4; 52:7–15; 55:4; Jeremiah 23:5–6; 33:15–16; Daniel 2:44; 7:27; Micah 4:1–8; 5:2–5; Zechariah 9:9–10; 14:9, 16–17.
3. Isaiah 9:6–7; 33:17, 22; 44:6; 60:21; Jeremiah 23:5; Daniel 4:3; 7:14, 22, 27; Micah 2:13; 4:6–7, 5:2.
4. Isaiah 35:10; 54:14; 60:18; 61:3; 66:12; Jeremiah 31:12–13; Micah 4:4.
5. Psalm 110:1; Matthew 22:44; 26:64; Mark 12:36; 14:62; 16:19; Luke 20:42; 22:69; Acts 2:33–34; 5:31; Romans 8:34; Ephesians 1:20; Colossians 3:1; Hebrews 1:3, 13; 8:1; 10:12; 12:2; 1 Peter 3:22.
6. Psalm 72:8–11; Isaiah 2:4; 11:2; 18:1–7; 19:16–25; 42:1; 45:14; 49:6, 22; 59:18–19; 60:1–14; 61:9; 62:2; 66:18–19; Jeremiah 3:17; 16:19–21, 49:6, 39; Ezekiel 38:23; Amos 9:11–12; Micah 7:16–17; Zephaniah 2:11; 3:9; Zechariah 8:20–23; 9:10; 10:11–12; 14:16–19.
7. Isaiah 56:7; 66:20–23; Jeremiah 33:18; Zechariah 14:16, 21; Malachi 3:3–4.

# Bibliography

Anderson, Sir Robert. *The Coming Prince*. London: Hodder & Stoughton, 1909. Premillennial.

Augustine. *The City of God*. Translated by Marcus Dods. Vol. 2 of *A Select Library of the Nicene and Post-Nicene Fathers of the Christian Church*. Edited by Philip Schaff. 1886. Reprint, Grand Rapids: Wm. B. Eerdmans Publishing Co., n.d. Amillennial.

Berkhof, Louis. *The Second Coming of Christ*. Grand Rapids: Wm. B. Eerdmans Publishing Co., 1953. Amillennial.

Blackstone, W. E. *Jesus Is Coming*. New York: Fleming H. Revell Co., 1908. Premillennial.

Campbell, Donald K., and Jeffrey L. Townsend, eds. *A Case for Premillennialism: A New Consensus*. Chicago: Moody Press, 1992. Pretribulational and premillennial.

Chafer, Lewis Sperry. *Systematic Theology*. 8 vols. Dallas: Dallas Seminary Press, 1948 Reprint (8 vols. in 4), Grand Rapids: Kregel, 1993. Pretribulational and premillennial.

Couch, Mal, ed. *Dictionary of Premillennial Theology*. Grand Rapids: Kregel Publications, 1996.

Darby, J. N. *Will the Saints Be in the Tribulation Period?* New York: Loizeaux Brothers, n. d. Pretribulational and premillennial.

Dyer, Charles H. *World News and Biblical Prophecy.* Wheaton, Ill.: Tyndale House Publishers, 1993. Pretribulational and premillennial.

Feinberg, Charles L. *Millennialism: Two Major Views.* 3d ed. Winona Lake, Ind.: BMH Books, 1985. Pretribulational and premillennial.

Gundry, Robert H. *The Church in the Tribulation.* Grand Rapids: Zondervan Publishing House, 1973. Posttribulational and premillennial.

Hamilton, Frank. E. *The Basis of the Premillennial Faith.* Grand Rapids: Wm. B. Eerdmans Publishing Co., 1942. Amillennial.

Harrison, Norman B. *The End: Re-thinking the Revelation.* Minneapolis: Harrison Service, 1941. Midtribulational and premillennial.

Hodge, Charles. *Systematic Theology.* 3 vols. New York: Charles Scribner's Sons, 1887. Postmillennial.

Hoekema, Anthony A. *The Bible and the Future.* Grand Rapids: Wm. B. Eerdmans Publishing Co., 1979. Amillennial.

House, H. Wayne, and Thomas Ice. *Dominion Theology: Blessing or Curse? An Analysis of Christian Reconstructionism.* Portland, Oreg.: Multnomah Press, 1988. A critique of current postmillennialism.

Huebner, R. A. *The Truth of the Pre-tribulation Rapture Recovered.* Millington, N.J.: Present Truth, 1973. Pretribulational and premillennial.

Ironside, H. A. *The Great Parenthesis.* Grand Rapids: Zondervan Publishing House, 1943. Pretribulational and premillennial.

Kemp, Karl. *Mid-week Rapture.* Shippensburg, Pa.: Companion Press, 1991. Midtribulational.

Kromminga, D. H. *The Millennium.* Grand Rapids: Wm. B. Eerdmans Publishing Co., 1948. Amillennial.

Ladd, George E. *The Blessed Hope.* Grand Rapids:Wm. B. Eerdmans Publishing Co., 1956. Posttribulational and premillennial.

LaHaye, Tim. *No Fear of the Storm.* Sisters, Oreg.: Multnomah Press, 1992. Pretribulational and premillennial.

Lightner, Robert B. *The Last Days Handbook.* Nashville: Thomas Nelson Publishers, 1990. Pretribulational and premillennial.

Miller, Earl. *The Kingdom of God and the Kingdom of Heaven.* Meadville, Pa.: By the author, 1950. Premillennial.

Murray, G. L. *Millennial Studies.* Grand Rapids: Baker Book House, 1948. Amillennial.

Ockenga, Harold John. "Will the Church Go through the Tribulation? Yes." *Christian Life*, February 1955, 22, 66. Posttribulational and premillennial.

Pache, René. *The Return of Jesus Christ*. Translated by William S. LaSor. Chicago: Moody Press, 1955. Premillennial.

Pentecost, J. Dwight. *Things to Come*. Grand Rapids: Zondervan Publishing House, 1958. Pretribulational and premillennial.

Peters, George M. H. *The Theocratic Kingdom*. 3 vols. Reprint, Grand Rapids: Kregel Publications, 1952. Posttribulational and premillennial.

Reese, Alexander. *The Approaching Advent of Christ*. London: Marshall, Morgan, & Scott Co., n. d. Posttribulational.

Ryrie, Charles C. *Basic Theology*. Wheaton, Ill.: Victor Books, 1986. Pretribulational and premillennial.

_____. *The Basis of the Premillennial Faith*. New York: Loizeaux Brothers, 1953. Pretribulational and premillennial.

_____. *Come Quickly, Lord Jesus*. Eugene, Oreg.: Harvest House Publishers, 1996. Pretribulational and premillennial.

_____. *Dispensationalism*. Rev. ed. Chicago: Moody Press, 1995. Pretribulational and premillennial.

Scofield, C. I. *Addresses on Prophecy*. New York: A. C. Gaebelein, 1910. Pretribulational and premillennial.

Smith, Wilbur M. *World Crises and the Prophetic Scriptures*. Chicago: Moody Press, 1951. Pretribulational and premillennial.

Snowden, James H. *The Coming of the Lord*. New York: Macmillan Publishing Co., 1909. Postmillennial.

Stanton, Gerald B. *Kept from the Hour: Biblical Evidence for the Pretribulational Return of Christ*. Rev. ed. Miami Springs, Fla.: Schoettle Publishing Co., 1991. Pretribulational and premillennial.

Walvoord, John F., and John E. Walvoord. *Armageddon, Oil and the Middle East Crisis*. Rev. ed. Grand Rapids: Zondervan Publishing House, 1990. Pretribulational and premillennial.

John F. Walvoord, *Major Bible Prophecies*. Grand Rapids: Zondervan Publishing House, 1991. Pretribulational and premillennial.

_____. *The Millennial Kingdom*. Grand Rapids: Zondervan Publishing House, 1959. Pretribulational and premillennial.

_____. *The Prophecy Knowledge Handbook*. Wheaton, Ill.: Victor Books, 1990.

Pretribulational and premillennial.

_____. *The Rapture Question.* Rev. ed. Grand Rapids: Zondervan Publishing House, 1979. Pretribulational and premillennial.

_____. "Will the Church Go through the Tribulation? No." *Christian Life,* February 1955, 23, 67, 78. Pretribulational and premillennial.

Wilkinson, Samuel H. *The Israel Promises and Their Fulfillment.* London: John Bale, Sons & Danielsson, 1936. Premillennial.

Willis, Wesley R., and John R. Master, eds. *Issues in Dispensationalism.* Chicago: Moody Press, 1994. Pretribulational and premillennial.

Wood, Leon J. *Is the Rapture Next?* Grand Rapids: Zondervan Publishing House, 1956. Pretribulational and premillennial.

Wyngaarden, Martin J. *The Future of the Kingdom in Prophecy and Fulfillment.* Grand Rapids: Zondervan Publishing House, 1934. Amillennial.

Zuck, Roy B. *Basic Bible Interpretation.* Wheaton, Ill.: Victor Books, 1991. Pretribulational and premillennial.

_____. ed. *Vital Prophetic Issues.* Grand Rapids: Kregel Publications, 1995. Pretribulational and premillennial.

# Scripture Index

**Genesis**

| | |
|---|---|
| 1 | 63 |
| 1–11 | 81 |
| 1:1 | 60, 61 |
| 1:26–27 | 63 |
| 2:16–17 | 64 |
| 3 | 65 |
| 3:1–7 | 64 |
| 3:14 | 64 |
| 3:15 | 65, 142 |
| 3:16 | 65 |
| 3:17–19 | 65, 204 |
| 3:22–24 | 65 |
| 4:1–6:6 | 65 |
| 4:12–15 | 168 |
| 6:3/17/19–20 | 66 |
| 7:7–9 /10/11/12 | |
| 20/23/24 | 66 |
| 8:1–14/15–19 | 66 |
| 9:1–7 | 67 |
| 9:5–6 | 204 |
| 9:8–17 | 67 |
| 10 | 67 |
| 11:1–9 | 71 |
| 11:4 | 67 |
| 11:7/9/10–32 | 68 |
| 11:28/31 | 72 |
| 12–50 | 78 |
| 12 | 71 |
| 12:1 | 71 |
| 12:1–3 | 68, 72 |
| 12:3 | 73 |
| 12:7 | ix, 74 |
| 12:10–20 | 96 |
| 13 | 75 |
| 13:14–17 | 76 |
| 15:4/5/6 | 76 |
| 15:7 | 72 |
| 15:8–17 | 76 |
| 15:13–14 | 78, 96 |
| 15:18 | 77 |
| 15:19 | 73 |
| 15:18–21 | 115, 198 |
| 15:19–21 | 77 |
| 16:1–4 | 72 |
| 19 | 75 |
| 25:1–4 | 72 |
| 25:7–8 | 73 |
| 26 | 77 |
| 26:3–5 | 77 |
| 28:13–15 | 78 |

**Exodus**

| | |
|---|---|
| 1:1–7/8–14 | 97 |
| 5:1–12:42 | 97 |
| 12:40 | 96 |
| 14:26–31 | 73 |
| 15:19 | 73 |
| 20:13 | 67 |
| 25 | 53 |

**Leviticus**

| | |
|---|---|
| 16 | 114 |
| 23:9–14 | 156 |
| 25:1–9 | 112 |
| 27 | 53 |

**Numbers**

| | |
|---|---|
| 1–4 | 79 |
| 13–14 | 79 |
| 15:32–36 | 67 |
| 32:9–13 | 79 |

**Deuteronomy**

| | |
|---|---|
| 5:17 | 67 |
| 17:14–17 | 84 |
| 28:1–68 | 79 |
| 28:64 | 89 |

| | |
|---|---|
| 28:64–67 | 85 |
| 30:3 | 142 |
| 30:6/9/7 | 143 |

**Joshua**
| | |
|---|---|
| 1:1–6 | 75 |
| 7:4/5 | 75 |
| 13:1–17 | 75 |
| 15:8 | 181 |
| 18:16 | 181 |
| 21:43 | 75 |

**Judges**
| | |
|---|---|
| 21:25 | 80 |

**1 Samuel**
| | |
|---|---|
| 1:1–24:22 | 80 |
| 15–31 | 81 |
| 16–17 | 80 |
| 16:1–13 | 81 |
| 25:1 | 80 |

**2 Samuel**
| | |
|---|---|
| 2 | 81 |
| 2:4 | 81 |
| 3:1 | 81 |
| 4:7 | 81 |
| 5:1–3 | 81 |
| 7:10–16 | 142 |
| 7:12–16 | 82 |
| 7:13/14 | 201 |
| 7:16 | 115 |

**1 Kings**
| | |
|---|---|
| 1–2 | 81 |
| 1:7/9–10/28–53 | 83 |
| 2:10–12 | 84 |
| 4:29–34 | 84 |
| 6:21–32 | 53 |
| 9:3–5/6–9 | 84 |
| 10:14–29 | 84 |
| 10:20 | 102 |
| 10:26–11:8 | 84 |
| 11:9–13/41–43 | 85 |

**2 Kings**
| | |
|---|---|
| 17:1–6 | 85, 99 |
| 17:5–6 | 73 |
| 18:9–11 | 99 |
| 18:13–19:14 | 99 |
| 19:15–34/37 | 99 |
| 24:10–14 | 99 |
| 24:18–25:21 | 86 |

**2 Chronicles**
| | |
|---|---|
| 9:19 | 102 |
| 36:22–23 | 115 |

**Ezra**
| | |
|---|---|
| 1–2 | 86 |
| 1:1–4:5 | 104 |
| 1:1–4 | 115 |
| 3:1–3/4/5/7–13 | 87 |
| 4:1–2/3/4–5 | 87 |
| 5:1–6:18 | 104 |
| 5:1/3–17 | 87 |
| 5:13 | 115 |
| 6:1/6–12 | 115 |
| 7:11–26 | 115 |

**Nehemiah**
| | |
|---|---|
| 1:1–6:15 | 104 |
| 2:1–8 | 116 |
| 6:15 | 88, 116 |
| 11:1 | 88, 116 |
| 11:30 | 181 |

**Job**
| | |
|---|---|
| 1:6–12 | 27, 62, 132 |
| 1:12 | 191 |
| 2:1–6 | 62 |
| 2:1–7 | 27, 132 |
| 2:6 | 191 |
| 19:25–26 | 154 |

**Psalms**
| | |
|---|---|
| 2 | 143 |
| 2:1–3 | 172 |
| 2:4–6 | 143, 147, 172 |
| 2:6 | 198 |
| 2:7 | 143 |
| 2:8–9 | 200 |
| 2:9 | 143, 149 |
| 2:10–12 | 200 |
| 2:11–12 | 143 |
| 11:7 | 154 |
| 17:15 | 154 |
| 24 | 147 |
| 24:7–10 | 155 |
| 47:8 | 142 |
| 72 | 83, 147, 194 |
| 72:1/2 | 194 |
| 72:1–4 | 83 |
| 72:5–7 | 83, 194 |
| 72:7 | 200 |
| 72:8–11 | 83 |
| 72:8 | 11, 194 |
| 72:9 | 200 |
| 72:11 | 194, 200 |
| 89 | 194 |
| 89:3–4/29–37 | 82, 201 |
| 89:28–29 | 201 |
| 89:29 | 194 |
| 89:30–32 | 194 |
| 89:35–37 | 194 |
| 89:36 | 195 |
| 93:1–2 | 142 |
| 97:1 | 142 |
| 99:1 | 142 |
| 105:8–11 | 78 |
| 146:10 | 142 |

**Isaiah**
| | |
|---|---|
| 2:2 | 198 |
| 2:3/4 | 202 |
| 2:4 | 204 |
| 2:10–21 | 149 |
| 8:3–4 | 98 |
| 9:7 | 82, 200, 201 |
| 11 | 193 |
| 11:1–12:6 | 147 |
| 11:3–5 | 155, 193, 199 |
| 11:4 | 200 |

| | | | | | |
|---|---|---|---|---|---|
| 11:6–7 | 194 | 6:23 | 102 | 14:21 | 128 |
| 11:8 | 194 | 7:30–33 | 181 | 17:3–7/7–8/11–24 | 102 |
| 11:9 | 194, 202 | 16:4 | 128 | 20:33–38 | 174, 200 |
| 11:10–16 | 194 | 18–21 | 91 | 20:34–38 | 90 |
| 11:12 | 174 | 19:6 | 181 | 20:40 | 200 |
| 13:1–22 | 102 | 23:5 | 200 | 28:2/11–15/16–17 | 62 |
| 13:6/9/13 | 149 | 23:5–6 | 115, 175, 194 | 30:3 | 149 |
| 14:10 | 55 | 23:7–8 | 174 | 30:10–20 | 102 |
| 14:12–15 | 62 | 23:8 | 194 | 34:23–24 | 155, 195 |
| 14:22–27 | 130 | 25:1–11 | 86 | 36:24 | 200 |
| 17:12–13 | 102 | 25:11–12 | 110, 112 | 36:24–28 | 92 |
| 18 | 130 | 29:10/11 | 86 | 36:25–26 | 201 |
| 19 | 98 | 29:10–14 | 110 | 36:26–27 | 38 |
| 19:19–21/23–25 | 98 | 30:1–11 | 91 | 36:27/28 | 201 |
| 21:1–10 | 102 | 30:5–7 | 89 | 36:29–30 | 200 |
| 24:21 | 150 | 30:5–11 | 91 | 37 | 154–55 |
| 24:23 | 150, 199 | 30:7 | 128, 163 | 37:15–22 | 200 |
| 26:19 | 154, 162 | 30:8–9/18 | 90 | 37:21–22 | 195 |
| 29:18 | 204 | 30:9 | 195 | 37:21–28 | 92 |
| 33:24 | 204 | 30:18 | 90 | 37:23 | 114 |
| 34:8–9 | 150 | 31:8–9 | 90 | 37:24 | 154–55 |
| 35:1–2/6–7 | 198 | 31:14 | 200 | 37:24–25 | 195 |
| 35:5–6 | 204 | 31:8–14 | 92 | 37:25 | 155, 195 |
| 37:1–38:13 | 99 | 31:23–28 | 92 | 38–39 | 123 |
| 40:28 | 3 | 31:31–34 | 91, 115 | 38:5–6 | 124 |
| 45:23 | 55 | 31:33 | 201 | 38:8/11/14 | 123 |
| 47:1–15 | 102 | 31:33–34 | 202 | 38:15/18–23 | 124 |
| 53 | 19 | 31:34 | 201 | 39:2/4/12 | 124 |
| 54:1/5–10 | 200 | 31:36 | 91 | 39:25 | 200 |
| 57:20 | 102 | 32:35 | 181 | 39:25–28 | 175 |
| 59:20 | 147 | 33:14 | 200 | 40:1–46:24 | 202 |
| 60:5/11 | 200 | 33:16 | 194 | 40:38–43 | |
| 60:21 | 115 | 36:27–31 | 85 | 40–46 | 202 |
| 61:1–2 | 30–31, 121, 143 | 38:17–18 | 86 | 41–46 | 115 |
| 61:2 | 150 | 43:1–6 | 110 | 43:13–17 | 202 |
| 61:26 | 30 | 46:10 | 149 | 47:21 | 175 |
| 62:2–5 | 200 | 50–51 | 130 | 47:21–22 | 198 |
| 65:20 | 199, 204 | 50:1–51/58 | 102 | 48 | 175 |
| 65:20–21 | 209 | 50:39–40 | 131 | 48:1–28 | 198 |
| 66:12 | 200 | 51:8/29/37 | 131 | | |
| 66:24 | 181 | | | **Daniel** | |
| | | **Ezekiel** | | 1:1–3 | 99 |
| **Jeremiah** | | 7:19 | 149 | 1:5–21 | 100 |
| 3:18 | 200 | 13:5 | 149 | 2 | 101, 102, 109 |

| | | | | | |
|---|---|---|---|---|---|
| 2:28/29 | 100 | 9:25 | 112, 116 | *Obadiah* | |
| 2:32 | 102 | 9:25–26 | 115 | 1–20 | 150 |
| 2:34–35 | 193 | 9:26 | 118 | | |
| 2:39a | 109 | 9:27 | 35, 89, 105, 112, | *Micah* | |
| 2:42/44 | 192 | | 118, 121, 123, 174 | 4:3 | 204 |
| 2:44–45 | 193 | 10:1–12:5 | 102 | 4:4 | 200 |
| 2:48 | 100 | 10:2 | 112 | 4:6–7 | 150 |
| 2:48–49 | 99 | 10:14 | 114 | 5:2 | 88, 104 |
| 4 | 101, 102 | 11 | 97 | 5:2–5a | 121 |
| 4:17/25b/34b–35 | 145 | 11:1–35 | 97 | 5:4 | 195 |
| 5 | 73, 101, 109 | 11:14 | 114 | 5:10–14 | 150 |
| 5:28 | 103 | 11:21–35 | 104, 105 | | |
| 7 | 101, 102, 121, 192 | 11:36 | 97, 124, 133 | *Zephaniah* | |
| 7–8 | 109 | 11:36–39 | 127 | 1:7–18 | 149 |
| 7:1 | 102 | 11:36–45 | 97, 124–25 | | |
| 7:2 | 102 | 11:37 | 124 | *Zechariah* | |
| 7:2–4/5/6/7 | 101 | 11:38 | 124 | 3 | 150 |
| 7:5 | 103, 109 | 11:40–45 | 124, 127 | 3:1–2 | 62 |
| 7:6 | 104 | 11:44 | 130 | 3:10 | 200 |
| 7:7 | 10, 105, 106, 121 | 12:1 | 27, 32, 118, 123 | 4 | 159 |
| 7:8 | 123 | 12:1–2 | 154, 162, 163 | 4:3/2/6/11–12/14 | 159 |
| 7:13–14 | 143 | 12:3 | 200 | 10:8–12 | 200 |
| 7:23 | 105, 106, 123 | 12:11 | 105, 118 | 14 | 144, 150 |
| 7:23–27 | 105 | | | 14:1–3 | 125 |
| 7:24 | 10, 106, 122, | *Hosea* | | 14:1–5 | 150 |
| | 123, 135, 192 | 1:11 | 200 | 14:2–3 | 144 |
| 7:25 | 123, 193 | 2:14/23 | 200 | 14:4 | 197, 198 |
| 7:26–27 | 106, 193 | 3:5 | 195 | 14:4–9 | 144 |
| 7:27 | 195, 202 | 11:1 | 96 | 14:8 | 197 |
| 8 | 102, 109 | 12:9/13 | 96 | 14:9–11 | 195 |
| 8:3 | 103 | 13:4 | 96 | 14:10–11 | 198 |
| 8:3–4 | 109 | | | 14:16–19 | 199 |
| 8:5/8/9–14/21/22 | 104 | *Joel* | | | |
| 8:20–21 | 100 | 3:2 | 176 | *Matthew* | |
| 8:20 | 103, 109 | 3:10 | 204 | 2:13–14/15 | 96 |
| 8:23–27 | 104 | 3:18 | 197 | 3:11 | 158 |
| 8:24–25 | 105 | 3:20 | 195 | 5:22 | 179 |
| 9 | 109, 110 | | | 8:12 | 182 |
| 9:1 | 110, 112 | *Amos* | | 9:24 | 26 |
| 9:1–2 | 86, 109 | 5:18/20 | 150 | 11:21–24 | 182 |
| 9:4–19 | 86, 110, 111 | 8:9 | 150 | 13:24–31 | 199 |
| 9:20–23 | 111 | 8:10 | 149 | 13:43 | 200 |
| 9:20–27 | 102 | 9:11 | 150 | 13:47 | 102 |
| 9:24 | 112, 114, 117 | 9:13 | 200 | 13:47–50 | 199 |
| 9:24–27 | 109, 111, 119 | 9:13–15 | 195 | 16:2/3 | v |

| | | | | | | | |
|---|---|---|---|---|---|---|---|
| 16:21 | 146, 156 | **Mark** | | **John** | | | |
| 17:22–23 | 146, 156 | 1:8 | 158 | 1:1 | 148 | | |
| 18:8–9 | 179, 181 | 9:43/48 | 179 | 1:33 | 158 | | |
| 19:28 | 20, 146, | 9:47–48 | 181 | 3:1–21 | 41 | | |
| | 196, 198 | 12:40 | 182 | 3:2 | 37 | | |
| 19:39–40 | 91 | 13:3/5–26 | 89 | 3:3 | 37, 142, 145 | | |
| 20:17–19 | 146, 156 | 14:24 | 93 | 3:4 | 37 | | |
| 20:20–23 | 196 | 15:46 | 41 | 3:5 | 142, 145 | | |
| 22:13 | 182 | 16:9–11 | 45 | 3:16 | 168, 180 | | |
| 22:31–32 | 155 | 16:12–13 | 43, 45 | 3:18/36 | 180 | | |
| 23:37–38/39 | 88 | 16:14/19–20 | 45 | 5:28–29 | 155, 163 | | |
| 24 | 34 | | | 7:50–51 | 38 | | |
| 24–25 | 51 | **Luke** | | 11:11 | 26 | | |
| 24:1–2/3–12 | 88 | 1:31–33 | 82, 196 | 11:21–27 | 155 | | |
| 24:3 | 89, 196 | 1:32 | 201 | 12:32 | 180 | | |
| 24:3–25:46 | 146 | 1:33 | 195 | 14 | 21 | | |
| 24:4–28 | 89 | 3:16 | 158 | 14:1–3 | 157, 218 | | |
| 24:15 | 105 | 4:18–19 | 143 | 14:1–4 | 34 | | |
| 24:15–22 | 89, 174 | 10:18 | 191 | 14:2–3 | 20, 21 | | |
| 24:21 | 33, 118, | 12:47–48 | 182 | 14:3 | 28, 212 | | |
| | 123, 163 | 14:13–14 | 155 | 14:17 | 35 | | |
| 24:21–22 | 128 | 16:19–31 | 172, 177, | 17:24 | 29, 212 | | |
| 24:29–30 | 146 | | 183 | 19:39 | 37 | | |
| 24:31 | 28 | 16:27–28 | 177 | 19:39–40 | 41 | | |
| 24:36 | 196 | 16:29/31 | 178 | 20:11–13/15 | 42 | | |
| 24:40–41 | 34 | 17:34–36 | 34 | 20:11–17 | 45 | | |
| 24:42 | 196 | 21:8–28 | 89 | 20:16 | 42 | | |
| 25 | 51 | 22:19 | 203 | 20:19 | 44 | | |
| 25:1–13 | 50, 51 | 22:20 | 93 | 20:19–23 | 45 | | |
| 25:21 | 57 | 22:29–30 | 196, 198 | 20:24–27 | 43 | | |
| 25:30 | 182 | 22:30 | 173 | 20:24–28 | 44 | | |
| 25:31–46 | 36, 176, 199 | 23:43 | 178 | 20:25–27 | 43 | | |
| 25:41 | 13, 63, 132, | 23:53 | 41 | 20:26–29 | 45 | | |
| | 164, 179, 181 | 24:11–12 | 42 | 21:1–14 | 45 | | |
| 25:46 | 180, 181 | 24:13–35 | 43, 45 | | | | |
| 26:28 | 93 | 24:15/16/17–27 | 43 | **Acts** | | | |
| 27:51–53 | 156, 157 | 24:30–31 | 43 | 1:3–9 | 45 | | |
| 27:59–60 | 41 | 24:33 | 44, 45 | 1:6–7 | 197 | | |
| 28:2–4 | 41 | 24:34 | 43, 45 | 1:11 | 26, 147 | | |
| 28:5–8 | 42 | 24:36–37 | 44 | 2:30 | 82 | | |
| 28:8–10 | 45 | 24:36–43 | 45 | 5:3 | 190 | | |
| 28:9 | 43 | 24:39 | 43, 44 | 7:55–56 | 45 | | |
| 28:11–15 | 41 | 24:43/44–47 | 44 | 8:12 | 197 | | |
| 28:16–20 | 45 | 24:50–53 | 45 | 9:3–7 | 45 | | |
| 28:20 | 25 | | | 10:38 | 190 | | |

| | |
|---|---|
| 14:22 | 197 |
| 15:13–18 | 146 |
| 15:14/16–18 | 147 |
| 17:1–9 | 22 |
| 17:11 | vi |
| 19:8 | 197 |
| 20:25 | 197 |
| 22:17–21 | 45 |
| 23:11 | 45 |
| 26:18 | 190 |
| 28:23/31 | 197 |

**Romans**

| | |
|---|---|
| 1:4 | 46 |
| 5:1 | 52 |
| 5:8 | 168, 180 |
| 8:1 | 52 |
| 8:25 | 220 |
| 8:28–39 | 4–5 |
| 8:29–30 | 5 |
| 8:33–34 | 52 |
| 8:34 | 25, 46 |
| 8:35–39 | 52 |
| 8:38–39 | 5 |
| 11:11–16 | 146 |
| 11:13–32 | 197 |
| 11:17–21 | 146 |
| 11:17–24 | 147 |
| 11:20–27 | 114 |
| 11:23–24/25–27 | 147 |
| 11:26 | 175 |
| 11:26–27 | 93, 147 |
| 11:13–32 | 197 |
| 12:1–2 | 221 |
| 14:10/12 | 55 |
| 14:10–12 | 170 |

**1 Corinthians**

| | |
|---|---|
| 1:7 | 220 |
| 1:18 | 180 |
| 3:10 | 53 |
| 3:10–15 | 53, 169 |
| 3:11–15 | 53 |
| 5:5 | 190 |

| | |
|---|---|
| 6:3 | 13 |
| 6:14 | 157 |
| 7:5 | 190 |
| 9:24–27 | 54, 169 |
| 11:25 | 93 |
| 11:26 | 203 |
| 12:12–13 | 158 |
| 12:13 | 37 |
| 15 | 220 |
| 15:5/6/7 | 45 |
| 15:12 | 157 |
| 15:14–19 | 39 |
| 15:18 | 26 |
| 15:19 | vii |
| 15:20/23 | 157 |
| 15:24 | 197 |
| 15:35–38/42–44 | 40 |
| 15:50 | 39 |
| 15:51 | 156 |
| 15:51–52 | 197 |
| 15:51–53 | 26, 157 |
| 15:51–54 | 40 |
| 15:51–55 | 220 |
| 15:52 | 28 |
| 15:53 | 159 |
| 15:58 | 220 |

**2 Corinthians**

| | |
|---|---|
| 2:11 | 190 |
| 3:6 | 93 |
| 4:14 | 157 |
| 5:6 | 159 |
| 5:8 | 25, 178 |
| 5:10 | 51, 52, 169 |
| 5:11 | 52 |
| 5:19/20/21 | 168 |
| 11:2 | 50, 51 |
| 11:14 | 190 |
| 12:4 | 178 |
| 12:7 | 190 |

**Galatians**

| | |
|---|---|
| 1:12 | 45 |
| 3:17 | 96 |

**Ephesians**

| | |
|---|---|
| 2:12 | 180 |
| 4:27 | 190 |
| 5:22–24 | 50 |
| 6:11 | 190 |
| 6:12 | 28 |

**Philippians**

| | |
|---|---|
| 1:23 | 159 |
| 3:11 | 27 |
| 3:20 | 220 |
| 3:21 | 27, 45, 159 |

**Colossians**

| | |
|---|---|
| 1:13 | 142 |
| 1:13–14 | 145 |
| 2:3 | 3 |
| 2:15 | 191 |
| 3:4 | 29 |

**1 Thessalonians**

| | |
|---|---|
| 1:3/5/8–9 | 23 |
| 1:9 | 33 |
| 1:10 | 23 |
| 2:17–3:5 | 22 |
| 2:19 | 23 |
| 3:6–9 | 22 |
| 3:13 | 23 |
| 4 | 18 |
| 4:13 | 24 |
| 4:13–17 | 219 |
| 4:13–18 | 21, 23, 29, 34, 157, 197 |
| 4:14 | 24, 26, 157 |
| 4:15 | 26, 39 |
| 4:15–18 | 25, 36 |
| 4:16 | 23, 26, 37, 39, 158 |
| 4:17 | 29, 156 |
| 4:18 | 36, 219 |
| 5 | 34 |
| 5:1–10 | 23 |
| 5:3 | 182 |
| 5:4/8 | 34 |

| | | | | | | | |
|---|---|---|---|---|---|---|---|
| 5:9 | 33, 182 | 9:27–28 | 141 | **Jude** | | | |
| 5:23 | 23 | 9:28 | 203, 220 | 6 | 14, 62, 132, 182 | | |
| | | 10:16 | 93 | 9 | | | 27 |
| **2 Thessalonians** | | 10:26–27 | 182 | 14–15 | | | 147 |
| 1:8–9 | 180 | 11:9 | 76 | | | | |
| 1:9 | 182 | 11:10 | 76, 214 | **Revelation** | | | |
| 2 | 34–35 | 12:23 | 199 | 1 | | | 125 |
| 2:3 | 35, 132, 133, 150 | 12:24 | 93 | 1:3 | | | 213 |
| 2:4 | 124 | 13:5 | 25 | 1:4 | | | 213 |
| 2:6–7 | 35 | 13:14 | 214 | 1:6 | | | 212 |
| 2:8 | 133 | | | 1:7 | | | 148 |
| 2:8–9 | 132, 150 | **James** | | 1:8 | | | 213 |
| 2:9 | 190 | 4:7 | 190 | 1:11 | | | 125 |
| | | 5:7–8 | 220 | 1:12–20 | | | 45 |
| **1 Timothy** | | | | 1:17 | | | 213 |
| 1:20 | 190 | **1 Peter** | | 1:20 | | | 125 |
| 2:4 | 168, 180 | 1:10–11 | 30 | 2–3 | | 126, 213 | |
| 2:6 | 169 | 1:11 | 19 | 2:1/4 | | | 125 |
| 3:6 | 62 | 1:11–12 | viii | 2:7 | | | 213 |
| 5:15 | 190 | 3:18 | 168 | 2:8 | | | 213 |
| | | 5:8 | 189 | 2:9 | | | 190 |
| **2 Timothy** | | | | 2:10 | | 126, 190 | |
| 2:12 | 173, 197, | **2 Peter** | | 2:13 | | | 190 |
| | 198, 212 | 2:1 | 169 | 2:16/20 | | | 126 |
| 2:26 | 190 | 2:4 | 62, 132, 181, 182 | 3:3 | | | 147 |
| 4:1 | 197, 199 | 2:17 | 182 | 3:10 | | | 126 |
| 4:6/8 | 19 | 3:3–4 | 61, 150 | 3:10–11 | | | 147 |
| 4:8 | 49, 221 | 3:4 | 61 | 3:21 | | 198, 212 | |
| | | 3:5–7 | 150 | 4–5 | | | 127 |
| **Titus** | | 3:6–7 | 207 | 4:3 | | | 211 |
| 2:12 | 220 | 3:7 | 67 | 5:10 | | 198, 212 | |
| 2:13 | 15, 220, 221 | 3:9 | 168 | 6 | | | 127 |
| | | 3:10 | 207 | 6–18 | | 119, 170 | |
| **Hebrews** | | 3:10–12 | 67 | 6:2/3–4/5–6 | | | 127 |
| 2:14 | 190 | 3:11/12 | 208 | 6:7–8 | 127, 128, 129 | | |
| 6:2 | 182 | 3:11–12 | 219 | 6:9–11 | | | 128 |
| 7:25–26 | 46 | 3:13 | 208, 214 | 6:16 | | | 128 |
| 7:27 | 203 | 3:14 | 220 | 6:16–17 | | | 149 |
| 8 | 93 | | | 6:17 | | | 128 |
| 8:6 | 93 | **1 John** | | 7:1–8/9 | | | 33 |
| 8:7–13 | 93 | 3:2 | 27, 42, 45 | 7:9–17 | 33, 128, 160 | | |
| 9:15 | 93 | 3:2–3 | 219 | 7:14 | | 118, 123 | |
| 9:26 | 203 | | | 8 | | | 128 |
| 9:27 | 5, 167 | | | 8:6–9:21 | | | 28 |

8:7/8–9/10–11/   129
8:12   10, 129
9:1   10
9:1–11   129
9:13–16   129, 130
9:16   137
9:20–21   130, 131
9:26   117
11   159
11:1–6   159
11:2   116
11:5/6   159
11:7–10/12–13   160
11:15   129
11:15–19   28
11:16–14:13   129
12:6   116
12:7–9   27
12:7/8/9   132
12:9   190, 191
12:9–10   132
12:10   28, 62, 190
12:11   118
12:12   34, 132
12:17   34, 161
13   133
13:1   102, 133
13:4   127
13:5   116, 118, 133
13:6/7/8/11   133
13:15   160
13:15–16   191
13:17   133
14:9–11   183
15–16   129
16   32, 33
16:1   129
16:2/3/4/8–9/10   130
16:9/11/21   176
16:14   130
16:16   125, 171
16:17–21   170
16:18/19/20   130
16:21   130, 131, 132
17   136

17:1   102
17:1–3/12   135
17:15   102
17:16–17   13, 135
18   130
19   131
19–20   162, 189
19:7   50
19:7–9   51, 171
19:10   213
19:11   148, 189
19:11–16   148
19:11–21   161
19:11–20:15   189
19:12   148
19:13   148
19:14   149
19:15   33, 149, 171
19:16   145, 149
19:17   171
19:17–21   118
19:18/19   171
19   189
19–21   209
19:20   133, 171, 172, 179
19:20–21   164
19:21   171
20   189
20:1–3   132, 172, 187
20:1–6   187, 189, 191
20:1–7   196
20:2   190
20:3   163, 172, 190
20:4   34, 173, 187, 191
20:4–6   36, 161, 162, 163, 191
20:5   162, 189
20:6   57, 173, 198, 212
20:7–8   163
20:7–9   200
20:7–10   132
20:10   13, 63, 133, 164, 172, 179, 180, 183
20:11   177, 207

20:11–15   162, 164, 172, 177
20:13–14   183
20:14–15   180
21   209
21–22   76
21:1   177, 207, 208
21:1–8   210
21:2   208
21:3/4/5   209
21:6   210, 213
21:7   210
21:8   179, 210
21:9   210
21:10   208
21:11/12   210, 211
21:13   210
21:14   210, 211
21:14–16   208
21:16   210, 211
21:17/18   211
21:18–19   208
21:19–20   211
21:21   208, 211
21:23   208, 211, 213
21:26/27   211
22   214
22:1   212
22:2   211, 212, 213
22:2–3   208
22:3–4   212
22:5   57, 198, 208, 212
22:6   212, 213
22:7   213, 214
22:8–9   213
2:9   212, 213
22:10/11   213
22:12   213, 214
22:13/14   213
22:14   208, 213
22:17/18–19   213
22:19   208
22:20   214
22:21   214

# Subject Index

—A—

Abraham, 71–78
  and God's plan, 68, 71
  Abrahamic Covenant, 68–69,
    72–78
Abyss, 172
Adam and Eve, 63–65
Alexander the Great, 103, 104
Alexandrian school of theology, 185,
  188, 216
Amillennarian views, 74, 76, 162, 185–
  86, 188–92
  and resurrection, 153
  of Daniel, 113, 117
Angels
  at second coming, 149
  creation of, 61–62
  fallen, 62–63
  judged by church, 13–14.
  *See also Michael; Satan*
Annihilationism, 180
Antichrist, 97, 105, 118, 123, 127,
  132–33, 135, 160, 161
  judgment of, 171–72
  revealed, 35

Antioch, school of, 216
Antiochus (as type of Antichrist), 97,
  104–5
Apostate church, in end times, 13
Ark, 65–66
Armageddon, 2, 121–39, 171
Artaxerxes Longimanus, 116
Assyria in prophecy, 12, 98–99
Augustine, 216–17
  on millennium, 187, 188–89
  on prophecy, 9

—B—

Babel, Tower of, 67–68
Babylon, 12
  destruction, 130–31
  in prophecy, 99–104
  Israel in, 86–88
Baptism of the Holy Spirit, 158–59
Beast (Revelation), 135, 164
  commerce and, 133
  judgment of, 171–72
  worship of, 173, 182–83
Belshazzar, 101

Bible, as Word of God, *viii–x*, 215–16
Body, in resurrection.
    *See Resurrection body*
Book of Daniel, 10
Book of life, 164
Bowl judgments, 129–30
Bush, George, 134

—C—

Calvin, John, 217
Catastrophes, in Revelation, 127
Chafer, Lewis Sperry, 93–94
Christ. *See Jesus Christ*
Christ's return. *See Second coming*
Church, 135
    avoidance of prophecy, 7–8
    end time events, 136
    in Revelation, 125–27
    New Covenant and, 93
    professing church, 13, 131, 136
    prophecy on, *xii*, 12–13, 125–27
Clement, 188
*Come Quickly, Lord Jesus*, 32
Coming of Christ. *See First coming;*
    *Second coming*
Coming ruler, 122–23
Covenants, 91
    Abrahamic, 68–69, 72–79
    Davidic, 81–85
    Mosaic, 78
    New, 91–94
Creation, time of, 61, 63–64
Cyrus the Great, 115

—D—

Daniel, 99–116, 127
    Christ in Daniel, 113–14, 115
    forgery claim, 109, 113
    interpretation, 112–14
    Israel's prophetic years, 109–19
    Jeremiah's prophecy, 109–10, 116–17
    prophetic accomplishments, 114–16
Darius I, 115
Davidic Covenant, 81–85

Day of the Lord, 149–50
Dead, in Christ, 158
Death
    Rapture and, 22–24, 25–26
    soul and, 153
Demons, 62–63, 129, 132, 172.
    *See also Angels*
Descendant of David, 81–82, 145
Devil. *See Satan*
Disbelief in prophecy.
    *See Prophecy, unbelief*
Dispersions, of Israel, 85–89
Divine inspiration of Bible.
    *See Bible, as Word of God*
Dominion theology, 187
Dragon. *See Satan*
Duesterdieck, Friedrich H.C., 191

—E—

Egypt, in prophecy, 12, 95–98
Eleventh horn (of Daniel), 123
End times. *See Great Tribulation;*
    Judgments; Millennium; Rapture;
    Second coming
Ephesus, church in (Revelation),
    125–26
Eternal punishment, doctrine of,
    178–84
    Epistles, 182
    Gospels, 180–81
    Revelation, 182–3
    Roman Catholic view, 179–80
Eve. *See Adam and Eve*
Evolutionary theories, 60–61, 63–64

—F—

Fallen angels. *See Angels, fallen*
False prophet (Revelation), 133, 164
    judgment of, 171–72
Final world war, 125.
    *See also Armageddon*
First coming, 142
    in Old Testament prophecy,
    19–20, 30–31

Flood, biblical, 65–68
Four beasts (empires) of Daniel,
    101–7, 192–93
Fourth beast (of Daniel), 123

—G—

Gehenna, 181
Gentile world, prophecy on, 9–10, 11.
    judgment at Second coming,
    175–76. See also Nations
God
    as seen in Bible, 3–5
    as creator, 60–61
    foreknowledge, 3–5
    human freedom, 4–5
    plan for salvation, 3–4, 59–68
    sovereignty over nations, 107
Gog and Magog, 123, 124
Great Tribulation, 13, 32–33, 97, 123,
    124, 134, 149, 150, 159–60,
    172, 173, 176, 182–83
    catastrophes, 127–28
    martyrs in, 33–34, 160–62
    Satan in, 34
    temporal judgments, 170–71.
Great White Throne, 177–78, 183
Greece in prophecy, 12, 104–5
Gulf War, as Armageddon, 2

—H—

Hades, 171–72, 177, 178, 180
Harlot (Revelation), 135
Hell, 132
    as eternal punishment, 178–84
    bible terms for, 180–82
Hodge, Charles, 187
Holy Spirit, as restrainer of evil, 35

—I—

Inspiration of Bible. See Bible, as Word
    of God
Interpreting prophecy.
    See Prophecy, interpretation
Israel, 135

490 prophetic years, 109–19
Abrahamic covenant, 68–69, 72–79
    as cast off, 146–47
    as focus of prophecy, x
    attacked, 123–24
    Davidic Covenant, 81–85
    dispersions, 85–89
    end time events, 89, 139
    in Babylon, 86–88
    in Egypt, 95–98
    judgment of, 173–75
    messianic line, 80–85
    Mosaic covenant, 78
    New Covenant, 91–94
    nuclear threat, 2–3
    persecution of, 73
    promise of the land, 75–78
    prophecy on, 11, 12
    regathering, 89–94
    restoration, 89

—J—

Jesus Christ
    as judge, 51–56, 169–70
    misunderstood, 20
    Nathan's descendant, 85
    on resurrections, 155
    predicts own death, 20, 30
    prophesies his rejection, 146
    reign of Christ, 149–50
    resurrection, x, 40, 41–47.
    See also Second coming
Jews
    and prophecy, 9–10, 30–31
    in millennium, 188–89, 217.
    See also Israel
Joachim of Fiore, 187
Joseph of Arimathea, 37, 41
Jude, Second coming in, 147
Judgment seat, of Christ, 51–56
Judgments, x–xi, 167–84
    Christ on cross, 168–69
    believers, 51–56, 169–70
    end time judgments, 169–78

evil beings, 172
gentiles, 175–76
living Israel, 173–75
millennial saints, 178
raptured believers, 51–56
rejected, 131–32
temporal judgments, 167–68, 170–71
Tribulation martyrs, 160–62, 173
wicked, 163–64, 177–78
world armies, 171

—KL—

*Kept from the Hour*, 31–32
Kingdom, millennial.
    *See Millennial kingdom*
Kliefoth, Theodor F.D., 191–92
LaHaye, Tim, 32
Lake of fire, 171, 177, 183
Laodicea, 126
Last judgment, 167.
    *See also Judgments*
Last trumpet, 28–29
Lazarus, 177–78
Life after death, in Bible, 14
Luther, Martin, 217

—M—

Maccabees, 180
Man of lawlessness. *See Antichrist*
Man of sin. *See Antichrist*
Mark of the beast, 133.
    *See also Beast (Revelation)*
Martha, 155
Martyrs
    fifth seal, 128
    in Tribulation, 33–34, 36
    resurrection of, 160–62
Mary Magdalene, 41–42, 156
Medo–Persians, in prophecy, 12, 103–4, 115–16
Messianic prophecy, 80–85
Michael, role of, 27–28

Midtribulational view of Rapture, 32
Millennial kingdom, 143, 176, 185–205
    subjects of, 199–200
Millennial saints, 178
Millennium, 150, 189–90
    geographic change, 197–98
    government in, 198–201
    life in, 203–4
    New Testament prophecy, 196–97
    Old Testament prophecy, 192–95
    purpose of, 204–5
    theological views on, 185–92
    worship in, 201–4
Mosaic Covenant, 78–79

—N—

Nations, 135
    end time events, 137–38
    origin of, 67
Nebuchadnezzar, 99–101, 102
New Covenant, 91–94
    church and, 93
    with Israel, 200–201
New Jerusalem, 208–13
New world order, 207–8
Nicodemus, 37, 41
*No Fear of the Storm*, 32
Nuclear weapons, and prophecy, 3

—O—

Old Testament prophecy
    concept of kingdom, *x*
    introducing God's master plan, 59–68
    limitations, 121
    misunderstanding in, 19–20, 30–31
    on gentile world, *x–xi*.
    *See also Prophecy*
Old Testament saints, 37, 38
Olivet Discourse, 146
Origen, 188

—P—

Palestinian land claim, 78
Partial–Rapture position, 32
Peace treaty (of Daniel), 123–24
Pentecost, J. Dwight, 31
Pergamum, church in, 126
Philadelphia, church in, 126
Plato, and prophecy, 9
Postmillennialism, 74–75, 186–87
Posttribulation views of Rapture,
    32–36, 160–62
Predestination, 3–5
Premillennialism, 74–75, 185
Pretribulational view, of Rapture,
    32, 35
Pre–wrath Rapture view, 32
Professing church, in end times, 13
Prophecy
    as divine revelation, *xi*, 5,
        215–16
    church. *See Church, prophecy on*
    current events, 1–2
    early Christian views on, 31
    focus on Christ, *x*
    fulfilment, 7, 114–16, 215–16
    gentiles.
        *See Gentile world, prophecy on*
    God's plan for world, 95–107
    Israel. *See Israel, prophecy on*
    literal interpretation, 8–10, 216–17
    misinterpretation, 217–18
    practical application, 24, 218–20
    significance of, 14–15, 215–21
    unbelief, 5–6
    world history, 12.
    *See also Messianic prophecy;*
        *Old Testament prophecy*
Prophecy, interpretation, 7–15
    history, 9–10
    natural vs. literal meaning, *x*
    obscure passages, 10–11
    symbols, 10
*Prophecy Knowledge Handbook, The,* 11

Protestant Reformers' teaching on
    prophecy, 9
Purgatory, doctrine of, 179–80

—R—

Rapture, 12–13, 29, 126, 135, 176,
    219–20
    church as bride, 50–51
    death and, 22–24, 157–59
    different views on, 32–36
    disbelief in, 49–50
    imminence, 29–36
    importance, 17, 36–38
    Jesus' first revelation, 20–21
    judgment of believers, 51–56
    Michael in, 27–28
    preceding Second coming, 21, 31,
        34–35, 147–48, 150–51
    revealed to Paul, 21–27
    salvation views and, 37–38
    transformation at, 26–27, 40, 157
*Rapture Question, The,* 31
Reign of Christ, 149–50, 197–204
Resurrection
    of believers, 25–26
    of Jesus Christ. *See Jesus Christ,*
        *resurrection*
    of martyrs, 160–62
    of New Testament saints, 156–57
    of Old Testament saints, 154–55,
        162–63
    series of resurrections, 26
Resurrection body, 26–27, 39–47
    individual identity, 42–43
    Jesus' body, 41–46
    transformation, 40
Resurrections, in New Testament,
    155–64
    Jesus' teaching, 155–56
    Old Testament saints, 162–63
    Rapture resurrection, 157–59
    restorations to life, 157
    token resurrection, 156–57

two witnesses, 159–60
wicked, 163–64
Resurrections, in Old Testament, 154–55
Resurrections, order of, 153–65
Revelation, 10
  on Rapture, 36
  prophecies in, 125–31
  Second coming in, 147–49
Roman Catholic teaching on prophecy, 9–10
Roman Empire, 12
  in prophecy, 105–7
  revival, 106–7
  ten–nation confederacy, 121–22
Ryrie, Charles C., 32

—S—
Saints, at Second coming, 149.
  See also Resurrection
Salvation, Rapture and, 37–38
Sardis, church in, 126
Satan, 163–64
  as dragon, 161, 172
  end time, 13
  fall of, 62–63
  Great Tribulation and, 34, 132
  judgment of, 172
  prophecy on, xi
  second coming and, 132–33
  world dictator and, 13
Second coming, 2, 128, 134, 141–51
  judgments in, 167–84
  martyrs and, 161–62
  New Testament prophecy, 145–49
  Old Testament prophecy, 141–45
  Paul's approach, 18–19
  separate from first, viii–ix
  timing, 17–19
  trumpet of God, 28–29
  vs. Rapture, 31, 147, 148, 150–51.
  See also First coming; Jesus Christ
Seven churches (lampstands) in Revelation, 125–27

Seven–sealed scroll, 127–28
Sheol, 177, 180
Smyrna, church in, 126
Solomon's kingdom, 83–85
Stanton, Gerald B., 31–32
Stott, John R.W., 180
Symbols, in prophecy, 10
Syrian leader, 104–5

—T—
Ten horns (of Daniel), 121–22
Ten–nation confederacy, 121–22, 192–93
Theonomy, 187
Things to Come, 31
Thyatira, 126
Transformation, of the body, 40.
  See also Resurrection body
Tree of Life, 212, 214
Tribulation. See Great Tribulation
Trumpet judgments, 128–29
Trumpet of God, 28–29
Twelve apostles, in millennium, 198
Twentieth century, pace of events, 1
Two witnesses (Revelation), 159–60

—UV—
Unbelief in prophecy.
  See Prophecy, unbelief
United Nations, 133
United States of Europe (proposed), 107
Universalism, 180
Unsaved. See Eternal Punishment, doctrine of; Judgments
Valley of Jehoshaphat, 176

—WXYZ—
Warfield, Benjamin B., 192
Water of life, 212
Whitby, Daniel (postmillennialist), 186–87
World armies, judgment on, 171
World–church movement, 134–35

World Council of Churches, 135
World government, 133–34

World ruler (Daniel), 124–25, 127,
133, 135
judgment of, 171–72